Eastern Europe and the World Economy

To the women in the profession
of economics and social sciences

Eastern Europe and the World Economy

Challenges of Transition and Globalization

Edited by

Iliana Zloch-Christy

Edward Elgar
Cheltenham, UK • Northampton, MA, USA

Published by
Edward Elgar Publishing Limited
8 Lansdown Place
Cheltenham
Glos GL50 2HU
UK

Edward Elgar Publishing, Inc.
6 Market Street
Northampton
Massachusetts 01060
USA

A catalogue record for this book
is available from the British Library

Library of Congress Cataloguing in Publication Data

Eastern Europe and the world economy: challenges of transition and globalization / edited by Iliana Zloch-Christy.
Includes bibliographical references and index.
1. Europe, Eastern—Economic conditions—1989– 2. Europe, Eastern—Economic policy—1989– 3. Economic stabilization—Germany (East) 4. Privatization—Germany (East) I. Zloch-Christy, Iliana, 1953–
HC244.E22318 1998
339.5'0947—dc21 97–35422
CIP

ISBN 1 85898 695 8

Printed and bound in Great Britain by Bookcraft (Bath) Ltd

Contents

Figures

Tables

Contributors

Gabor Bakos, Institute of Economics, Hungarian Academy of Sciences, Budapest, and International Research Center for Japanese Studies, Kyoto, Japan.

Jozef M. van Brabant, United Nations, New York.

Karoly Foldes, Institute of Economics, Hungarian Academy of Sciences, Budapest.

Franklin Pitcher Johnson, Jr, founder and partner, Asset Management Company, Palo Alto, and Lecturer, Graduate School of Business, Stanford University, California.

Robert T. Kudrle, Professor of Economics and Director, Freeman Center for International Economic Policy, University of Minnesota, Minneapolis.

Thomas D. Lairson, Department of Politics, Rollins College, Winter Park, Florida.

John McHale, Department of Economics, Harvard University.

Ken Morita, Faculty of Economics, Hiroshima University, Japan.

Randall E. Newnham, Department of Political Science, Pennsylvania State University, Reading, Pennsylvania.

Lucjan T. Orlowski, Department of Economics, Sacred Heart University, Fairfield, Connecticut.

Gillian Youngs, political scientist and consultant, Hong Kong.

Kazuo Zaiki, Faculty of International Studies, Hiroshima University, Japan.

Iliana Zloch-Christy, economist and independent consultant; former faculty associate, Department of Economics, Harvard University, and Senior Associate Member, St. Antony's College, Oxford, UK.

Abbreviations

BIS	Bank for International Settlements
CAP	Common Agricultural Policy
CE	Central Europe
CIS	Commonwealth of Independent States
CMEA	Council for Mutual Economic Assistance
CPE	centrally planned economy
(D)ARPA	(Defense) Advance Research Projects Agency
DME	developed market economy
EBRD	European Bank for Reconstruction and Development
EC	European Community
EFTA	European Free Trade Association
EIB	European Investment Bank
EU	European Union
EVCA	European Venture Capital Association
FDI	foreign direct investment
FFT	First Fundamental Theorem (of welfare economics)
GATT	General Agreement on Tariffs and Trade
GDP	gross domestic product
GNP	gross national product
IBRD	International Bank for Reconstruction and Development
IEO	International Economic Organization
IFC	International Finance Corporation
IGC	Inter-governmental Conference
IMF	International Monetary Fund
ITS	International Trading System
JDB	Japan Development Bank
MITI	Ministry of International Trade and Industry
NEDO	New Energy Development Organization
NTBs	non-tariff barriers
OECD	Organization for Economic Cooperation and Development
R&D	research and development
SAR	Special Administrative Region

SF	structural funds
SFT	Second Fundamental Theorem (of welfare economics)
UN	United Nations (Organization)
UNCTAD	United Nations Conference on Trade and Development
WTO	World Trade Organization

Preface

This book is based on contributions by East European and Western scholars to one of the most interesting topics of current economic development – the problems of transition in Eastern Europe in comparative perspective and in the framework of the global world economy. Some of the chapters in the book were presented at the IV Annual Meeting of the European Association of Comparative Economic Studies in Grenoble, France, 12–14 September 1996, and at the International Studies Association Conference on Globalism and Regionalism, held in Tokyo, Japan, 20–22 September 1996. However, this study is not, and was never intended to be, a 'conference proceedings' book. My intention as editor has been to produce an integrated and coherent book, and I do hope that readers will react positively to this attempt in their judgement of how far I have succeeded.

The work on this book was a particularly interesting and personal experience for me. I wanted to invite as many female colleagues as possible to contribute. I failed to realize that, because the women in our profession still remain a considerable minority, in many cases they are confronted with financial constraints in their endeavour to pursue their scholarly work.

The study was completed during my scholarship at Harvard University, where I benefited from the institution's fascinating intellectual atmosphere and seminars at the Department of Economics, at the Center for International Affairs, at the JFK School of Government, and elsewhere. I would like to acknowledge also the stimulating discussions with János Kornai and Jeffrey Sachs. I owe special thanks to Ronald J. Hill for his excellent copy editing and to Ethna Frayne for technical assistance. My colleague Wolfgang Weigel provided helpful advice. Edward Elgar and his staff made a speedy publication possible.

ILIANA ZLOCH-CHRISTY

Harvard University, Cambridge, MA, December 1996

Vienna, April 1997

Introduction

Iliana Zloch-Christy

One of the most fascinating issues of contemporary world politics are developments in Eastern Europe and the former Soviet Union.[1] And one of the most interesting trends in the world economy is globalization. The transition in the East European region in comparative perspective and in the framework of the global world economy is the subject of this study. The main goal of the proposed book is to assess the transition problems and to establish a basis for better understanding of the directions in which economic and political changes are expected to develop and for assessing their scope.

The main questions addressed in the study are:

1. What is the present stage of economic development in Eastern Europe and what have been the trends in the world economy since the early 1990s?
2. What are the main trends in the changes of global and regional development strategies, government policies, privatization, foreign investments and external balance?
3. What is the current situation and what are the prospects for economic and political relations of Eastern Europe with the European Union, the World Trade Organization and the rest of the world?

1. The terms 'Eastern Europe' and 'post-communist Europe' are used as synonyms. Eastern Europe is defined in political rather than geographical terms, namely, the former Soviet Union and the European countries which were under Soviet domination after 1945. The terms 'West', 'Western countries', 'industrialized countries' and 'developed economies' are used to designate the economies that constitute the membership of the OECD. Please refer also to the individual authors' descriptions of the countries involved in their analyses.

4. What are the main challenges to business and government activities in shaping economic development (discussed in regional and global aspect)?

In preparing the volume I have invited the participation of colleagues who hold a wide range of views and belong to different nationalities: Eastern Europe, Belgium, Ireland, UK, US and Japan.

The study is organized in four parts as follows. The first part addresses the challenges of transition and globalization from the perspective of the developed economies. It includes contributions from two American scholars – Thomas D. Lairson, on the USA's competitiveness policy and on the formation of policy involving government support for high technology; and Robert T. Kudrle on the economic nationalism policies of the industrialized countries. Part II turns specifically to a discussion of the issues of transition from the perspective of the Eastern European economies and includes the following contributions: the Irish-American economist, John McHale, attempts to analyse the privatization in the region in its distributional dimension; the Japanese scholars Ken Morita and Kazuo Zaiki, focus on privatization in Poland in comparison with Chinese privatization; the Hungarian economist Karoly Foldes addresses issues of systematic changes and integration compatibility in his country. Part III discusses specifically the relations between the international organizations and the transitional economies in Eastern Europe. The chapter by the Polish-American economist Lucjan T. Orlowski analyses the economic conditions for accession to the European Union. This is followed by a detailed overview and assessment of the relations with the World Trade Organization by the United Nations Secretariat economist Jozef M. van Brabant. Part IV addresses selected aspects of transition, regionalism and globalization. It includes a chapter based on my work on the role of industrial policy in Eastern Europe. The Hungarian economist Gabor Bakos in his chapter attempts to answer the question whether Japanese experience in economic development might be useful for the East European economies. These are followed by a chapter by the American entrepreneur and scholar Franklin P. Johnson, Jr, on the role of venture capital in shaping economic development. The American scholar Randall E. Newnham addresses, in his chapter, political aspects of economic linkage policies of Germany and Japan, and this is followed by a chapter completing the fourth part and written by the British scholar Gillian Youngs on the political economy of transition in Hong Kong. The conclusion summarizes the main findings of the study.

Part I

The Developed Economies

1. Charting the Future: Industrial Governance Structures and the Political Economy of High Technology in the USA

Thomas D. Lairson

1. OVERVIEW

The increasing pace of technological change and the rising level of global economic competition have recently created a heated political and theoretical debate over the relative merits of markets and government in the generation of economic growth.[1] Similarly, the emergence and success of government-managed economies in Asia have prompted questions about whether a strong governmental role helps, hinders or is irrelevant to success. Efforts to expand the government's role in promoting high technology provoke intense criticism or praise. Some condemn any notion of an affirmative government role, while others assert that government support is crucial to competitive success.[2] When the government, in the form of the

1. The author would like to thank David Skidmore for his many contributions to this project and Richard Foglesong for his helpful comments on an early draft of this chapter. Thanks are also due to Rollins College for its support of this research.
2. For examples, see Peter Passell, 'High Tech Industry is Hard to Help', *New York Times*, 2 February 1993, p.B5; 'When the State Picks Winners', *The Economist*, 9 January 1993, pp.13–14; 'Uncle Sam's Helping Hand', 2 April 1994, pp.77–9; Otto G. Lambsdorff, 'Fascination with the Immediate', *International Economic Insights*, March–April 1993, pp.6–9; Linda Cohen and Roger Noll, *The Technology Pork Barrel* (Washington, DC: Brookings, 1993); Harold Brown and John Wilson, 'A New Mechanism to Fund R&D', *Issues in Science and Technology*, Winter 1992–93, pp.36–41; Lewis Branscomb, 'Toward a U.S. Technology Policy', *Issues in Science and Technology*, Summer 1991, pp.50–55. For an overview of the political

(Defense) Advanced Research Projects Agency ([D]ARPA),[3] acts to supply capital, provide for basic research or organize R&D consortiums among private firms, or serves as an information conduit, is it helping, hurting or just squandering money? More generally, are there times when state action is the best and even the most effective way to resolve problems in the development of high-technology industries?

The effort to debate these matters and answer such questions is mired in a theoretical conundrum created by four theoretical weaknesses: (1) difficulties in conceptualizing the relationship of market and non-market institutions in entire economies or industries; (2) failure to understand how and why the governance structure of an industry changes; (3) misunderstandings about the circumstances in which non-market institutions (such as government) contribute to economic growth; and (4) a lack of clarity in defining the prerequisites for effective government involvement in encouraging such growth. Consequently, what is missing from the debate are the conceptual tools that will permit us to clarify how industries actually function, why and how the arrangement of institutions in an industry changes, and the ability to sort out when and how governments can be effective and important.[4]

The most significant theoretical weakness lies in the way we have thought about the relationship of markets and government: namely, by pitting the tow against one another as explanatory factors. On one side of this debate are the 'statists' who press for government intervention

debate in the early 1980s see Richard E. Foglesong, 'The Politics of Industrial Policy in the United States', in Richard E. Foglesong and Joel D. Wolfe, *The Politics of Economic Adjustment* (New York: Greenwood, 1989), pp.27–43. A more recent investigation of industrial policy is Otto Graham, Jr, *Losing Time: The Industrial Policy Debate* (Cambridge, MA: Harvard University Press, 1992).

3. When first created in 1958, this agency was named the Advanced Research Projects Agency. In 1972 the name was changed to the Defense Advanced Research Projects Agency, and in 1993 changed back to the Advanced Research Projects Agency. Our research spans these name changes, hence our reference to (D)ARPA.
4. Even the most sophisticated work in this area is based on essentially *ad hoc* theoretical categories: see Martin Fransman, *The Market and Beyond: Information Technology in Japan* (Cambridge: Cambridge University Press, 1990); David Gibson and Everett Rogers, *R&D Collaboration on Trial* (Boston, MA: Harvard Business School Press, 1994); Kenneth Flamm, *Creating the Computer* (Washington, DC: Brookings, 1988). For largely atheoretical work on DARPA see Jeffrey Rayport, *DARPA* (Cambridge, MA: Harvard Business School Case, 1990); and Burton Edelson and Robert Stern, *the Operations of DARPA and its Utility as a Model for a Civilian ARPA* (Washington, DC: Johns Hopkins Foreign Policy Institute, 1989).

to ensure technological competitiveness. 'Free marketeers', on the other hand, argue that governments cannot surpass markets in 'picking' winners. Each of these perspectives fails to understand that it is the varying *relationships* among firms, industry associations, government and other institutions that define the most important level of analysis for understanding the development of high technology. The concept of industrial governance structure directs our thinking and observation towards these institutional arrangements. As a consequence of ignoring this concept, existing research has failed to define how the various institutions of an industry are arranged and how this can be changed by the particular circumstances of an industry. Most importantly, there is an insufficient basis for a theoretically grounded explanation of how and why non-market institutions become essential elements in the growth and development of an industry.[5]

The purpose of this research is to fill these theoretical gaps and examine an important but largely ignored instance of government–business cooperation: the (Defense) Advanced Research Projects

5. There are some important perspectives from international political economy that support the approach adopted in this research. Chalmers Johnson, *MITI and the Japanese Miracle* (Stanford, CA: Stanford University Press, 1982) opens the door to a consideration of the relationship of institutions; John Zysman, *Governments, Markets and Growth* (Ithaca, NY: Cornell University Press, 1983), and Laura D'Andrea Tyson and John Zysman, 'Developmental Strategy and Production Innovation in Japan', in Chalmers Johnson *et al.* (eds), *Politics and Productivity: How Japan's Development Strategy Works* (New York: Ballinger, 1989), pp.59–140, consider the way markets are conditioned by the institutional settings in a society; Daniel Okimoto, *Between MITI and the Market: Japanese Industrial Policy for High Technology* (Stanford, CA: Stanford University Press, 1989), offers a nuanced sense of relationship between governments and markets; Robert Wade, *Governing the Market* (Princeton, NJ: Princeton University Press, 1990), articulates and tests arguments for an affirmative government role in economic growth; Michael Piore and Charles Sabel, *The Second Industrial Divide* (New York: Basic Books, 1984), and David Friedman, *The Misunderstood Miracle* (Ithaca, NY: Cornell University Press, 1988), press the case for seeing industrial arrangements as a product of broad political struggles and outcomes; finally, David Yoffie, 'Introduction: From Comparative Advantage to Regulated Competition', in David Yoffie (ed.), *Beyond Free Trade: Firms, Governments, and Global Competition* (Boston, MA: Harvard Business School Press, 1993), pp.1–25, suggests how we may distinguish among different forms of industry structure, national institutions, government policies and firm behaviour, and then recombine these to understand outcomes. Beyond these works lies a vast and growing literature from microeconomics, sociology and technology policy largely unknown to students of international political economy. This research has been incorporated into the theoretical material below.

Agency. We seek a sounder framework from which to draw judgements about how, when, and to what purpose government aid to industry should be encouraged. This study defines in some detail the theoretical approach and outlines one important case: the effort by (D)ARPA to accelerate innovation in semiconductors and computer architecture in the Very Large Scale Integration (VLSI) programme from 1978 to 1983. We show how (D)ARPA actions rearranged the governance structures for these industries and contributed to the creation of networks of innovators.

2. THE THEORETICAL FRAMEWORK

Understanding the political economy of state–firm relations in high technology requires a new theoretical understanding of how actual industries develop and change.[6] There are four main theoretical tasks. First we shall provide a model that captures the main lines of variance in the way governance structures of different industries are organized. Second, we shall show how environmental circumstances in an industry help to generate different configurations of institutions in a governance structure. Third, we shall specify circumstances of governance structure failure where government involvement can reduce transaction costs and/or resolve collective action problems that hinder or prevent effective adaptation. Finally, we define the criteria that make an effective government response politically possible. Development of this theoretical perspective permits us to pose questions, offer interpretations and understand outcomes in ways that otherwise would be impossible or at least unlikely.

A governance structure is composed of the organization and forms of relationship among the various institutions in an industry. In addition to producer firms, this web of relationships ties together associations of producers, banks, suppliers and distributors, worker organizations, universities and research organizations and various levels and agencies

6. Much of the research done by economists into technology and innovation has long ago dropped the dualism of markets and governments: for two of many examples see Jurgen Hausler *et al.*, 'Contingencies of Innovation Networks: A Case Study of Successful Interfirm R&D Collaboration', *Research Policy*, vol.23 (1994), pp.47–66, and Giovanni Dosi *et al.* (eds), *Technology and Enterprise in a Historical Perspective* (Oxford: Clarendon Press, 1992).

of government. These institutions are directed towards coordinating transactions and interaction among firms and among other governance institutions so as to enhance the main goals of firms. These can include efficiency and profitability, reducing transaction costs, supplying capital, reducing uncertainty, stabilizing prices and costs, organizing and directing innovation, and defining and defending political interests.

The notion of structure is crucial, since it focuses attention on the way the decisions of individual firms are influenced by the broader set of relationships in which they are enmeshed. By treating the governance structure as a whole, rather than the individual firm, as the unit of analysis, we can examine and explain the patterns of industrial development that emerge from the collective decisions taken by apparently independent actors and the unintended outcomes resulting from the interaction of various institutions. The concept of governance structure alerts us to the fact that industrial competitiveness is not determined by market forces alone, but rather by the strategic relationships that evolve among the diverse institutions of an industry. And this concept also points us toward the crucial notion of *governance failure* – not simply market failure – as the point of access for government involvement.

On the basis of the concept of industrial governance structures, we develop a series of propositions that contribute to resolving the key theoretical weaknesses identified above and which focus on defining an effective role for the state in the promotion of high technology industries.

(1) Governance structures vary across industries and through time in the same industry. Much of this variance can be described using a three-dimensional model that captures differences in structure.

How has the concept of governance structure been understood by others? Not surprisingly, there are important differences in the way governance structures have been conceived. Most neo-classical economists have treated the organization and forms of relationship in an industry in terms defined almost exclusively by market exchange. But if we adopt a theoretically precise definition of markets, many of the most important elements of governance structures are excluded. If the concept of market is made so elastic as to include any form of exchange and bargain, its theoretical power is greatly diminished. For purposes of this discussion, a market is a system of arms-length exchanges free of power or coercion (voluntary), which each party is free to renew or not, and in which neither party can influence the price. This definition conforms to that of a free market in a situation of perfect competition.

An industry whose governance structure is defined by markets would be devoid of institutions, except for markets themselves, and the latter would be composed of the continuing system of transactions. No agreements between or among firms could exist outside markets and none could affect price. Furthermore, the internal structure of the firms would need to be very simple, composed of one decision maker and workers engaged in market transactions with firms. Finally, individual firms would supply internally or would purchase in markets all capital, materials, information and technology.

For industries not defined by perfectly competitive markets, the organizational structure of firms, arrangements among firms, and the relationship of firms to supporting institutions define the relationships of governance structures. The key theoretical proposition is that markets are but one of several relationships that compose a governance structure.

Scholars, often working from a sociological perspective, have identified five general types of institutions that come together to produce governance structures: markets, firm hierarchies, supportive hierarchies; formal and informal inter-institutional arrangements such as clans, networks, alliances and associations; and state hierarchies. Governance structures differ in the ways these institutions are related and combined.[7]

One approach to understanding differences in governance structures identifies several ideal types that might exist, distinguished by the extent to which one type of institution is dominant.[8] These include: market-dominant, in which arms-length exchange based on autonomous market prices overwhelms all other relationships. Commodity futures might provide an example. A second ideal type is dominated by firm hierarchies: here, relationships within the industry are controlled

7. See Leon Lindberg, John Campbell and J. Rogers Hollingsworth, 'Economic Governance and the Analysis of Structural Change in the American Economy', in John Campbell, J. Rogers Hollingsworth and Leon Lindberg (eds), *Governance of the American Economy* (Cambridge: Cambridge University Press, 1991), p.29.
8. Campbell *et al.*, *Governance*, p.32.

by large complex firms that have only limited contact with each other; a classic oligopoly and monopoly are examples. A third ideal type is based on the way different hierarchies are mixed together: a combination of firm and association hierarchies could be based on the leadership of one dominant firm or could be multilateral in origin; classical notions of corporatist systems in which firm cooperation in apportioning market share and controlling prices is aided by an intra-industry organization or association are examples of such a governance structure. A fourth general type is characterized by extensive systems of cooperating among firms and between firms and a dense system of supportive organizations: examples might include the emergence of widespread strategic alliances between firms, combined with information networks, R&D alliances and cooperative arrangements with universities. A fifth type would be directed by some active form of state involvement in which the government was responsible for investment and perhaps production: examples would include early stages in the jet aircraft and computer industry in the USA, when the government supplied capital and markets for development of these goods.[9]

Remembering that we define governance structures in terms of the *relationships* among institutions, and drawing on existing research, we define three forms of relationship among governance institutions: (1) market-based forms of exchange; (2) political leadership; and (3) cooperation. Conceptualizing variance can be done by translating

9. See ibid., pp.29–32, for elaboration of the notion of various types of governance structure. A similar approach is adopted by John Dunning, *The Globalization of Business* (New York: Routledge, 1994), pp.315–29. Another approach, used by Kitschelt, sees somewhat similar categories for differentiating governance structures: he defines such structures in terms of whether markets, firms, centralized structures or teams of organizations are the central actors: see Herbert Kitschelt, 'Industrial Governance Structures, Innovation Strategies, and the Case of Japan: Sectoral or Cross-National Comparative Analysis', *International Organization*, Vol.45, no.4 (Autumn 1991), pp.453–93. Additional work on governance structures is to be found in J. Rogers Hollingsworth *et al.* (eds), *Governing Capitalist Economies* (Oxford: Oxford University Press, 1994); Gary Pisano, 'The Governance of Collaboration', *Research Policy*, vol.20 (1991), pp.237–49. Strategic alliances are discussed in John Hegendoorn and Jos Schakenraad, 'Leading Companies and Networks of Strategic Alliances in Information Technologies', *Research Policy*, vol.21 (1992), pp.163–90. Networks are examined by M. Callon *et al.*, 'The Management and Evaluation of Technological Programs and the Dynamics of Techno-Economic Networks: The Case of AFME', *Research Policy*, vol.21 (1992), pp.215–36, and C. Freeman, 'Networks of Innovators: A Synthesis of Research Issues', *Research Policy*, vol.20 (1991), pp.499–514.

Figure 1.1. Dimensions of variance in governance structures

The Impact of Markets

High: free market transactions for capital, labour, materials, services and finished products; high level of competition among many firms; no protection from foreign competition

Moderate: limited impact from associations such as unions; some limited market power by firms; limited protection from foreign competition; limited government management of prices (direct or indirect)

Low: significant protection from foreign competition; market-sharing agreements among firms; a single dominant producer creates monopoly effects; many buyers, few producers; market collusion in fixing prices

Source of Governance Structure

What institutions provide the political leadership for the formation of governance structures?

Individual firms: firms themselves, acting alone, resolve problems through hierarchies

Firm association: governance structures are created and maintained largely by organized groups of firms or by a dominant firm

State leadership: the government plays the primary role in organizing and preserving the governance structure

Complexity and Density of Institutional Cooperation

Low complexity: relationships are *ad hoc* and intermittent; all are bilateral; very few non-firm institutions

Moderate complexity: many formal and informal arrangements persist through time and reform with some frequency; significant number of bilateral alliances among firms and non-firm institutions

High complexity: many formal alliances and networks persisting through time; multilateral arrangements of firms and other institutions; many networks of communication and information flow

these different forms of relationship into three dimensions that register the ways each can differ. The three dimensions include the level of impact of markets; whether individual firms or collective leadership are the primary source of the governance structure; and the level of complexity and density of cooperation among governance institutions. These dimensions can be summarized as shown in Figure 1.1.

Bifurcating and combining the three dimensions generates an eightfold table of possible cells. Representation in two-dimensional space is best seen by looking at the front (Figure 1.2) and rear (Figure 1.3) of the cube. The vertical dimension represents the degree of market impact (High to Low); the horizontal dimension represents the source of governance leadership (Collective to Individual Firm); and the depth dimension represents the level of cooperation among governance institutions (Dense and Complex to Simple and Limited). The face of Figure 1.2 represents the Dense and Complex end of the cooperation continuum.

Figure 1.2 Representation of governance variance (cube front)

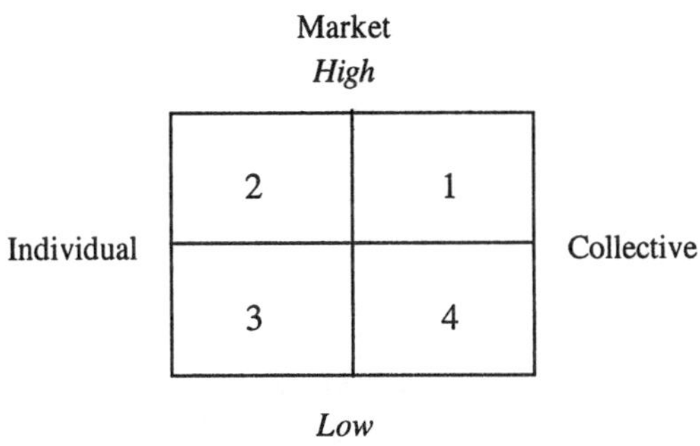

The face of Figure 1.3 represents the Simple and Limited end of the cooperation continuum.

If we see Figures 1.2 and 1.3 as the front and back of a cube representing the three dimensions, we generate eight cells or sub-cubes. These cells represent eight ideal types of governance structure:

Cell 1: Dense and complex forms of cooperation among governance institutions, collective leadership and high market impact. This may be the prototypical situation of a mature high-technology

Figure 1.3 Representation of governance variance (cube rear)

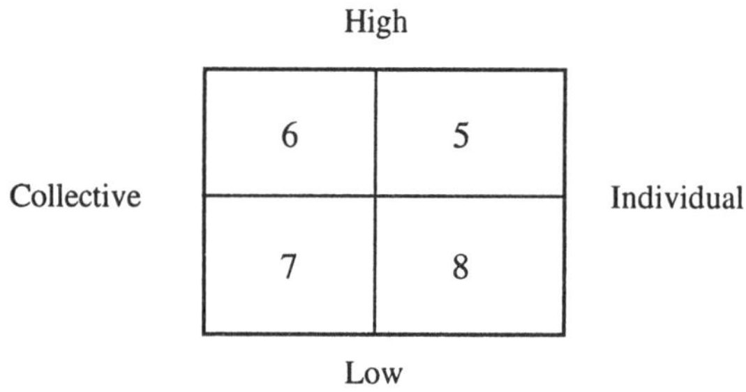

industry, with a mixture of many networks among firms and supportive institutions, a combination of collective leadership drawn from networks and the state, and strong market forces. There may be more examples of this in Japan and Taiwan than in the US.

Cell 2: Dense and complex relationships, leadership by individual forms, and high market impact. Here many bilateral strategic alliances exist but the hierarchical structure of individual firms gives substance and direction to industry governance, and market impact is high. The semiconductor industry in 1980 may be an example.

Cell 3: Dense and complex relationships, individual firm leadership, and low market impact.

Cell 4: Dense and complex relationships, collective leadership, and low market impact.

Cell 5: Simple and limited cooperative relationships among governance institutions, leadership from individual firms, and high market impact. This, of course, is the case of perfect competition typically used to understand all industries.

Cell 6: Simple and limited cooperative relationships, collective leadership, and high market impact. The dairy industry operates with exchange transactions and substantial industry associations combined with significant state involvement, but also in a high market-impact environment;

Cell 7: Simple and limited cooperative relationships, collective leadership, and low market impact. This may characterize the aircraft industry, where firms have little cooperative interaction and markets have less power because of firm size, but the state provides significant leadership in governance;

Cell 8: Simple and limited cooperative relationships, leadership by individual firms, and low market impact.

This typology of governance structure variance has the merit of treating more systematically the criteria of other scholars' thinking. But this is only the beginning. In a later version of this research, we shall explore the micro-level and contextual features of especially interesting governance types. This includes high-technology industries and focuses on the microprocesses of policy networks, information-processing networks, and shared beliefs and practices. At present, we want to understand why variation in governance structures occurs in different industries, and why in a single industry change of governance structure can take place over time.

(2) Variance in governance structures is the consequence of different industry conditions and changes in these conditions over time.

Why should variance in governance structures occur, either across industries or in a single industry through time? Several answers have previously been given to this question. Some have seen governance structures as the result of the basic motivation of decision makers in firms: a search for efficiency prompts a calculation of various arrangements for lowering transaction costs. This search leads to a trial-and-error process that eventually yields greater efficiency through different forms of governance structure. Another perspective focuses on firm motivation in terms of the need to control markets and competition, to counteract the power of labour unions and to displace on to the public some of the costs of conducting business.[10]

More complex arguments seek to understand the arrangement of governance structures beyond hierarchies through understanding the

10. These two views focus almost entirely on the origins of hierarchies: see Oliver Williamson and William Ouchine, 'The Markets and Hierarchies Program of Research', and Charles Perrow, 'Markets, Hierarchies and Hegemony', both in Andrew Van De Ven and William Joyce (eds), *Perspectives in Organization Design and Behavior* (New York: Wiley, 1981), pp.347–406. A further elaboration of the efficiency perspective is found in Albert Chandler, *The Visible Hand: The Managerial Revolution in American Business* (Cambridge, MA: Harvard University Press, 1977).

impact of broad environmental forces. One related approach has examined the size of the firm, the size of demand at the firm level, technological complexity and the rate of change in technology.[11] Unfortunately, this promising approach has related these factors only to different types of industries rather than to different types of governance.

Research that corrects this problem focuses on how the search for efficiency and reducing transaction costs is affected by the nature of technology in the industry. Kitschelt argues that one dimension defining the nature of technology is the tightness by which the elements of technology are coupled together, while the other is the level of complexity of the technology. A four-fold table generates the following relationship between technology and governance:

- A combination of linear, low-complexity and loosely coupled technology tends to generate market governance arrangements.
- Linear but tightly coupled technology systems generate corporate hierarchies as governance.
- Complex systems that are loosely coupled generate teams as the basic feature of governance.
- Complex and tightly coupled systems generate centralized governance structures.[12]

This effort to understand how the attempt to minimize transaction costs (and maximize efficiency) leads to different forms of governance structure depending on the nature of a sector's technology is a very important theoretical advance.

And yet it has important weaknesses. The image of a trial-and-error process based in calculations of firms driven by efficiency and conditioned by technology is not wrong but incomplete. Each of the hypotheses linking technology and governance contains considerable uncertainty about the forms of governance structure that should emerge. For example, in situations of complex interactive and loosely

11. J. Rogers Hollingsworth and Leon Lindberg, 'The Governance of the American Economy: The Role of Markets, Clans, Hierarchies, and Associative Behavior', in Wolfgang Streeck and Philippe Schmitter (eds), *Private Interest Government: Beyond Market and State* (London: SAGE, 1985), p.225.
12. Herbert Kitschelt, 'Industrial Governance Structures, Innovation Strategies, and the Case of Japan: Sectoral or Cross-National Comparative Analysis', *International Organization*, vol.45, no.4 (Autumn 1991), pp.460–75.

coupled technology systems (such as software, artificial intelligence or biotechnology) the expected governance structure is a system of teams drawn from a combination of public infrastructure and private business. But this leaves unanswered the question of the nature and scope of the public infrastructure, the mechanisms for turning externalities into public goods and allowing firms to capture profits, whether capital markets will supply funds at the right time, and whether collective-action problems can be resolved so as to permit innovation clubs to forms.[13]

Research on the sources of variance in governance structures has two general weaknesses: the focus on minimizing transaction costs is too restrictive for understanding the array of choices in and between governance institutions, and the number of factors seen to be active in affecting choices needs to be enlarged. Minimizing transaction costs is a useful concept for understanding intra-firm choices involving markets and hierarchies; but it is much less effective in thinking about inter-firm and firm-supporting institutional cooperation.

We argue that the variance in governance structures can better be understood in relation to a broader set of industry characteristics: the nature and rate of change in the technology of product and production; the level of domestic and international competition; the position of the industry in the product cycle; the length of the product cycle; the sources of capital and the culture of risk aversion; the ratio of R&D to sales and profits; and the size of economies of scale. Taken together, these factors make up the basic environmental context of the firms in an industry and affect their individual and collective choices.

Driven by goals of profitability, expansion and survival, firms acting alone, together and in relation to other industry institutions generate patterns of organization and exchange as they attempt to cope with the problems produced by the operation of the industry. The basic causal model is depicted in Figure 1.4.

The basic characteristics of the industry generate problems that increase transaction costs or require collective action for their

13. Another example comes from situations of complex interactive and tightly coupled technology (nuclear power, space technology, aircraft, mainframe computers, telecommunications). This technology calls for a governance structure based on state-planned R&D and state-provided markets. Once again, the boundary between public and private is unclear. Space technology creates a market for externalities that show a profit, whereas aircraft can themselves become an object of private profit.

Figure 1.4 Basic causal model

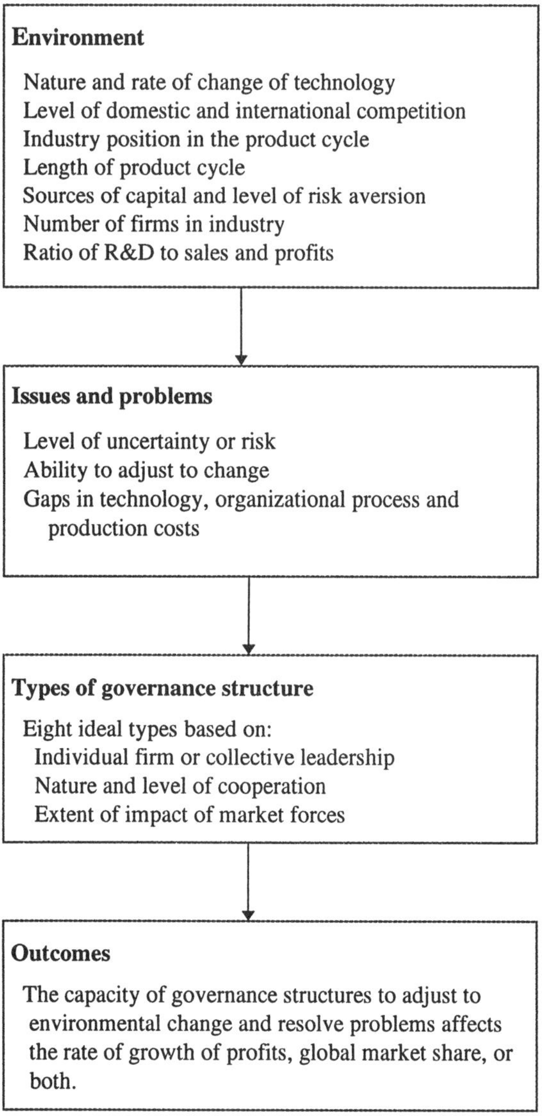

resolution, or both. Governance structures emerge through trial and error in an effort to cope with these difficulties. We posit a series of relationships between environmental circumstances and the configuration of governance structures. In particular, we are interested in the impact of technology and technological change on the level of cooperation among governance institutions.

(3) The special characteristics of high technology industries frequently generate problems that require cooperation among firms and between firms and other governance institutions. This cooperation may be very difficult for firms to organize owing to problems associated with collective action.

There are good reasons to understand high-technology industries as having distinct characteristics. High-technology industries are constantly faced with designing arrangements within firms and across governance institutions that resolve problems of raising capital in the face of high risk and uncertainty, obtaining and processing information, making choices about research and products, and engaging in especially high levels of continuous innovation.[14] These circumstances often strain and surpass the capacities of individual firms which frequently cannot individually organize the resources needed to achieve their goals. The most effective means for resolving these problems is a complex arrangement of markets and intra-institutional cooperation. This is because cooperation permits pooling resources, spreading risks, widening information flows and leveraging uncertainties. But the possibility of cooperation among otherwise competing firms and with other institutions faces the problem of collective action, that is the ability of interdependent actors to organize together (see Figure 1.5).[15]

14. For a discussion of some of these problems, see AnnaLee Saxenian, 'The Origins and Dynamics of Production Networks in Silicon Valley', *Research Policy*, vol.20 (1991), pp.423–37; Leonard Lynn *et al.*, 'Linking Technology and Institutions: The Innovation Community Framework', *Research Policy*, vol.25 (1996), pp.91–106; David Angel, *Restructuring for Innovation* (New York: Guilford Press, 1994); and W. Brian Arthur, 'Increasing Returns and the New World of Business', *Harvard Business Review*, July–August 1996, pp.100–109.
15. The classic text on this theme is, of course, Mancur Olson, *The Logic of Collective Action* (Cambridge, MA: Harvard University Press, 1965). For an updating of this research and a very useful critique see Todd Sandler, *Collective Action* (Ann Arbor: University of Michigan Press, 1992).

Figure 1.5 Basic causal process: High-tech industries

Industry characteristics

This industry typically combines high risk and uncertainty; large capital needs; rapid technological change and shortened product cycles; extreme levels and rates of continuous innovation; high ratios of R&D to sales, profits and unit production costs; and high levels of domestic and international competition. May also be prone to cyclical over-capacity and large losses at the bottom of the cycle.

Issues and problems

These characteristics create problems with maintaining innovation in view of large capital demands, rapid change, high R&D needs and large swings in profits. Individual firms and the entire industry face difficulties of recovering fixed costs, organizing information streams, and integrating information in a context of rapid change and uncertainty. This high risk and uncertainty can lead to difficulties in funding innovation projects to maintain the competitiveness of individual firms and national industries.

Governance structure

These circumstances tend to push governance structures towards arrangements that minimize the impact of markets and competition. Information becomes a vital input for decisions but is usually privatized and hoarded by individual firms. Complex and dense networks and alliances emerge among firms and with institutions such as universities. The high volume of exchange outside markets creates problems of coordination and integration. High demand for public goods is undermined by the proprietary needs of firms and intense competition. A variety of collective action problems are created by the need for cooperation and the obstacles to cooperation.

Outcomes

The tendency to resolve problems outside markets undermines firm and industry dynamism. Government action to supply public goods and resolve collective action problems must retain the market discipline of firms for competitive success.

What forces move actors in a governance structure to cooperate and what barriers exist to this cooperation? We argue that as the resources needed for competition expand relative to firm size and capabilities, the need for cooperation among governance institutions increases, but, even in situations where all members of a group will benefit from cooperation, this may not be forthcoming. There are several reasons for this result. When the benefit of collective action approximates to the characteristics of a public good, the probability increases that cooperation to provide that good will not take place.[16] Thus, the ability of the actors in a governance structure to cooperate in solving some problem is undermined by the public quality of the benefits. Each actor will fail to contribute voluntarily, hoping that others will provide the good.

However, we argue, even more stands in the way of collective action in a group of otherwise competing actors. First, when the value of the public good is uncertain - that is, when its value cannot be known with sufficient confidence - the probability of collective action to provide this good is low.[17] Second, when members of a group place a significantly different value on the benefits of collective action, its probability declines. And third, when members of the group are competing for the benefits of the collective action, fear of defection and of relative gains by others will inhibit the capacity for cooperation.

(4) Government intervention is most needed and effective when the existing governance structure fails. This intervention should be directed at overcoming collective-action problems and organizing appropriate cooperation. The ability of government to act successfully depends on a series of specific conditions.

High-technology industries may be especially susceptible to long periods of intense demands on individual firms and therefore generate needs for complex and varied permutations of governance over time. Firms and other actors in an existing governance structure may often fail to cooperate sufficiently to form institutions adequate to solve these

16. A special but important case is externalities, which involve situations where benefits are available for some actors but no practical means of compensation to the provider can be arranged.
17. An example is basic research or development of technology that advances beyond incremental change.

problems.[18] The ability of state actors to resolve collective action problems and organize cooperation among governance institutions depends on the answers to four questions. First, can government decision makers define choices in terms of a social welfare beyond that of individual firms or industries? This might include some combination of an extended time horizon, calculating positive externalities, recognizing the need for public goods or some other element of problem-resolution found in governance structures. Second, can government actions alter the nature, timing, or both, of choices in other governance institutions from those that would come in any case? Specifically, does government involvement alter outcomes? Third, can state actors become involved at early stages of technology development, perhaps through a variety of access points? Are there ways for state actors to engage in substantial and continuing consultation with firms about decisions? And fourth, does state involvement have political legitimacy, or is the state role a deeply contested matter.[19]

Theoretical Summary

In brief, we want to investigate a series of processes involving the role of government as an element in the governance structure of high technology industries. At various points in the developmental history of high technology industries, the basic elements of competition, uncertainty, risk and R&D expenditures reach thresholds where the demands and problems are beyond the capacities of individual firms. In these circumstances, some form of cooperation is the most effective mechanism for sharing costs and risks and leveraging uncertainties. But because of the public goods benefits deriving from cooperation, difficulties in estimating the nature and size of these benefits, and the

18. This is but one of many ways in which governance structures can fail. More generally these are situations where functional needs and problem solving are not adequately met by the existing arrangements among governance institutions. The standard concept of market failure is subsumed under the broader concept of governance failure. Market failure is loaded in favour of the primacy of markets for the organization of production and resolving all functional needs. This term perpetuates the conclusion that we can analytically isolate the impact of markets from that of other institutions; only when markets fail can we look to other institutions for help. The argument here is that markets, hierarchies, non-market institutions and governments are always necessary elements of governance, albeit in different configurations. Thus, it is *governance structures* that fail.
19. This list recasts the argument found in Okimoto, *Between MITI and Market.*

competitive relations among firms, cooperation is very difficult. A state actor, in a position to recognize both the positive externalities and the positive benefits to the industry from cooperation, is the most effective source for resolving problems of collective action and providing leadership that facilitates cooperation, collaboration or both. The success of the effort depends in part on organizing the governance structure so that cooperation does not mute the impact of markets and competitive pressures and yet resolves the difficulties.

3. APPROACH TO STUDYING (D)ARPA

The examination of several cases of (D)ARPA involvement in high-technology development permits us to consider the entire spectrum of relationships postulated by our theory. We will focus on three: (1) the nature of industry circumstances and the ability of the existing governance structure to cope with the existing difficulties; (2) the role of (D)ARPA in identifying what we would call governance-structure failures, in resolving collective action problems that prevent cooperation, and in reorganizing the governance structure; and (3) the outcome of the effort, focusing on the relationships in the governance structure and the ability of (D)ARPA to play an essential (or ineffective or damaging) role.

The methodology for this research will be based largely on interviews with participants and the published reports of (D)ARPA activity. Each case will be examined using the following set of questions drawn from the theory:

1. What are the basic features of the industry governance structure; that is, how can we describe the relationships among industry institutions in terms of our categories of markets, political leadership and cooperation? This can be done in terms of such matters as the number and size of firms, the competitive environment, the nature and role of industry associations, the nature and role of non-profit institutions and the nature and role of state involvement.
2. What are the main characteristics of the industry's operations? This can be examined in terms of such measures as the ratio of investment and R&D expenditures to sales and profits; the position

of the industry in the product cycle; the length of the product cycle; the rate of technological change; and levels of risk and uncertainty.

3. How are industry characteristics (and changes in characteristics) related to specific problems faced by the industry?
4. In what ways does the existing governance structure succeed or fail in addressing these problems? Which problems remain?
5. What public goods could be supplied to help resolve the problems? What are the barriers to collective action by firms and non-profit institution?
6. How do (D)ARPA officials relate to the industry? What role has (D)ARPA played in the past?
7. How did (D)ARPA officials understand the problems in the industry; was it from a narrow perspective of military use or from a perspective reflecting ideas of governance structure?
8. What is the relationship between (D)ARPA actions and the resolution of collective action and the supply of public goods?
9. What was the result of (D)ARPA involvement? Was the public good supplied and did it matter for the development of the industry? How did (D)ARPA actions alter the industry governance structure; did this provide the new governance structure with new adaptive capabilities?

We are interested in the pre-intervention phase, the (D)ARPA intervention, and the post-intervention consequences as these relate to the theoretical concepts and propositions.

Why (D)ARPA?

(D)ARPA is a small but influential agency located in the Department of Defense. Created in 1958 in the wake of the Sputnik crisis, (D)ARPA was designed to coordinate and direct a series of high-risk and innovative research projects, such as those in space development, ballistic missile defence and nuclear test detection. The goal was to perpetuate US technological superiority in areas with direct application to defence capabilities. This often meant interaction with industry, universities and research agencies to examine potential technological breakthroughs and demonstrate the feasibility of certain technologies. (D)ARPA's special responsibilities, its position at the intersection of government and business, and the importance of industrial capabilities for technology development meant that (D)ARPA programmes frequently had 'dual use' implications. That is to say, (D)ARPA projects very often involved technology with military and commercial applications; moreover, developing a technology for defence purposes was many times linked to developing it for commercial purposes. This dual-use element of (D)ARPA activity became increasingly relevant in the 1970s and after.

During this time, (D)ARPA was re-designed to shift its focus away from projects and applications to an emphasis on generic technology.[20]

(D)ARPA operates with a small staff and budget ($2 billion+ in the 1990s) and cultivates a *modus operandi* of informality, quick decision making, and rapid adaptation to changed circumstances. Operating without any research laboratories of its own, (D)ARPA has sponsored advanced R&D, defined research priorities, funded projects and coordinated information flows among its constituencies in government, business, research and academia. This activity can take many forms, with (D)ARPA funds often contingent on commitments from outside government, or risk-taking that demonstrates feasibility so as to reduce risks for commercial activity, or team-building, or communication and idea-clearing, or serving as a gatekeeper whose involvement sparks actions by others.[21]

The results of these activities are varied but involve interesting contributions to high-technology development. Perhaps most important was (D)ARPA's role in the development of the computer and semiconductor industries.

> In computers, in particular, DARPA's contribution was nothing short of dazzling. The agency funded research that developed the concept of the personal computer and the menu- and icon-driven software that went into the first Apple Macintosh. It supplied grants, and, later, the venture capital to fund development of artificial intelligence and parallel processing computers. In fact, in the late 1960s it designated four research institutions – Stanford, Berkeley, Carnegie-Mellon, and MIT – as academic centres for the study of computers and computing; using agency seed money, DARPA virtually single-handedly created the United States leadership in computer

20. Burton Edelson and Robert Stern, *The Operations of DARPA and its Utility as a Model for a Civilian ARPA* (Washington, DC: Johns Hopkins Foreign Policy Institute, 1989); US Congress, Office of Technology Assessment, *Defense Conversion: Redirecting R&D*, OTA-ITE-552 (Washington, DC: US Government Printing Office, May 1993), pp.121–43.
21. This catalogue is drawn from Rayport, *DARPA*.

sciences. (The four DARPA-funded centres would train, directly or indirectly, nearly every computer sciences expert in the nation). As MIT's provost [and former Director of the CIA], John Deutsch, has said, 'The computer strength of the United States came out of DARPA'.[22]

These accomplishments also include the creation of ARPANET, and the associated technologies of packet switching and time-sharing, which provided the prototype of the Internet, and extend to such areas as CAD systems and RISC chips. Many of the same conclusions could be reached about (D)ARPA's role in the development of materials science.

A brief look at one major (D)ARPA activity – that directed toward the VLSI (Very Large Scale Integration) problem – helps illustrate how the theoretical perspective of this paper can be applied.[23] This strategic intervention by (D)ARPA in the computer and semiconductor industry came during the period 1976–84. (D)ARPA's main concern at the time was the promotion of rapid technological advances by the USA, as a strategic goal in the cold war with the Soviet Union. This meant that any sluggishness in the USA innovation was a problem to be solved and led to a focus on related weaknesses in the semiconductor and computer industries as a whole. Studies of these industries indicated the goal of rapid advances in integrated circuit (IC) design and computer capability was being stymied by slowing rates of innovation.

The computer–semiconductor industry at that time was composed of many firms, but with dominance of computer markets by IBM. Although decisions, developments and results in the computer industry were substantially internalized within one firm – IBM – the semiconductor industry contained many independent firms competing and interacting through market relations. Generally, governance relations were based in firms and markets, with little inter-firm cooperation. Profit levels were high and the growth of demand strong. The ties between academic and industrial research were weakening and government funding for academic research was declining. Academic

22. Ibid., p.7.
23. The (D)ARPA VLSI programme was distinct from, though related to, the VHSIC (Very High Speed Integrated Circuit) programme in the Department of Defense. For example, VLSI promoted developments with commercial applications and encouraged open communication of results. For a somewhat critical review of VHSIC, see Leslie Brueckner, *Assessing the Commercial Impact of the Very High Speed Integrated Circuit Program*, BRIE Working Paper 5 (Berkeley, CA, 1984).

research was less important for industry developments; in particular, academic work was less able to engage in feasibility studies and cutting-edge research because of the expense of purchasing equipment. The bulk of microelectronics R&D was done in forms and most of that was devoted to making incremental improvements to existing technology. The dominant interaction relationship among firms was based on 'closed proprietary systems', that is, systems that worked only for one system and which were unavailable for use by other firms. The combination of academic–industry separation, reducing funding to academia, incremental R&D and a 'closed proprietary' culture meant that the rate of innovation was slowing down and little attention was being devoted to advances from new architecture designs.[24] The dominance of firms and markets and the associated competitive climate, created substantial barriers to collective action aimed at overcoming these difficulties.

(D)ARPA officials saw many interesting and potentially important ideas relating to VLSI in the academic community and in firms, but also saw the lack of resources to pursue these ideas. The strategy developed by (D)ARPA was to create an infrastructure that would 'facilitate learning, implementation and propagation of VLSI technologies and research of key academic centres on actual VLSI technologies'.[25] Initially, this involved using ARPANET to support rapid and extended innovation, to supply facilities to promote the development and production of new and experimental semiconductor device technologies, and to provide new CAD technologies to assist quick development. A system of cooperation was organized around four

24. Many of these conclusions were made in a RAND study commissioned by (D)ARPA in 1976 and completed in 1977: see Richard Van Atta, Sidney Reed and Seymour Deitchman, *DARPA Technical Accomplishments, Volume II: An Historical Review of Selected DARPA Projects* (Alexandria, VA: Institute for Defense Analysis, 1991). An example of industry innovation weakness comes from IBM, which developed the Reduced Instruction Set Computer (RISC) microprocessor in 1976. This microprocessor was much faster than previous ICs but IBM chose not to move towards commercial development because RISC undermined existing IBM hardware and software systems: see Jonathan Khazam and David Mowery, 'The Commercialization of RISC: Strategies for the Creation of Dominant Designs', *Research Policy*, vol.23 (1994), p.90. (D)ARPA officials concluded over several years that industry innovation weaknesses were also shown by Xerox PARC's failure to turn its Alto into a commercial computer, and AT&T's failure to move the UNIX on to a workstation platform.
25. Van Atta *et al.*, *DARPA Technical Accomplishments, Volume II*, p.17-5.

universities, the Jet Propulsion Laboratory, Xerox PARC, several semiconductor firms, the National Bureau of Standards and the National Science Foundation. This network supported the rapid development, production and testing of VLSI chips. These arrangements were later extended from facilitating the development of sub-micron semiconductor technologies to supporting rapid advances in computer architecture and capabilities.

(D)ARPA's interest in a new computer architecture came in four areas: (1) RISC; (2) parallel processing; (3) systolic arrays; and (4) symbolic processing. The most important outcome was the effort to leverage advances in RISC, software and high resolution screens into the creation and commercialization of networked computer workstations. Using resources provided by (D)ARPA to Stanford University, computer scientists there conceived, designed and built the first version of the Stanford University Network (SUN) between 1979 and 1981. The problem of developing an effective software was met through (D)ARPA efforts to obtain and further develop the UNIX system from AT&T's Bell Laboratories. This provided a software based on an open architecture with networking and multi-tasking capabilities. Additionally, high-resolution graphics displays were provided through (D)ARPA efforts.

> By the end of 1981 the project had distributed roughly twenty work-stations around the Stanford campus, at an estimated cost of $10,000 dollars each. Each provided computing power approaching that of a $100,000 dollar VAX 780 at about a tenth of the cost.[26]

(D)ARPA encouraged the commercialization of the system, which became SUN Microsystems in 1982, and supplied the funds to several universities to purchase SUN workstations. This company has become a major global player in computer development and innovation. Between 1985 and 1987, SUN made a new technological leap by incorporating RISC technology developed under (D)ARPA's auspices.[27]

What impact did (D)ARPA efforts have? First, (D)ARPA rearranged much of the governance structures for the computer and semiconductor industries: the academic community was reintegrated; a new cross-

26. Ibid., p.17-B-7.
27. This story is told in detail in ibid., pp.17-1- 32; 17-A-1 - A-4; and 17-B-1 - B-14.

industry communications network was created and nurtured; and an additional basis for intra-industry cooperation was promoted through the open architecture emphasis and the reduction of single proprietary systems. Second, (D)ARPA provided a critical intervention at the point of governance structure failure and in the face of barriers to collective action by other governance institutions. Third, (D)ARPA intervention contributed to significant technological advances in the semiconductor industries at a pace and in a manner that almost certainly would not have come in the absence of such intervention. (D)ARPA played the key role in the creation of an innovation network within the integrated circuit and computer industries. This innovation network increased the rate of innovation and led to the creation of several new firms and much greater industry dynamism.

4. CONCLUSIONS

The theoretical perspective offered in this paper helps to illuminate and give meaning to the events of the case study of (D)ARPA and VLSI. Though in no sense a 'test' of the theory, this exercise does establish a basis for further research. We identified a problem - slowing rates of innovation - emerging from failures in the existing governance structures in semiconductors and computers. The highly competitive setting, combined with large R&D costs, contributed to a focus on incremental changes in existing technology. And the presence of many firms, with a shared expectation of operating in an exclusive, proprietary environment, created barriers not only to more rapid innovation but equally to collective action to solve this problem. (D)ARPA, a specially situated unit of the state, was positioned to recognize the problem and to act to resolve it. (D)ARPA was at the intersection of information and communication about the situation in both industries; it was able to formulate a strategy with high credibility based on these contacts and past successes; and it moved to provide the public goods needed to advance these industries. The effect of these actions was to reconstruct significant elements of the governance structures of these industries and thereby increase the pace of innovation.

Very little detailed research exists on (D)ARPA and essentially no work using theoretical categories based in political economy. We believe the approach in this paper offers a rethinking of business–government relations and highlights a significant actor in high technology development. Furthermore, our theoretical perspective advances the ability to understand industrial governance structures and identifies, in a nuanced way, an affirmative and essential role for state actors in the relationships among the institutions in an industry. But this perspective demands comparative investigation: additional (D)ARPA cases; other USA cases such as Microelectronics and Computer Technology Corporation (MCC); cases from Europe, such as the Joint European Submicron Silicon Initiative (JESSI); from Japan, such as VLSI and HDTV; and from the formation of strategic alliances among firms. To date, we have lacked a theoretical perspective that permitted comparison of such diverse instances of business–government cooperation.

2. Economic Nationalism and the Global Economy

Robert T. Kudrle

1. INTRODUCTION

Economic discrimination based on the nationality or jurisdiction of the actor continues to play a very important role in the global economy. Until quite recently, of course, it was *expected* that non-nationals would be treated differently from nationals - whether real persons or corporations. Under what circumstances is it in a state's interest to discriminate in favour of its own citizens (or residents) and firms or activities taking place within its territory and when is it damaging?[1] When is it theoretically possible but either technically unfeasible or offensive to other international actors? This chapter seeks some summary and approximate answers to those questions based on a specific conception of the national interests.

This chapter will consider a broad range of economic issues. To do this, much detail must necessarily be sacrificed. None the less, many major problems will be considered. The analysis focuses on the goals and policies of the industrial countries, but some of the analysis may be relevant to other states as well.

The investigation turns upon a definition of economic nationalism. Although a search of the literature revealed no definition that could be of service here, economic nationalism can be defined as any official practice that distinguishes between domestic and foreign economic agents for purposes of applying economic policies.[2]

1. For some purposes, it is important to draw a distinction between a citizen and a permanent resident. For simplicity, the distinction will not normally be made in this paper.
2. It will be noted immediately that the definition does not involve private economic

Several approaches to the problem might be attempted. The one employed here links two summary schemes developed from a consideration of national goals and the policies of economic nationalism. The first simplification aims to capture the national goals that should plausibly guide public policies if such policies really serve the national interest. The second summarizes an endless list of discriminatory policies into a manageable set of policy clusters. Governments practise economic nationalism by determining who is allowed to participate commercially on the national territory and in what spheres, by controlling international trade and by the discriminatory manipulation of other policies, typically to favour nationals over non-nationals.[3] By approaching the subject in this way, many issues can be treated straightforwardly.

The rational choice approach to foreign policy favoured by the author seeks a set of national goals that appear fundamental in two respects: they cannot be further reduced or summarized and they appear to be universal among modern states. The three goals are prosperity,[4] security and autonomy (Kudrle and Bobrow, 1982), and all are equally important. The physical safety of an individual can often be assumed after capitulation to a foreign power and such a defeat need not lead to a decline in the material standard of living for the vast majority of the country's citizens. What is necessarily lost is the ability to be *maître chez nous*, an extremely important goal for most polities. A group must be self-conscious in its desire for autonomy. Beyond that, its ambitions may range from, at minimum, a desire to remain self-conscious to, at maximum, an attempt to avoid any foreign influence. A desire for autonomy then is very closely akin to a sense of nationalism.[5]

nationalism, whether based on xenophobia or on profit-seeking collusion; moreover, it does not involve official discrimination in such closely related areas as permitted foreign political activity.

3. An increasingly important issue with which this paper will not deal is extraterritoriality, the practice of attempting to apply domestic law in foreign countries. Critics would claim that extraterritorality involves an inappropriate *failure* to discriminate between domestic and foreign.
4. 'Prosperity' in this paper is measured by the size of the national pie and not how it is sliced. All economic change creates differential gains and in most cases actual losers. The usually correct assumption by the latter that they will not be compensated after a change – even though they could be – underlies much of the political opposition to economic change in general and globalization in particular.
5. A nation is defined by Yael Tamir (1995 p.425) as 'a community whose members

This way of presenting the three national goals defends their irreducibility, but do others belong on the list? A fourth goal – standing – has also been suggested, but while the regard of non-nationals for one's own nation may be important it appears less universal than the others.[6]

The sufficiency of the list can be further challenged. Many would question the absence of a specific concern for the environment, but that concern in the industrial countries stems mainly from the contribution of the environment to material welfare rather than for its own sake. Hence – for the present at least – it can be treated under the rubric of prosperity.

Some might assert that, just as altruism appears important as a source of collective utility within a polity, a parallel motivation internationally should also be recognized. Several countries in northern Europe spend as much on foreign assistance as they do on national security, and any tangible gain from such assistance is difficult to discern. On the other hand, the percentage of GDP devoted to aid by most of the larger countries has dropped precipitously since the end of the cold war. It may be that, at some future time, the welfare of non-nationals will be important enough in national policy that a descriptively accurate array of goals must include it, but such inclusion would now seem premature.[7]

Viewed from the standpoint of economic theory, the three goals of prosperity, security and autonomy can be considered to be collective

share feelings of fraternity, substantial distinctiveness, and exclusivity, as beliefs in a common ancestry and a continuous genealogy...They thus seek to secure for themselves a public sphere where they can express their identity, practice their culture, and educate their young.' Although such concerns lie beyond the scope of this essay, the failure of state boundaries to align with groups desiring autonomy poses an important problem in international relations. The concept of autonomy is further discussed in Kudrle, 1991, pp.402–3.

6. The strongest case for the independent importance of standing can be made for nations that are well placed to gain recognition or influence in the first place. In most cases, this appears to be largely the province of the major states. Bobrow and Kudrle (1991) refer to the same goal as 'assertion'.
7. Assistance to those within the nation-state can be made conditional upon certain recipient behaviour, while, because of nominal state sovereignty, the international analogy breaks down. For example, it could be plausibly argued that even if *all* of the foreign assistance of the major powers had been devoted to India over the past 40 years, less material advance would have occurred than if the Indian government had undertaken certain fundamental reforms that would arguably have been unacceptable to the majority of Indians. Whatever the truth of such an argument, any plausibility provides a barrier to substantially increased international assistance.

goods pursued by foreign policy. Moreover, the goals must be traded off against each other, otherwise, for example, there would be no limit on the level of defence spending that a country would establish in the face of danger unless it could be shown that additional resources had zero (or negative) defence relevance.[8] Nevertheless, there is no presumption that a policy's stated relation with a national goal should be taken at face value. Leaving incompetent policy design aside, modern approaches to policy determination stress the extend to which specific interests may advance their own private objectives (income being the chief among them) by cloaking their quest in claims about the national interest. Even policies that do clearly serve national goals operate in a world of increasing interconnectedness. Economic nationalism by a country may either increase or decrease its own welfare while leaving the rest of the world either unchanged or poorer. In some cases economic nationalism may even be an element of a larger policy that increases the welfare of other states. Therefore, this study will attempt not only to match policy clusters with national goals but also to evaluate the effects on other states and their likely reactions.

2. FACTOR ACCESS AND DISCRIMINATION IN DOMESTIC TREATMENT

International economics is distinguished by the immobility of at least some factors of production. But that immobility is itself subject to policy influence. Capital has become highly mobile in recent decades, while labour has remained largely within its original national territory. Land does not move.

One cluster of economic nationalist restriction aims to control factor participation - either labour or capital - in the domestic market.

8. During the height of the cold war most US opponents of American defence expenditure did not argue that most expenditures above the levels actually experienced had zero or negative defence significance, although that was the precise line of attack adopted by some critics of some programmes, for example the Strategic Defense Initiative ('Star Wars').

Labour

Immigration

The easiest policy of economic nationalism towards the influx of labour for economic (or any other) purpose is simply to prevent it.[9] The grounds for such practice include an antipathy towards the general behaviour of outsiders, doubts about their loyalty in times of national crisis and their competition with specific parts of the pre-existing economy. The last factor suggests that immigration will attract opposition even if it serves some conception of the national interest.

Economic theory is predicated on the notion that voluntary trade enriches both parties. Textbooks therefore make observations such as that 'trade in goods, labour services and capital have broadly similar motivations and results' (Krugman and Obstfeld, 1994, p.155). Yet the calculation of national gains in even the simplest models that employ only two homogeneous factors, labour and capital, turns heavily on who 'us' is. Johnson (1967) demonstrated that immigration is beneficial for the original inhabitants of a country as a group if their capital:labour ratio differs from that of the newcomers. However, assuming that the newcomers bring less capital than the average per capita endowment, and in the absence of economies of scale, wages are driven down, so those living on labour earnings alone are clearly hurt by the inflow unless they receive some of the augmented earnings of domestic capital. Moreover, if the migration is permanent and 'they' become 'us' then the lower marginal product of labour also pulls down the average product of labour which translates directly into lower per capita income.[10] A parallel set of calculations can be done for the country of emigration.

9. Indeed there are many historical examples of individuals or groups even being denied the right of residence and economic participation granted by a previous government.
10. If the newcomers bring in a greater endowment of capital per person, then the country as a whole becomes more capital-rich; temporary migration of the 'package' enriches the pre-existing citizenry as a group and permanent migration (when 'they' become 'us') raises per capita income yet more. The latter case helps illuminate the logic of special immigration rules for the wealthy for which Canada has become well known and which are also found in US regulations. An influx of unusually productive 'human capital' may be analyzed similarly.

Complex as it is, such analysis is only the beginning of a consideration of the impact of labour mobility on prosperity and public policy in this area, as in most others, is not dominated by coherent concerns about prosperity in any case.

Temporary or permanent immigration is an important policy issue in virtually every modern country. In theory, labour services can be obtained without permanent residence or citizenship. The German 'guest worker' (*Gastarbeiter*) programme of the 1960s aimed to realize gains from trade in labour services for both seller and purchaser. The worker's marginal product (wage) is higher in the new area, and non-marginal increments of the new labour supply raise national income beyond the wage bill paid to the incoming workers.[11] In fact, the male guest workers established families with Germans and with female immigrants, and the German government subsequently found many migrants impossible to repatriate. As Max Frisch put it so memorably, 'we sought labour power - people came'.[12] France has had a somewhat similar experience with North Africans.

Discrimination by nationality may affect earning opportunities within the receiving country. The temporary work programme in Germany and some other countries confined work opportunities to specific tasks: this was consonant with the purpose of bringing in workers only to meet narrowly defined needs. The United States and some other countries allow foreign students pursuing degrees to engage only in limited income earning activities. In general, countries allow permanent residents essentially full access to domestic employment opportunities, with only a few exceptions. Historically, citizenship has been necessary to gain security clearances for defence-related jobs in many countries, but that criterion has diminished in importance in some countries, including the United States (Executive Order 12968, 5 August 1995). Access to regulated professions in some USA states is sometimes restricted to citizens, although such restrictions have been widely attacked as completely indefensible.

11. This is the standard marginal productivity theory upon which much of conventional microeconomics is built. National income in the sending country may go down with permanent emigration because, instead of trading labour services in the course of which people work abroad and send remittances home, permanent migration may reduce the resource base. In the real world, the cases blur: temporary workers spend part of their income in the local economy, and permanent migrants make remittances.
12. Cited in Franz, 1981, p.596 (my translation).

Part of the opposition in Europe towards permanent migrants undoubtedly rests on cultural grounds, but the non-return of the unskilled *Gastarbeiter* may also contain a threat to prosperity resulting from the taxation and expenditure practices of the modern welfare state – a critical issue not included in simple economic models. The original plan was regarded as particularly favourable for the receiving country because some major social investments, notably basic education, had been borne elsewhere. Yet when those same 'bargain' workers stay long enough to receive social benefits for themselves and their families, the calculation may change dramatically. Borjas's research on recent USA experience (1994) reveals that unskilled immigrants appear to take more from the economy in social benefits than they pay in taxes; moreover, their productivity does not rise quickly over succeeding generations. Although no entirely comparable research has been done in Europe, welfare benefits are higher there than in the USA and unemployment is chronically higher, so the mechanisms may operate even more strongly there.

Other factors can be placed on the positive side of the ledger and could tip the policy towards permissiveness on grounds of prosperity. With constant or increasing returns to scale, a non-marginal increment of migrant labour will add more to the economy than it takes in wages, and newcomers help divide the cost of genuinely public goods.[13] Most analysts do not find these factors to be very powerful for the USA however, and one suspects they are less likely to tip the analysis for Europe or Japan, where population density is already much higher. Permanent immigration by the unskilled almost certainly lowers prosperity for previous residents as a group.

By a parallel argument, the migration of the especially productive[14] not only raises national income but also adds more to tax revenue than is obtained in services. Unless there are sharp diseconomies of scale, the prosperity of the receiving state is increased and opposition to their migration must rest on other grounds. In most cases, the newcomers could not plausibly detract from national security, and opposition to the

13. Such goods (defence research, weather forecasting) that a group of any size can benefit from equally account for only a small and probably decreasing part of a modern state's expenditure: see note 11.
14. Tanzi (1995) uses the term 'especially talented'. It should be noted that the same argument applies to the especially wealthy, if their immigration changes the locus of their investments: see note 10.

migration of highly productive persons appears in nearly all states to rest on cultural grounds related to autonomy. To pick an extreme example, Japan appears not only to have rejected the migration of the unskilled but has shown no interest in attracting the extraordinarily able either. '"Japaneseness" has long been regarded not so much as a matter of race but rather as a reflection of qualities that are inbred, even divine, and that cannot be acquired by others' (Weiner, 1995, pp.63–8). The effect of the newcomers on autonomy could be regarded as an 'externality' of their simply being in the country. Externalities are unmarketed positive or negative spillovers to the rest of the society that result when economic agents pursue their own ends.

Permanent labour migration is likely to change the average productivity of the citizenry. Thus, while national income increases, the market distribution of that income will change along with the generation and disposition of tax revenues with unchanged public policies. Moreover, if the migrants become citizens or otherwise gain political rights exercised in part on the basis of economic self-interest, the distribution of income may be further affected by additional policy changes.[15]

Overall, immigration, depending on its magnitude and origin, will present a threat to autonomy that differs greatly according to the type of receiving country, but immigration by the unskilled is likely to threaten the prosperity of any welfare state. These effects do not depend on the formal granting of citizenship but could be exacerbated by it because that status always brings greater political rights.[16]

Emigration

The desire to leave a country may be variously motivated, but the most recent attempts to prevent outward migration have a declared rationale of economic loss unacceptable to the abandoned state. Walter Ulbricht justified the Berlin Wall on the basis of the state's investment in the

15. And because all distribution changes involve changed incentives, such policy changes may in turn change total income and its growth path as well.
16. Thus, while immigration by the unskilled is likely to lower average income in the receiving country and especially to disadvantage unskilled domestic labour in its market impact, a political alliance with the newcomers could actually raise the final incomes of the unskilled.

emigrant's human capital as did the Soviet Union when it refused to allow its citizens to migrate without paying an impractically high tax.[17]

Although the exact status of the right to emigrate under international law is subject to some dispute, some countries, including the United States, have regarded it as a fundamental human right since the middle of the nineteenth century, and no major state now practises general control of emigration (Hanum, 1987).

Implications

The control of immigration will remain that part of economic nationalism least dominated by narrow calculations of economic prosperity. If that were the only objective, the rich countries would be competing with each other for the most talented people in the world. Even crowded countries could easily absorb a substantial number of persons whose contribution to the economy would be many times what they would ever consume. In the future, such competition may make it difficult for each polity to engage in what it would regard as appropriate income redistribution because the objects of high taxation could escape to other jurisdictions. In fact, very little of this has yet been observed. One would expect to see it first in North America and especially in the European Union where barriers to labour mobility have completely disappeared, while tax and expenditure policies remain entirely in the hands of the individual states (Kudrle, 1996).

The net uncompensated flow of human capital that now takes place among the developed countries is quite modest, and what frictions have arisen have come from the differential market earnings - not from official actions. Thus, however minor, the difficulties result from openness and not from economic nationalism. Quite a different problem appears from the perspective of countries that are not the primary focus of this study. India, for example, makes large human capital transfers every year (Bhagwati and Wilson, 1989), but these persons also make great contributions to the home country in the form of remittances, technology transfers, business contacts and political influence abroad (Weiner, 1996).[18]

17. There were other declared grounds for blocking departure, especially the possible leakage of state secrets.
18. While the failure of the richer countries to import more unskilled labour from the poorer could be seen as a failure to help alleviate their population problems, the relative numbers suggest that this argument cannot be taken very seriously. While

Capital

Portfolio Investment

In standard economic analysis, international trade in capital services (inter-temporal trade) starts with the same presumption of mutual gain as other forms of trade. Where the borrowing is a public obligation, however, this result turns on the use of the resources borrowed to increase the productivity of the receiving country. Otherwise - just as with domestic public borrowing - succeeding generations will be worse off.

The difference between borrowing from home and from abroad comes when the bills cannot be paid - by either private or official debtors. In the past the USA and other countries have used the inability to pay back loans as sufficient reason to intervene in a state's internal affairs, and, while such interventions are no longer recognized as appropriate, the inability to make debt payments has the potential to bring a country to the door of the International Monetary Fund with a consequent loss of autonomy in setting national economic priorities. This loss of autonomy would be so unacceptable to the higher-income countries that they have not come close to risking it, as many poorer ones did as recently as a decade ago. Borrowing from abroad within the range observed for the developed countries does not therefore represent a significant threat to autonomy (or security).

Countries have frequently restricted the outflow of portfolio capital. Under fixed exchange rates uncontrolled outflows made official defence of a currency's value more difficult. Even under the present regime of flexible rates, the free movement of capital creates problems of exchange rate instability which may sometimes seriously inconvenience the government.[19] Although the control of foreign lending lowers national income, the direct losses are mainly to upper income persons, while much of labour may actually be better off. In recent years, however, most governments - even those representing labour - have

some specific developed countries may have played the role of demographic safety valve for some small developing countries, the maximum number of unskilled workers ever absorbed by any single developed country or by developed countries as a whole is minuscule when compared with the numbers of persons added to the poorer countries each year. And 'crowding' is not those countries' principal deficiency in any case: see Olson, 1996.

19. These difficulties should not be exaggerated, however (Krugman, 1996, p.169).

concluded that virtually any restriction on portfolio capital hinders the flexibility necessary to take maximum advantage of direct investment and trade.

Direct Investment Inflow

Foreign direct investment (FDI) raises many of the same issues as borrowing and lending, along with many others. Incoming foreign direct investment (IFDI) implies both foreign control of domestic enterprise and, in nearly all cases, at least some non-nationals resident in the host country do exercise that control. Such investment is properly regarded as a package of internationally mobile resources, and a voluminous literature has been developed on its economic costs and benefits (Caves, 1986).

Historically most states have been hesitant about IFDI. Some countries, notably France and Canada, have at various times in the past attempted to screen all incoming investment (Safarian, 1993, pp.79–287). In the first decades after the Second World War Japan sought the technology of the multinationals through licensing. The precise mix of autonomy and prosperity motives underlying Japanese behaviour is unclear. Japan's need for capital and overseas marketing expertise had to be balanced against the loss of autonomy that IFDI would have implied: the increased integration of foreigners into the Japanese economy. This would have meant the introduction of management behaviour towards competitors, complementary firms and labourthat was almost certainly thought to be socially disruptive. Many of these same concerns motivated European policy-makers, particularly in France, but the cultural gap was smaller, and the need for the resources of multinational corporations was greater. Most particularly, many in Europe saw disruptive USA business practices as necessary to spur productivity growth. In Canada, the experience with screening from 1974 to 1985 accompanied slow growth and was ultimately abandoned.[20]

The increased economic interdependence within and among firms and the relationship of those connections to the development and transmission of technology has rendered obsolete many previous views

20. It is most unlikely that the screening *caused* the slow growth because evidence that the screening limited direct investment significantly is very weak: see Kudrle, 1995b.

about picking and choosing among discrete pieces of IFDI. In general, whatever was true in the past, a general posture of openness towards IFDI would now appear to be warranted on prosperity grounds for virtually any country, and nearly all recent empirical studies suggest a positive effect of an FDI inflow on the economic welfare of the recipient country (Dunning, 1985; Kudrle, 1991; Graham and Krugman, 1995).

Most countries have blocked IFDI into a number of specific sectors: most frequently controlled are transportation, communications, public utilities, natural resources, land, and defence industries. The record indicates that most of these restrictions were originally justified on the basis of national security.[21]

The ease with which liberalization of IFDI, including that in most restricted sectors, took place throughout the industrialized world in the 1980s suggests not only that defence no longer justified such restrictions, but that in many cases it may never have been more than a pretext for protection. For example, many public utilities around the world were recently opened to foreign investors as part of large-scale privatization accompanying broader market-oriented reforms. Resistance to reform came mainly from the national producers of equipment used in these industries that could no longer be given non-transparent preference (McGowan and Thomas, 1989).[22]

Continuing restrictions on foreign ownership of broadcasting and sometimes other mass media are often justified on grounds of autonomy. Canada, for example, has declined to bargain with foreigners (including especially the United States in their bilateral Free Trade Agreement or in the subsequent trilateral agreement including Mexico) on ownership of what it calls its 'cultural industries', including broadcasting, sound and visual recording, film making and distribution, and all forms of publishing. As many critics have pointed out, however,

21. The most comprehensive international survey of such restrictions among the industrial countries, was prepared nearly a decade ago; for a more complete analysis than can be presented here, see Kudrle, 1993.
22. National security is typically much more directly involved in national discrimination in water transport where subsidies to shipbuilding, restrictions on the nationality of crews, and restrictions on foreign ownership are frequently bound together in a complex package. At least in the case of the United States, however, present arrangements attempt to deliver a measure of naval readiness with extraordinary inefficiency. Reforms measures frequently involve the complete abolition of discrimination in foreign ownership of USA shipping (White, 1988, pp.101–15).

restrictions on foreign ownership are neither necessary nor sufficient to control content in the way that would preserve a distinctly Canadian viewpoint (Globerman and Vining, 1984).

In the United States, which has historically had no general screening and controlled sectors coinciding largely with federally regulated industries, the Exon–Florio Amendment to the Trade Act of 1988 gave the president power to block IFDI on 'national security' grounds just as other countries were considerable liberalizing their IFDI restrictions. When examined closely, however, the rationale for exclusive ownership by nationals of even defence-relevant industry becomes suspect. First, far from driving the civilian economy from 'spin-offs' as it once did, innovative military technology is now very likely to 'spin on' from successful developments in the non-military sector. This problem is posed by 'dual-use technologies' which increasingly dominate because of the much larger size of civilian markets and the limited military aspirations of one of the most important high-technology players, Japan.

As Moran has argued persuasively and influentially (1990, 1993), an attempt to ensure national dominance by wholly nationally-owned firms in all aspects of advanced technologies with military relevance would be extraordinarily expensive and probably impossible – even for the United States. Instead, an objective of maintaining access to all militarily-relevant goods and services should be the aim, and in some circumstances this may involve the encouragement or even the requirement of foreign direct investment (Moran, 1990; Graham and Krugman, 1995, pp.162–9).

Critics of foreign ownership express concern over the integrity of information and the national control of technologies and products developed. The former issue turns largely on the security clearance of persons actually involved in technology and product development, while the latter is governed by national export control laws and a coordinating group called the New Forum. If the participation of foreign-owned firms in military R&D and production created special security risks, this could be regarded as a negative externality. In fact, little of this problem has been discovered – at least for the United States (United States General Accounting Office, 1996).

If the integrity of information can be assured and there is agreement on legal control of technologies and products, there seems little reason to bar interpenetration of the military production bases of close allies

(Kudrle and Bobrow, 1996).[23] Such simultaneous cooperation recognizes that a foreign monopoly of a military-relevant technology is dangerous and that an attempt by any country - including the USA - either to monopolise or completely duplicate such technologies on domestic soil would be unfeasible, both economically (excessively expensive) and politically (other countries would not condone such sales-limiting behaviour at their expense).

In fact enticement, rather than rejection, may become a serious international relations problem if countries increasingly believe that non-marketed benefits accrue from having advanced-technology foreign firms operating in the local territory (Ostry, 1992; Ostry and Nelson, 1995). This issue is closely related to problems of strategic trade policy and government subsidies for R&D, to be discussed later in this chapter. Some but not all problems of either positive and negative discrimination are overcome by adopting the twofold objectives of the OECD for foreign investors: freedom of establishment and domestic treatment (Hoekman, 1992).

Direct Investment Outflow

Outgoing foreign direct investment (OFDI) has historically been subjected to various controls, mainly derived from an attempt to control the capital involved, although it has virtually disappeared in recent years except for the shunning of pariah states. When OFDI was construed largely as a capital flow, the arguments against a free outflow from a nationalist perspective were cogent: corporate taxes could shift corporate decisions away from an investment pattern than would be optimal from a national point of view. Domestic investment yielded a return equal to the gross earnings of capital, but foreign investment only to its net earnings - because in the former case the tax revenue accrues to the home country treasury while in the latter case it disappears into a foreign coffer (Caves, 1982, pp.226–37). In recent decades, however, capital flow has increasingly been seen as only one of several economically significant components of FDI (Caves, 1982, pp.279–99) and not necessarily the most important. In particular, the home country can realize significant gains from an OFDI outflow

23. For a recent discussion that stresses the need for such understandings in the context of trade rather than investment, see Center for Strategic and International Studies, 1996.

despite the tax disadvantage.[24] Moreover, the proponents of a restrictive position in the United States became increasingly vulnerable to the argument that their scenario for national gain, however weak, rested heavily on a lack of retaliation. As the stock of FDI in the United States came to approximate USA FDI invested abroad, this became an unavoidable concern.

Implications

The previous arguments allowed for the possibility that some restrictions on the outflow of both portfolio and direct investment might increase national prosperity in some circumstances. Although the subject remains disputed, it may also be true that the closure of some sectors to IFDI may have contributed to greater national income in some countries in the past. None the less, most observers agree that attempting to calculate the gains and losses from firm- or industry-specific policy initiatives with respect to foreign direct investment by comparison with market outcomes would be extraordinarily difficult even in the absence of the retaliation that they would almost certainly trigger. In fact, nearly all the richest countries (and much of the rest of the world) are now more open to direct investment inflows and outflows than ever before (UNCTAD, 1995), and the OECD has just launched an initiative to gain formal agreement on basic rules to govern both restriction and enticement.

The contribution of restrictions on IFDI to the goals of autonomy and security appear generally suspect. No known evidence suggests that commerce in entertainment is less profit-driven when pursued by domestic rather than foreign owners. Security concerns must recognize the symbiosis between civilian and military technology, which often suggests encouragement of IFDI rather than blockage.

How do nationalist capital-control policies affect the prosperity of other economies? International economics teaches that a 'small' country can take essentially any action it chooses without affecting the rest of the world when it operates in competitive markets. In fact, the failure of most individual states to borrow or lend in portfolio markets would make little difference – particularly if they abstained from both

24. Most obviously, the multinational corporation may sell abroad at prices well above the opportunity cost of the resources employed in the home country (their value in their next best use).

at the same time, because any country's *net* position is typically very small relative to world capital markets. If the United States, France, Germany, the UK or Japan dropped out of one side or the other, however, the impact would certainly be felt. But it is a moot point, because such capital movements are the handmaiden of trade and direct investment, and these activities are really vital for every state.

Because multinational corporations are now regarded as vital conduits for the latest technology, official policies aimed at confining their activities to the home market would be regarded elsewhere as a sign of economic hostility - and one in which no modern state is likely to engage. On the other hand, all impediments to IFDI frustrate foreigners because they lower home country earnings, which is manifest in less favourable terms of trade (the ratio of export to import prices).[25] Where IFDI is not formally blocked, foreigners have an interest in making the domestic economy as open to newcomers as possible. This sometimes involves policy areas well beyond IFDI, as is illustrated by the 1990 USA Structural Impediments Initiative with Japan.[26]

3. DISCRIMINATION AIMED AT BUYERS AND SELLERS LOCATED ABROAD

The most important national discrimination in the past, and among the most important today, concerns government restrictions on private and public commerce with other states. Past and present restrictions apply to both imports and exports.

It must be noted immediately that most trade laws around the world consider only the territory from which a product is imported and not the nationality of value added. For example, the fact that the firm from which Belgian exports a certain product into Canada is wholly owned by Canadians (and perhaps has a large part of its payroll devoted to Canadian nationals temporarily in Belgium) will play no role in determining the duty payable. Thus, territorial policies result in a disadvantage for national factors of production that are producing imports for

25. And not, as economists never fail to point out, because they worsen the offended country's trade balance, which is likely to be only trivially affected.
26. The USA approached Japan on a broad range of issues: saving and investment, land policy, distribution arrangements, exclusionary business practices, cross-firm trading and financial agreements, and pricing policies (Ito, 1992, p.376).

the home country as well as for entirely foreign enterprises.[27] Such considerations may greatly complicate the calculation of national gains and losses from protection.

Discrimination Against Imports

Theory suggests a role for economic nationalism by 'large countries' in devising an 'optimum tariff'. When a country can affect the ratio of its exports-to-import prices by moderating its demand for imports, national welfare can be improved - sometimes even when foreigners retaliate (Johnson, 1953–54). At best, however, the nationalist gainers gain less than the rest of the world loses. In fact, the optimum tariff has never been more than a theoretical oddity: there is no evidence of any major country actually basing a national tariff policy on it (Krugman and Obstfeld, 1994, p.232).

In sharp contrast, the 'infant industry argument' has been used as a justification for much nineteenth and twentieth century tariff protection. Inevitably, the argument received its strongest support from important competing industries. Economists have demonstrated that even temporary protection to allow domestic industry to 'get on its feet' could be justified, a subsidy is superior to protection. Moreover, for infant industries really to be socially justified by the losses they impose on the purchase of goods they must be expected to generate non-marketed benefits to the broader economy beyond the earnings with the industry. If this were not so, and protection yielded long-run industry profits, private firms should be willing to bear the temporary 'infant's' losses.

The history of most countries, although not all, suggests that the infants fail to grow up, and temporary protection becomes permanent.[28] Japan, however, appears to have been an exception in many industries:

27. The crudeness of the system in terms of isolating nationality is further illustrated by the fact that protection is typically levied on the entire value of a product and not on its foreign value added. Duty is thus payable on that part of the import's content that may have been originally exported from the home country. Exceptions are included in special arrangements with developing countries such as the *maquiladora* system between the USA and Mexico where only the value added is subject to duty (Caves, Frankel and Jones, 1996, pp.186–7).
28. Many were alarmed when the GATT was modified in the 1960s by the general system of preferences which allowed developing countries protection otherwise unavailable. This seemed to ratify the idea that protection was a useful ingredient of development, a position that many economists viewed with great scepticism.

there, temporary protection often yielded industries that became internationally competitive over quite a short period of time (Ito, 1992, p.301).

Although Britain and some other countries embraced free trade for decades in the nineteenth century, many other countries, including the United States, did not. It was not until the Reciprocal Trade Agreements Act of 1934 that Congress developed a means of re-vectoring the politics of trade so that export interests *in general* were mobilized to combat import competing forces *in general* (Destler, 1995, pp.3–40).

Since the Second World War virtually all modern states have supported or acquiesced in ever freer trade, as export and import interests ascended. The GATT Rounds, based on the same political logic as the Reciprocal Trade Agreements, reduced the average tariff on manufactured goods from 40 per cent in 1947 to less than 4 per cent in 1994 (Caves, Frankel and Jones, 1996, p.219). But at the same time as this development was occurring the developed countries refined other measures that became known as 'administered protection'.[29] The GATT recognizes a number of exceptions to the lower national tariffs 'bound' by multilateral negotiation. Rapid surges of imports for whatever reasons can be countered by temporary protection, but so too can imports that are allegedly 'dumped' by private firms or that are subsidized by foreign governments. Many studies confirm that the politics underlying the operation of these mechanisms (which now exists in the USA, Japan, the European Community and a number of newly industrializing countries as well) push them strongly in the direction of serving uncompetitive firms and industries and against the interests of the sellers of imports and all users of the imported products. Most observers also agree that nearly all these restrictions in all countries lower the national income of the importing state.

In many countries, lingering conventional barriers are used alongside administered protection, not to preserve or build up industries, but simply to allow them to decline at a slower rate than would otherwise be experienced. Their trading partners typically see this as an unacceptable form of economic nationalism because it places burdens on them that they see as properly borne more fully by the importing state. If disruptive innovation arises from within a national economy, official

29. Regulatory measures concerning health, safety and the environment have also often been designed to maximize protective impact.

remedial action only rarely involves a sacrifice of profits by the innovating firm.[30]

Analytically respectable national interest arguments against 'dumping' and foreign subsidization stress the possibility that selling at below the full-cost can drive home firms out of a market, after which monopoly power could be exercised against the importing country. Japanese firms entering certain consumer electronics branches in the United States in the 1970s and 1980s were accused of such behaviour, but there was never any strong evidence of collusive price-raising following the demise of the US industry (Scherer, 1994, pp.78–87). More importantly, most economists believe that truly anti-competitive practices by foreign firms can be satisfactorily treated by the application of the country's competition laws without special discrimination against foreigners. The predatory pricing that is alleged to accompany 'dumping' could be attacked under Section II of the Sherman Act, Section 86 of the Treaty of Rome, and Japan's Fair Trade Act (Scherer and Ross, 1990, pp.483–8).

An emphasis on positive externalities provides one pillar for recent defences of nationalist protection called 'strategic trade policy', a line of argument that some claim to have destroyed the persuasiveness of free trade doctrines (Prestowitz, 1994). Some nationalist policy makers believe that certain, usually high-tech, industries will generate positive effects beyond the firms generating them; therefore protection is justified. Unlike the traditional infant industry case, however, only a handful of 'cutting edge' firms (at most) exist in a limited number of relevant industries and a small number of firms and (relevant) governments create a strategic 'game' in which winning and losing governments are well aware of the stakes and their performance in the game. The potential for international conflict inherent in such 'games' cannot be denied.

The other strand of strategic trade theory turns on economies of scale and accumulated output at the level of the firm. Through some form of protection that garners an especially large market for a national firm, the government may ensure that one of its firms gets ahead and stays ahead of foreign rivals, winning a long-run stream of profits to bolster

30. This statement is more completely true now than in earlier times. Such measures as retail practice maintenance, and, in the United States, the Robinson–Patman Act (now seldom enforced) suggest measures that appear aimed to soften competition by making rapid market penetration more difficult for innovators (Kudrle, 1995a).

national income. Such policies are 'strategic' for the same reason as in the first case.

Although the 'strategic trade' arguments developed in the 1980s were genuinely innovative, many economists who developed and tested them advise against their employment as national policy (Krugman, 1987). Retaliation by rival states can lead to destructive competition, but even without a direct foreign response many doubt whether states in general (and the United States in particular) have the economic and technical forecasting knowledge necessary to create national value rather than destroying it by providing protection for activities that fail more than they succeed. At all events, strategic trade theory is likely to lead to policies that fail to maximize global welfare.

Concerns about autonomy have frequently driven import policy. The consumption of desired foreign information and entertainment is believed to erode the collective sense of uniqueness, and the erosion can be considered an externality of that consumption. France (with the largest film industry of any Western country outside the United States) pushed successfully in the Uruguay Round to prevent trade in cultural products from being covered, while the United States pushed strongly for inclusion. Despite the temporary European victory, it appears that the protection of films and broadcasting through the use of quotas could at best serve as a short-term palliative. While some past policies have successfully pushed content in a nationalist direction, this was far more feasible when there were only a few choices of radio and television. Now, cable and satellite technologies have multiplied the number of choices so dramatically that, even if every channel (or package of channels) were obliged to offer the 50 per cent European content required by the EU, all viewers would, at any given time, face a plethora of non-European options (however the latter are defined) that is growing ever larger.

A similar situation will pertain in most of Asia. It seems reasonable to assume that, under current conditions, the only successful attempts to control national exposure to a huge volume of compelling foreign communication will be mounted by distinctly non-democratic governments. A typical citizen is simply unwilling to forgo very much choice in entertainment to serve the goal of autonomy - even when that goal is accepted as very important.

Which kinds of governments face the greatest challenges from trade and investment in cultural products, mainly emanating from the United

States? Some of the democratic states that have most agonized over the issue, notably Canada, have been those that by international standards are already most similar to the United States - doing so in an attempt to maintain those distinctions that remain. A society such as Japan must view the problem differently. US popular culture can scarcely provide any immediate or even medium-term threat to Japanese uniqueness. Over the longer term, however, the real cultural stakes are dramatically higher because there is so much difference to erode.

For Canada, Europe or Japan, government control of choice through protection appears to be a completely unviable option for retaining cultural autonomy. Even if cultural products are ultimately included in the GATT, however, the only viable option for national cultural support - subsidization of production - will remain an option. While any resulting exports of such subsidized production could be subject to countervailing duties, this retaliation could be invoked only if harm to import-competing industries in the receiving country could be demonstrated.

Much of the most severe trade discrimination against foreigners - quotas and outright import bans - invokes national security as its rationale. Historically, a whole range of industries around the world have successfully made the case that domestic production provides assurance in war and national emergency, but, as Moran (1990) and others have argued, stockpiling is vastly superior to protection for the provision of most of what the military uses in the short-run, while at the advanced end of military needs, an attempt to assure local production by domestic firms would be extraordinarily expensive and probably impossible - even for the United States.

Government purchasing may discriminate against foreigners while it allows the profit motive to animate private trading agents dealing with the same or similar goods. This kind of protection has been more pervasive and powerful than most other types, largely for technical reasons. Governments typically supply their goods and services under monopoly conditions, frequently either directly to the public or to providers which are themselves monopolies. This means that the historically outgunned commercial forces combating protection have typically been particularly mismatched in government procurement. Nonetheless, the logic of the GATT ultimately resulted in the government procurement code of 1981 to open foreign bidding for government purchases on a non-discriminatory basis (Schott, 1994, pp.66–76) that was considerably expanded in the Uruguay Round. The issue needs no special economic analysis because government purchases in most circumstances differ little in consequence from private purchases, and all the arguments for general openness apply in this case as well.

Discrimination Against Exports

Security issues surround the most systematic national controls on exports. During the cold war, the major anti-communist countries - essentially NATO plus Japan - cooperated in the 'Coordinating Committee' or 'COCOM' to prevent militarily-relevant goods and technologies from falling into enemy hands. Since the break-up of the Soviet Union and its empire, COCOM has developed into 'The New Forum' which attempts to keep the militarily relevant technology out of the hands of pariah states. Neither COCOM nor its successor have been entirely successful, partly because of disagreements among members about how much security was purchased at the cost of denial. Traditionally, the USA has been the most cautious of the group, and this caution has been claimed by critics of the US position to have sacrificed foreign sales - not only to other major industrial states but also to other countries, particularly in East Asia (Flamm, 1996, pp.22–5).

Another tool of nationalist export control is the embargo. Such activity gains effectiveness as the embargoing country dominates the supply of the good or goods embargoed or coordinates its activity with other potential suppliers (Mansfield, 1995). The ineffectiveness of the USA wheat embargo against the Soviet Union for its invasion of Afghanistan suggests both conditions. Sometimes embargoes take place for reasons of hostility unrelated to any immediate security threat: the Western refusal to trade with South Africa in the late 1980s provides an example - moreover, one which does not fit neatly with the three overarching goals posited at the beginning of this chapter. The policy was driven by altruistic idealism galvanized in the case of the United States by intensity of feeling by a significant part of the electorate and made very feasible by a very modest price in terms of prosperity.[31]

31. Some embargoes have been justified by prosperity rather than security. A prime example would be the USA refusal to sell soy beans to Japan in 1973 in an attempt to dampen inflationary pressure that the Nixon Administration was already combating with price controls (Cohen, 1994, p.201). The avoidance of inflation, just like the maintenance of social cohesion, is an important social goal that international

Implications

Nearly all documented trade protection around the world has lowered the national income of the countries practising it. Theoretical exceptions to what is generally the best policy - namely, of openness - have usually either not been attempted or been operationalized very poorly. Powerful interests within states have none the less seen their own economic positions ensured or enhanced by the same policies.

Import protection seems seldom to have favoured domestic over non-national interests by providing systematically more favourable access for foreign sources that are intensive in the labour or capital of the importing country. The explanation for this is not hard to find. Over most of this century tariffs have been set through negotiations between or among countries that refer to entire categories of goods traded from their own territories. No discrimination has typically been allowed among the outputs of specific firms or factories with a jurisdiction.[32]

The protection of 'cultural industries' appears increasingly impossible technologically and inconsistent with popular government. Finally, import protection to ensure military preparedness has become obsolete in an era of limited come-as-you-are wars. Some export controls can be justified for security reasons but merely diminish national income unless enforced multilaterally.

Import protection harms foreign interests more if the protecting state is large and the foreign sellers operate with market power, holding other factors constant. The smaller the importing country, the less its diverted demand will lower the prices of exports in other countries and, if the international industry is very competitive, the profits sacrificed per unit of rejected exports will be modest or negligible as well.[33] In a 'normal' case, say the import of a moderately profitable consumer

comity suggests should be pursued in a way that avoids shifting a disproportionate part of the policy's cost to a country's trading partners.

32. And virtually all tariff reductions have been done on a most-favoured-nation basis, which essentially gives the same access to a large number of countries. (Quotas *have* frequently been assigned to specific countries, typically in order to damage them proportionately to their sales when the quota is introduced.)
33. For example, if New Zealand elected to reverse its recent engagement with the international economy and set up a domestic steel industry, the country's low total demand coupled with the very low profitability of that industry would mean that the cost of new Zealand's folly would be borne almost exclusively by New Zealanders with little impact on its trading partners.

durable into a country of average size, the protection would generate losses to the importer but a substantial loss to foreign export industries as well. As a matter of simplicity and equity, the international trading system makes no distinction among states on the basis of size and the damage caused to other states by protection is (nominally) regarded as equally offensive whether practised by New Zealand or Japan.

The newest rationales for protection can really only be used by the largest actors, and 'strategic policies are inherently beggar-thy-neighbour policies'.

Other Policies that Result in Income Shifting

A tempting theoretical objective for economic nationalism is obviously 'to get the foreigner to pay'. The national goals posited earlier significantly do not include the unreciprocated welfare of non-nationals. Standard economic analysis follows this assumption: when additional income is collected from foreigners (including the payment of more taxes by foreigners than they receive in benefits), the net national gain is typically regarded as the fruit of good policy design.

Despite the possibility of aggregate national gain, evidence suggests that the classic instrument of protectionism, the tariff, has seldom been crafted with income-shifting in mind. Moreover, quantitative restrictions have not been administered in a way that maximizes national gain, either. The most popular device of the United States during the 1980s, the so-called 'voluntary export restraints' (VERs), allowed the scarcity value of foreign goods, notably automobiles, to be appropriated by foreign producers rather than by the American government. Because the amounts transferred were so large, observers have puzzled over US motivations. One important analysis suggests two possible motives: an attempt to 'buy off' foreign governments so as to prevent various kinds of retaliation, and an attempt to package the protection through a device that disguises its real effect as much as possible (Caves, Frankel and Jones, 1996, pp.291–2).

Another possible avenue of income shifting lies in policies to cartelize export sales. Although some countries have developed policies to encourage such activity while attempting to isolate collaboration in foreign sales from competitive sales at home, this is both theoretically unpromising and has not generally worked.[34] Raising price–cost margins through collusion abroad usually implies some collusion at home and Auquier and Caves (1979) have shown that, consistent with national wealth-maximization, those countries exporting the greatest share of their manufactured output in the late 1960s had the least stringent general competition policies. And yet the world has changed considerably in the period since then. The development of the European Union left no room for national versus intra-community differences and EU and US competition authorities achieved a landmark agreement on cooperation in 1991 that appears wholly inconsistent with further tolerance of discriminatory enforcement of competition policy (Tamura, 1994, p.114). In Japan, cartels for both internal and external trade have been far more prevalent than elsewhere in the developed world. The usual foreign complaint has not been about price discrimination against foreigners but domestic cartelization as a trade barrier to foreign penetration, a problem attacked by the USA Structural Impediments Initiative of 1990 (Ito, 1992, pp.204–5).

One lesson emerges from this summary of income-shifting policies reviewed in this section and previously: doubts about the efficacy of such policies in an interdependent world and a desire to avoid conflict frequently lead to cooperative compromises with other states on policies deemed acceptable if not optimal from a nationalist perspective.[35] While they have pursued income-shifting intermittently in the past, most governments do not appear anxious to defend opportunistic behaviour and seem generally willing to abandon it if other states pledge to do the same.

One form of national discrimination that appears unexceptionable concerns avoiding the appropriation of public subsidies by foreigners. States do not typically provide substantial and sustained uncompensated subsidies. For example, the British National Health Service was open for over three decades to all who were within the United Kingdom at a given time. Widespread documentation of a lack of

34. The best evidence on such an attempt concerns the US Webb–Pomerene associations sanctioned by 1918 legislation (see Fournier, 1932; Larson, 1970). These associations had as their principal *declared* purpose, not exploiting foreigners, but the realization of economies of scale in foreign marketing.
35. Such thinking is reflected in the convention of host country taxation of multinational profits at a level that nearly always exceeds the benefits provided to the firm, with the home country granting a tax credit or forgiving taxes altogether.

reciprocity abroad and opportunistic use of system by foreigners led to a system of fees for non-taxpayers early in the Thatcher period.

The very substantial subsidies given by the United States to citizens of other countries in the form of under-priced higher education may appear anomalous. Elites dealing with the issues might have recognized this subsidy as a particularly valuable form of foreign aid, however, with the cost dramatically reduced (perhaps even completely offset) by the excess of tax payments over public services consumed by those students who become long-term US residents.[36]

Perhaps the most important issue of this kind now facing the governments of the advanced countries concerns participation by foreign firms in research and development consortia and other contracts subsidized by national governments. Many have claimed that the United States has demonstrated more stringency on this issue than its trading partners, and evidence appears in such legislation as the Advanced Technology Programme (begun in 1991) and the Energy Policy Act of 1992 (Office of Technology Assessment, 1995).

American discussions have focused on two issues that should be separated analytically. One has to do with whether foreign participation should be limited to firms based in countries employing commercial practices that include participation in somewhat similar foreign programmes but may go well beyond them. Second, independently of the nationality of the participating firm, there is controversy about whether firms engaged in such activity should be obliged to perform certain activities in the United States in order to maximize the national benefit from the public expenditure. Presumed positive externalities provide the rationale for government activity in R&D in the first place, and in virtually all cases the benefits of the expenditures will spill over, not just beyond the participating firms, but also beyond the nation-state that funded the research. From this standpoint, is it not reasonable that the paying state should have the right to skew the resulting benefits as much in its own direction as it chooses?

The insistence on nationally-located activity might maximize externality benefits in some circumstances while national location could (if the tax system were operating efficiently) tend to equalize the fiscal

36. Those returning to their home countries will have established strong ties with the United States and over 70 per cent of all foreign-born PhDs remain in America (Bhagwati and Rao, 1996, p.51).

return to the paying state derived from foreign and national firms.[37] This kind of conditional nationalism could raise incomes both at home and abroad. Nonetheless, in some circumstances, firms conducting the subsidized activity entirely outside the subsidized state might produce the same national outcome more cheaply than firms subject to geographical restriction. The information requirements to make such distinctions appear formidable. They suggest than an internationally cooperative solution, with the major states allowing subsidized R&D activity to take place anywhere, could minimize international conflict.[38]

The discussion of discrimination on the basis of the nationality of a firm forces a direct consideration of what counts as a national firm. Reich (1990) argues that over time the nationality of firms will frequently become difficult to discern because of the national dispersion of stockholder and director identity. In response, Laura Tyson (1991) has stressed that ambiguity was seldom a problem in the early 1990s, and her point remains valid today. The current answer to the question 'is this a German firm?' will yield just about the same answer if the German national stockholding or director nationality threshold is 50 per cent or 80 per cent; Japanese nationality would be even more robust to such varying thresholds.

From the perspective of this study 'Who is Us?' can be answered unambiguously. All the citizens (and permanent residents) of a state are 'us'. Policy makers are challenged to discover what, if any, measures of economic nationalism might enhance their welfare. Reich makes a simple but important point: incoming direct investment makes domestic factors of production more productive, and a focus on the nationality of firms can lead to very misleading conclusions about what behaviour by which economic agents increases national economic welfare. His argument illustrates a broader phenomenon that this chapter has attempted to explore. In a world economy of complex interdependence, attempts to pursue nationalist economic policies in order to increase

37. Some data suggest that foreign firms located in the USA are making suspiciously low corporate income tax payments (Hufbauer, 1992, pp.115–19), but, as noted above, the international system (based on dozens of bilateral treaties) is designed to reward the activity-site country with the first option on such taxes.
38. With respect to eligibility, it appears that an agreement on national treatment – at least among the OECD countries – would be a vastly superior solution to an attempt by national governments (or even individual agencies) to qualify firms on the basis of specific behaviour by their home countries (see various chapters in Beltz, 1995).

national prosperity may fail for at least three reasons. First, they may be based on technical misunderstandings encouraged by special interests: most observed protection falls unambiguously into this category. Second, they may be based on formally possible models of national enrichment but fail for lack of sufficient information or government competence combined with the ceaseless pressure of special interests similar to those in the first case. Third, the pursuit of special national advantage will normally be resisted by a country's trading partners.

4. GENERALIZATIONS AND CONCLUSIONS

The thrust of the foregoing arguments can be quite easily summarized. As a practical matter, national governments in the global economy should eschew most elements of economic nationalism if their only objective is increased prosperity as this is usually defined. The major exception lies in the fundamental question 'Who is Us?' - not in Reich's sense, but in the sense of controlling the population for which national prosperity is to be defined. For all modern welfare states, this implies great caution about any outflow of unskilled labour. Such persons will take more from the economy than they contribute in the short run, and some evidence suggests that the advance of their families towards average productivity takes place slowly. From a similarly narrow view, based only on prosperity, a substantial increase in highly skilled migration appears appropriate for the opposite reasons. Concerns about national autonomy that focus on a unique identity based on a shared heritage may none the less negate such considerations.

Except for the necessity to control immigration, the prosperity-maximizing policy for a nation-state in an interdependent global economy looks much like that for a region within such a state.[39] The state should maximize trade, attempt to attract investment and attempt to ensure that tax collection from foreigners at least matches the provision of government goods and services to them. On the other hand, opportunism in attempting to keep capital at home or to export the tax burden

39. This assumes that the level of net subsidy to the region from the central government is modest.

will almost certainly lead to retaliation that may well be mutually destructive. Although states may be justified in restricting the beneficiaries of government subsidies to local production, uncertainties and the potential for conflict suggest that agreed mutual forbearance might be a better solution - unless it leads to reduced enthusiasm by governments for such support and hence to a lower total effort.

Adding security concerns to those of prosperity implies perhaps less of a shift towards economic nationalism for most states today than ever before. The end of the cold war combined with dazzling changes in largely civilian-driven technology suggests increasing need for co-operation to promote collective security and the avoidance of expensive duplication of technology. The latter would probably prove impossible in any case, even for the United States. Cooperation will continue to play a crucial role in policies of denial towards pariah states.

National autonomy will be continually reconsidered as interdependence increases. The nominal sovereignty of most states will be challenged much less than their effective autonomy, and the preservation of national uniqueness will continue to vex policy makers and citizens alike. Subsidies to continue the production and dissemination of national culture will necessarily receive increasing emphasis at the expense of attempts to force consumption through protection, however. The latter will be tolerated neither by trading partners nor by the defending country's own public.

Overall, an investigation of the logic and scope of policies based on economic nationalism suggests an important continuing role, yet one quite narrowly circumscribed and frequently abandoned for more constructive policies of cooperation with other members of the global community.

BIBLIOGRAPHY

Auquier, A.A. and R.E. Caves (1979). 'Monopolistic Export Industries. Trade Taxes, and Optimal Competition Policy', *Economic Journal*, **89** (September), pp.559-81.

Beltz, Cynthia (1995). *The Foreign Investment Debate* (Washington, DC: AEI Press).

Bhagwati, Jagdish and Milind Rao (1996) 'The U.S. Brain Gain - at the Expense of Blacks?', *Challenge*, March/April, pp.51–4.

Bhagwati, Jagdish and John D. Wilson (eds) (1989). *Income Taxation and International Mobility*, (Cambridge, MA: MIT Press).

Bobrow, Davis and Robert T. Kudrle (1991). 'Mid-Level Power Strategies for Changing International Niches: Experience in the "Old World Order"', *Journal of East Asian Affairs*, vol.5, no.1 (Summer/Fall), pp.237–70.

Borjas, George J. (1994). 'The Economics of Immigration', *Journal of Economic Literature*, vol.32 (December), pp.1667–1717.

Caves, Richard E. (1982). *The Multinational Enterprise and Economic Analysis* (Cambridge, Cambridge University Press).

—— (1986). *The Multinational Enterprise and Economic Analysis*, 2nd edition (Cambridge: Cambridge University Press).

——, Jeffrey Frankel and Ronald W. Jones (1996). *World Trade and Payments: An Introduction*, 7th edition (New York: HarperCollins).

Cohen, Steven D. (1994). *The Making of United States International Economic Policy: Principles, Problems, and Proposals for Reform*, 4th edition (Westport, CT: Praeger).

Center for Strategic and International Studies (1996). *Making Transatlantic Defense Cooperation Work* (Washington, DC: The Center for Strategic and International Studies).

Destler, I.M. (1995). *American Trade Politics*, 3rd edition (Washington DC: Institute for International Economics).

Dunning, John H. (ed.) (1985). *Multinational Enterprises, Economic Structure and International Competitiveness* (New York: Wiley).

Flamm, Kenneth (1996). 'Controlling the Uncontrollable', *The Brookings Review* (Winter), pp.22–5.

Fournier, L. (1932). 'Purposes and Results of the Webb–Pomerene Law', *American Economic Review*, vol.22 (March), pp.18–33.

Franz, Wolfgang (1981). 'Employment Policy and Labour Supply of Foreign Workers in the Federal Republic of Germany: A Theoretical and Empirical Analysis', *Zeitschrift für die gesamte Staatswissenschaft/Journal of Institutional and Theoretical Economics*, vol.137, no.3, pp.596–611.

Globerman, Steven and Aidan Vining (1984). 'Bilateral Cultural Free Trade: The U.S.-Canadian Case', in Fred Thompson (ed.), *Canadian–U.S. Interdependence in the Cultural Industries*, proceedings of a Conference held at Columbia University, New York.

Graham, Edward M. and Paul R. Krugman (1995). *Foreign Direct Investment in the United States*, 3rd edition (Washington, DC: Institute for International Economics).

Hanum, Hurst (1987). *The Right to Leave and Return in International Law and Practice* (Dordrecht: Martinus Nijhoff Publishers).

Hoekman, Bernard (1992). 'Market Access and Multilateral Trade Negotiations: The Uruguay Round Services Negotiations', prepared for the National Bureau of Economic Research Conference 'The Political Economy of International Market Access' (7 February) (unpublished).

Hufbauer, Gary C. (1992). *U.S. Taxation of International Income: Blueprint for Reform* (Washington, DC: Institute for International Economics).

Ito, Takotoshi (1992). *The Japanese Economy* (Cambridge, MA: MIT Press).

Johnson, Harry G. (1953–54). 'Optimum Tariffs and Retaliation', The Review of Economic Studies, vol.21, pp.142–53.

——(1967). 'Some Economic Aspects of the Brain Drain', *Pakistan Development Review,* vol.7 (August), pp.379–411.

Krugman, Paul R. (1987). 'Is Free Trade Passé?', *Journal of Economic Perspectives,* vol.1, no.1.

—— (1996). 'First Do No Harm', *Foreign Affairs*, vol.75, no.4 (July/August), pp.164–70.

—— and Maurice Obstfeld (1994). *International Economics: Theory and Policy*, 3rd edition (New York: HarperCollins College Publishers).

Kudrle, Robert T. (1991). 'Good for the Gander? Foreign Direct Investment in the United States', *International Organization*, vol.45, no.3 (Summer), pp.397–424.

—— (1993). 'No Entry: Sectoral Controls on Incoming Direct Investment in the Developed Countries', in Lorraine Eden and Evan H. Potter (eds), *Multinationals in the Global Political Economy* (New York: St. Martin's, ch.10).

—— (1995a). 'Fairness, Efficiency, and Opportunism in U.S. Trade and Investment Policy', David Rapkin and William Avery (eds), *National Competitiveness in a Global Economy* (Boulder, CO: Lynne Rienner), ch.7.

Part II

The East European Economies

3. Post-communist Eastern Europe: Privatization and the Second Fundamental Theorem

John McHale

1. INTRODUCTION

This chapter concerns the goals of privatization programmes in post-communist economies. I will step back from the efficiency-based analysis that has dominated the literature on privatization, and consider arguments for giving weight to distributional goals. I will argue, somewhat controversially, I fear, that economic theory can be of help in guiding the choice of criteria for evaluating privatization options. I hasten to add that I shall not claim that economic theory can be used to make value judgements about the way to trade off equity for efficiency, but I shall try to make the case that theory has something to say about the policy situations where distributional issues can and cannot be ignored. I conclude that the choice of the initial distributional of previously state-owned property is one that makes distributional implications difficult to ignore.

The result from economic theory that I will focus on in particular is the Second Fundamental Theorem of Welfare Economics (SFT). This result, which provides one of the main pillars of theoretical support for the desirability of a market mechanism, is usually thought to have little practical relevance in established private-ownership economies for reasons that I outline below. I shall argue that if the SFT is *ever* to have practical relevance, however, it is during the privatization of a previously owned state economy. I conclude the typically useful role of the economist as analyst of – and advocate for – efficiency, is less compelling when the subject matter is the choice of the initial distribution of private-ownership rights in an economy.

The reformers who are guiding the difficult transitions from plan to market recognized early on that privatization is necessary for a successful outcome. They foresaw that the efficient restructuring of the distorted economies inherited from communism would require both market liberalization and privatization to give enterprises the incentives to respond efficiently to the new market signals.[1] Although it was clear that there are a number of competing goals that privatization is supposed to serve - maintain political support for reforms, raise revenues for the government, support the development of capital markets - the efficiency-based need to strip the control of enterprises from bureaucrats and politicians, and to put that control in the hands of long-run profit-maximizers,[2] has dominated the analysis of privatization policy.[3]

What advice should be given to a reformer seeking to maximize a social welfare function that is sensitive to the distribution of well-being as well as efficiency? To provide an initial answer to this question, my analysis begins in a world of perfect markets where considerations of distribution and efficiency can be separated. In that setting the special nature of the choice of the initial ownership structure is apparent. I will contend that even a purely economic analysis recommends that the evaluation of ownership options should be done from the perspective to general social welfare and not from a narrow efficiency perspective.

1. See, for example, the introduction to Gray (1996).
2. It is hoped that these new owners have some experience in running the type of firms that they own and control.
3. There is a huge literature that analyses privatization from an efficiency perspective. Some excellent examples are Boycko, Shleifer and Vishny (1995), EBRD (1993, 1994, 1995), Frydman and Rapaczynski (1994), and World Bank (1996). For models of the effects of privatization on firm behaviour, see Shleifer and Vishny (1994) and Boycko, Shleifer and Vishny (1996). Gray (1996, p.179) is explicit about the goals that privatization should serve, and distributional considerations enter only in so far as they place a political constraint on efficiency-oriented reforms:

> Programmes to privatize enterprises in transition economies should be evaluated in terms of three broad dimensions: the corporate governance mechanisms they create, the supporting institutions they foster, and the extent to which they create a self-sustaining economic and political reform process. Although some governments judge revenues to be an important goal of privatization, they are at best a secondary objective.

Although the neat separation between distribution and efficiency breaks down when we allow for market imperfections – how privatization is done does then matter for efficiency – I will argue that the basic insight about the relevance of distribution goals can still be valid.

The main arguments of the chapter can be summarized as follows:

- The fundamental theorems of welfare economics recommend the following division of labour in organizing economic activity: choose the initial distribution of endowment ownership so as to maximize social welfare (conditional on using a competitive market mechanism to allocate resources); and then actually use the competitive market mechanism to allocate resources.
- This has an analogue in a possible transition strategy: fully liberalize markets and use the privatization process (that is, the initial distribution of state-owned assets) to achieve distributional goals.
- Because of political constraints on the redistribution of property rights, the second fundamental theorem has little practical relevance in established private-ownership economics. By contrast, since the state owns the property at the outset of the transition, the set of politically feasible (or enforceable) distributions is larger, and the message of the second fundamental theorem – use the choice of initial ownership to achieve general social welfare goals – has more salience.
- The main alternative for achieving distributional goals is redistribution through the tax and transfer system. But because of the heavy demands for government spending and the narrowness of the tax base, the marginal social welfare loss of additional spending for redistributive purposes is very high during a transition. Thus there is also an *efficiency* rationale for using privatization to achieve distributional goals.
- This argument for focusing on distributional considerations when deciding between privatization options runs into two main objections. First, it is possible that it overstates the size of the set of politically feasible ownership distributions during a transition. And second, it wrongly supposes that efficiency can be separated from the structure of ownership. Thus there may be both limitations on the scope for using privatization to achieve

distributional goals and reasons to consider the efficiency implications of privatization options.

The rest of the chapter elaborates these arguments and is organized in four sections. In the next section, I argue that the fundamental theorems of welfare economics provide a *prima facie* case for focusing on distributional consequences of post-communist privatization. While I recognize that the practical relevance of these theorems is often limited, I contend that the second fundamental theorem has a particular saliency in the context of post-communist privatization. In Section 3, I discuss the efficiency–equity trade-off that arises when the lump-sum instruments required by the SFT are not available to policy makers. I argue that for various reasons this trade-off is especially severe in a transition economy. Therefore, economists - even in their traditional role as advocates of efficiency - might have reason to espouse the use of privatization to pursue distributional goals. Drawing on the Coase theorem, Section 4 takes up the main counter-argument: that the structure of ownership cannot be divorced from efficiency. Section 5 concludes the chapter.

2.1. THE FUNDAMENTAL THEOREMS OF WELFARE ECONOMICS

The two fundamental theorems of welfare economics provide important theoretical support for the desirability of the competitive market mechanism. The First Fundamental Theorem (FFT) formalizes Adam Smith's idea that the invisible hand of the market guides self-interested behaviour to produce good outcomes for society. It states that under certain assumptions - price-taking behaviour, non-satiated preferences, complete information and well-specified property rights - a competitive market equilibrium is Pareto efficient. The Second Fundamental Theorem states that, with some additional assumptions (notably that preferences and production sets are convex), any Pareto efficient outcome can be achieved as a market equilibrium with an appropriate initial distribution of endowments.

It has often been noted that an analysis based on the theorems suggests the following two-part strategy:

1. choose the initial distribution of endowments to maximize social welfare, conditional on using a competitive market mechanism to allocate resources.[4]
2. actually use a competitive market mechanism to allocate resources.

Part of the attractiveness of the theorems is that they tell us that allocative and distributive decisions can be separated. The market mechanism is used to allocate resources regardless of one's view of the best distribution of income. Using this idea, Musgrave (1959) envisaged a separation of responsibility between the allocative and the distributive branches of government. The allocative branch makes sure that

4. I assume that a social welfare function (SWF) is a criterion for ordering social states given certain information about these states. Social state x is ranked higher than social state y if the value of the SWF is higher for x than for y. While I refrain from assuming any particular SWF, I do place some conventional restrictions on the form it can take. First, I assume that social welfare is an increasing function of each person's utility. This embodies the assumption of welfarism - social welfare depends only on individuals' welfare - and ensures that the social ordering is consistent with the Pareto criterion. Second, I assume that the function is a symmetric concave (although not necessarily strictly concave) function of the utilities. This ensures that the reformer does not like the *in*equality of welfare, although the possibility that he is indifferent to it is left open. Third, I assume that the function is additively separable. This ensures that the increase in social welfare from increasing one person's utility is independent of the level of everybody else's utility. At one extreme of this class of SWFs is the classical utilitarian SWF. With this function, social welfare depends only on the sum of utilities and not at all on its distribution. At the other (egalitarian) extreme is the Rawlsian SWF, which equates social welfare with the utility of the worst-off individual

Ordering social states using such a function is an example of outcome-based evaluation; that is, the states are evaluated in terms of particular outcomes in those states (in these case, utility outcomes). An alternative way of ordering states is in terms of *processes*. The focus is then on the process by which the outcome is arrived at rather than the outcome itself. Examples of such process-based theories are Nozick's libertarian theory (see Nozick, 1974), and Marxian theories of exploitation.

In the context of post-communist privatization, an important argument for valuing the process by which outcomes come about has been given by János Kornai (1995 [1992]). Kornai emphasizes that a central feature of the transition is the movement from bureaucratically organized hierarchical interactions to market-motivated horizontal interactions. Value is placed on the *embourgeoisement* of society, where 'the bureaucratic, hierarchical stratification of society should be superseded by stratification according to property' (Kornai, 1995, p.81). To achieve this type of society, Kornai recommends that privatization should create *personal owners*, that is owners who are capable of personally controlling the use of their assets. To capture the importance of such 'sociological aspects' it follows that an evaluation of privatization options must go beyond the welfare-based analysis being used here.

markets work as they should: no monopolies, market-determined prices, well-specified property rights, and so forth, and the distributive branch determines the social welfare-maximizing distribution of endowments.

This suggests that a similar type of division of responsibilities might be appropriate in an economy going through a post-communist transition. A *liberalization agency* supervises the marketization of the economy;[5] and a *privatization agency* determines the initial distribution of private property. The mandate of the liberalization agency is to focus on efficiency, with the achievement of distributional goals left to its privatization counterpart.

Given the logic of this division of responsibility, it is surprising that most of the economic analysis of privatization options has focused on efficiency. Am I going wrong by trying to read too much practical relevance into the fundamental theorems? I think that most economists take the policy message of the FFT seriously.[6] Even though the theorem is based on strict assumptions, it is believed that markets often come sufficiently close to what are described by these assumptions to warrant the belief that market outcomes are quite efficient. Instead, it is the practical relevance of the SFT that is more often questioned. Besides the fact that this theorem requires even stricter assumptions than the FFT (as noted above), the practical relevance of the SFT is doubted for two further reasons: following Mas-Colell *et al.* (1995), I call these the *information* limitation and the *enforceability* limitation.

(1) The Information Limitation

The information limitation highlights that it is very difficult to know what distribution of ownership maximizes social welfare. To know what the best distribution of ownership is, we must first have complete

5. The responsibilities of this agency are defined broadly. In addition to ensuring free prices and free entry, they include the maintenance of a stable-valued medium of exchange, the enforcement of property rights and contracts, and the breaking up of monopolies.
6. For a recent critique of the practical relevance of the FFT see Stiglitz (1994). In particular, Stiglitz argues that market failure is common because of asymmetries of information between potential market traders.

knowledge about preferences, endowments and technological possibilities. Suppose someone is born with great intelligence and also is fortunate enough to get very little disutility from working. Given this person's natural advantages, it may be that her ownership share at the social optimum is relative low. Since her natural advantages give her a disadvantage when it comes to deciding about ownership, she has very little incentive to reveal private information about these advantages. The best we might be able to do is to infer information about this individual from her market behaviour - say, how much she works and what wage she earns - and to take income from her on the basis of these observations.[7] The problem, of course, is that because her treatment is conditional on her behaviour, her behaviour will be distorted in a way that harms efficiency.

This problem of information certainly is an obstacle to a complete ordering of alternative ownership distributions. Yet it may be possible to go a long way with a much rougher (or partial) ordering. For example, we might have enough information to conclude that a situation where a small group of managers and bankers owns almost everything is socially inferior to an approximately equal distribution of assets. The incompleteness of the information, then, need not completely block the application of the SFT.[8]

(2) The Enforceability Limitation

Although it is the information limitation that attracts the most attention, I do not consider it the main obstacle to the practical application of the SFT in an established private ownership economy. The main obstacle is

7. Through income and expenditure taxes, for example.
8. The literature on mechanism design takes a different approach to the information limitation. It looks for mechanisms that allow particular social functions to be implemented, namely mechanisms that get individuals to reveal the information that is needed to rank the alternative social states. Given the possibilities for such mechanisms, this delineates the class of implementable social welfare functions. Some social welfare functions are implementable and others not because the incentive to reveal information clearly depends on the social choices (for example, privatization choices) that are made on the basis of that information. The approach adopted here takes the social welfare function as given, and assumes that it is, at least partially, implementable, that is, there is enough information to rank at least some pairs of privatization options.

that the redistributions of property are usually not politically, legally – and perhaps even ethically – feasible. This point has been perceptively emphasized by Amartya Sen: following a discussion of the limitation on information Sen (1987, pp.37–8) notes:[9]

> There is a further problem that even if such information were available, the second part of the 'fundamental theorem' would be used only if it were politically possible to redistribute resources among the people in any way that would be required by considerations of social optimality. Even if the necessary lump-sum transfers were identifiable and also economically feasible, issues of political feasibility can be, obviously, extremely important when dealing with such fundamental matters as radical changes in ownership. Even though the invoking of the second part of the 'fundamental theorem' may often come from rather conservative quarters defending the market mechanism, that result can be of real use only as a part of some 'revolutionary's handbook', transforming the ownership of means of production before getting the market to do the rest.

I would argue that in addition to being a useful part of a revolutionary's handbook, the SFT is also a useful part of a *post-communist privatizer's* handbook. While Sen is surely correct to say that radical redistributions of ownership are not enforceable in an established private ownership economy, such redistributions are *exactly* what *must* take place during post-communist privatizations. Given any current distribution of property in an established private enterprise economy, the set of enforceable alternative distributions is likely to be small. There is strong *status quo* bias that obviates the relevance of the message of the SFT. In contrast, given that the private ownership rights to initially state-owned assets must be established *de novo*, the set of enforceable ownership distributions is likely to be considerably larger. Thus, although the SFT may not have teeth when private ownership rights have been long established – in other words, there are few, if any, feasible alternative distributions to choose from – it should have much greater relevance when all state-owned property in a previously communist economy must be given to *someone* in the private sector.

9. See also Sen (1983).

Some Formal Notation

In this section I briefly restate the main premises and arguments of the previous section more formally. My purpose here is obviously not to prove theorems, but to clarify the main concepts.

To keep things as simple as possible, I assume an exchange economy (that is, there is no production). There are I households and L goods. ω is an L-dimensional vector of the economy's total initial endowments. In a post-communist economy these endowments are initially owned by the state. The privatization agency must choose how to distribute these endowments so as to maximize social welfare in the new market environment. ω is an $L \times I$ dimensional matrix that represents a particular distribution of endowment ownership, so that ω_{l_i} gives the ith household's initial ownership of good l. I denote the set of physically possible distributions (given ω) as Ω.

An allocation of goods to households is given the $L \times I$ dimensional matrix x. And the competitive market equilibrium is denoted by (x^*, p^*), where p^* is a price vector such that total demand for good l by the I utility-maximizing households, x_l^*, equals the total initial endowment of good l, ω_l, for $l = 1, \dots, L$; that is, $x^* = \omega$.

Using this notation we can restate the two fundamental theorems as follows:

First Fundamental Theorem: x^* (the competitive market allocation) is Pareto efficient.

Second Fundamental Theorem: Any Pareto efficient outcome can be achieved as a competitive equilibrium by appropriately choosing ω from Ω.

As before, I assume that the privatization agency chooses ω to maximize social welfare where social welfare is a function of the utilities of the I households.[10] The utility of each household depends on its

10. I assume that the social welfare function provides a complete and transitive ordering of social states. By itself, the Pareto criterion provides only a partial ordering of states. According to this criterion, state x is superior to state y if everybody is at least as well off in x as in y and at least one person is strictly better off. If some people are better off in x than in y, and others are better off in y than in x, then x and y cannot be ranked by the Pareto criterion. One way of interpreting *Arrow's impossibility theorem* is as a generalization of this result. Under certain unrestrictive conditions, it

final (that is, post-market-trading) allocation of goods. This allocation for the *i*th household is given by the *L*-dimensional vector x_i^*, and is a function of the initial distribution of endowments ω. Thus, $u_i = u_i[x_i^*(\omega)]$, for all $i = 1, \ldots, I$. The (two-part) strategy for making the best use of resources can now be stated as a single social welfare maximization problem:

$$\underset{\omega \in \Omega}{\text{Max}}\ S = f\{u_1[x^*_1(\omega)], \ldots, u_I[x^*_I(\omega)]\} \tag{1}$$

The initial distribution that maximizes social welfare (conditional on using a competitive market mechanism) is denoted ω^*.

In any economy, the full set of physically possible distributions, Ω, is unlikely to be *politically enforceable*. Problems of political enforceability are probably especially severe in an established private ownership economy. In such an economy, the government typically finds it difficult to redistribute property rights even marginally. Given that the state owns practically all the property at the beginning of the transition, however, the initial distribution of ownership does not place the same limitation on a post-communist economy.

Letting $\Omega^E \subset \Omega$ denote the subset of enforceable initial distributions, I make the following assumptions:

(i) Given the initial distribution of ownership in an established private ownership economy, Ω^E is small. This greatly circumscribes the practical relevance of the SFT.
(ii) Given that the state initially owns all the property in a post-communist economy, Ω^E is large. Therefore, the message of the

is not possible to find a non-dictatorial welfare function rule that provides a complete and transitive social ordering using information about ordinal non-comparable utilities alone. When the information is enriched (most importantly in the direction of inter-personally comparable utilities), the set of social welfare functions expands. For example, when utilities are cardinally measurable and utility units (but not necessarily utility levels) are comparable across individuals, the utilitarian social welfare becomes a possibility. As noted above, in this chapter I will not assume any particular social welfare function. I do, however, assume that one exists, and I place some restrictions on it. Implicitly, then, I am assuming that the utility information is richer than the ordinal non-comparable utilities of the standard general equilibrium framework.

SFT – choose the initial ownership structure to maximize social welfare – has practical relevance.

Figure 3.1 diagramatically represents these assumptions in a two-household economy. The utility possibility frontier (UPF) gives the maximum utility that Household 2 can achieve for any given utility of Household 1. Each point of the frontier is Pareto efficient: in other words, it is not possible to make one of the households better off without making the other worse off. From the FFT, we know that a competitive market equilibrium is on the UPF. And from the SFT, we know that any point on the frontier is achievable as a competitive market equilibrium with an appropriate choice of initial ownership. The two-part strategy then simply involves choosing the point on the frontier that maximizes social welfare (which, to repeat, is implemented by choosing the initial ownership distribution and then allowing

Figure 3.1 Welfare-maximizing distribution

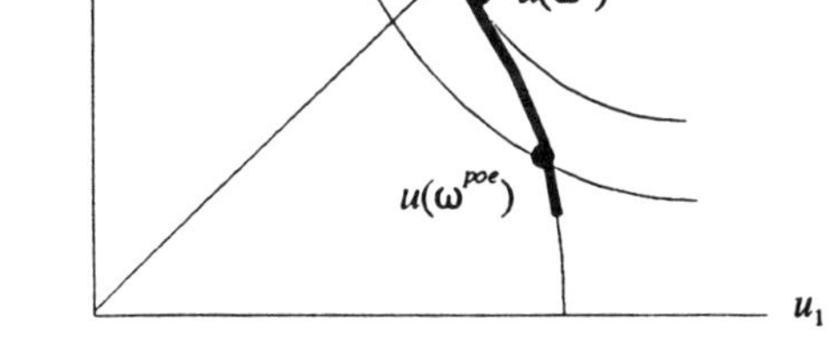

Point $u(\omega^{poe})$ is the single distribution of welfare that is feasible in the established private ownership company. The dark portion of the UPF represents the set of welfare distributions that are assumed to be feasible when there are no existing private property rights. As drawn, the enforceability constraint is not binding for the post-communist economy: that is, $\omega \in \Omega^E$.

completely free trade in goods). $u(\omega^*)$ denotes the social welfare-maximizing distribution of utilities. It is given by the point of tangency of the highest possible social indifference curve and the UPF.[11]

When Ω^E is a proper subset of Ω, then not all points on the UPF are feasible through the mechanism just described. If, in a private-ownership economy, the government cannot redistribute private property rights, then the feasible distribution of welfare will be the single point $u(\omega^{poe})$, corresponding to the status-quo property distribution, ω^{poe}. Because the government does not have to respect existing private-property rights in a post-communist economy, the set of feasible welfare distributions is assumed to be larger, say the heavy line in Figure 3.1.

Enforceability Limitations During a Transition

In Sections 2.1 and 2.2, I argued that, given the *status quo*, the set of enforceable new ownership structures is larger in a post-communist economy than in an established market economy. Since the state owns the property at the outset of a transition, there are no existing property rights that must be respected.

An obvious criticism of this argument is that it underestimates the enforceability limitations on ownership structures during a transition. In other words, it wrongly supposes that the reformers have complete discretion over who the new private owners of the previously state-owned property will be. With this in mind, it is useful to distinguish two (not necessarily mutually exclusive) groups of people who can block particular ownership distributions:

(1) *Stakeholders.* These are people who receive rents from their association with specific assets prior to privatization. The size of these rents after privatization depends on what is done with this assets, and also who the new owners of the assets are.

(2) *Potential owners.* As their name suggests, these are people who are in the running to receive previously state-owned assets. I assume that they do not have the power to guarantee themselves any particular

11. A social indifference curve is a set of utility combinations that yield the same level of social welfare. Given the assumptions about the social welfare function made earlier, these curves will be downward-sloping and convex.

allocation of assets, but that coalitions of potential owners can block particular ownership distributions.

Boycko *et al.* (1995) show very clearly what limitations on privatization options can confront post-communist privatizers. Reviewing the early privatization experience in Russia, they show how various groups - managers, workers, local government officials, the public and others - could block certain privatization options. For privatization to proceed, these groups needed to be bought off in some fashion. One group that had considerable power to block privatizations which they did not like were managers. Accepting their power, Russia's privatizers overcame manager opposition by allowing them to obtain large stages in enterprises at bargain prices. Survey evidence for Russia shows that, on average, 70 per cent of the equity of privatized large and medium-sized firms is owned by insiders; of that, 17 per cent is owned by managers (Lieberman and Rahuja, 1995).

The ability of various groups to block privatizations which they do not like varies across countries, and depends, it appears, on the history of pre-transition reforms (Frydman and Rapaczynski, 1995). Although the Gorbachev enterprise reforms in Russia nominally gave workers influence in enterprise decision making, the *de facto* influence went to the managers. In Poland, however, workers' councils acquired significant influence during the 1980s, and they have been able to continue to wield influence during the transition to block privatizations which they do not like. The former Czechoslovakia also provides another interesting example. Paradoxically, because the country did not go through a stage of reform socialism, the government was in firm control at the beginning of the transition, and was able to formulate and implement quickly a complicated equal-access voucher privatization programme.[12]

If the blocking power of these groups is large enough, the set of enforceable distributions that the privatization agency has to choose from is much more restricted than I have assumed, and the potential for achieving social welfare objectives via the two-part strategy is reduced.

Enforceability and Time: A Possible Argument for Gradualism

In considering the set of enforceable ownership distributions I have not

12. See Frydman and Rapaczynski (1994), Gray (1996), and World Bank (1996).

mentioned the effects of the passage of time. This may have struck the reader as an odd omission, since time has been central to the debate about optimal transition strategy. This debate is usually framed in terms of the relative merits of gradualist and 'big bang' strategies of reform.[13]

An obvious way to add a time dimension in the context of the set-up in Section 2.2 above is to allow the set of enforceable distributions to be a function of time (that is, $\Omega^E = \Omega^E(t)$). I think it is natural to suppose that Ω^E expands with time. At the outset of the transition, various groups are able to block many of the physically possible distributions. It takes time for the government to overcome this opposition, and to implement its preferred ownership distribution.[14]

The Russian privatization discussed above provides an interesting example. The designers of the privatization programme believed that the politicization of enterprise decision making had huge efficiency costs, and therefore delaying privatization allowed the inefficiencies to persist. To privatize – and thereby depoliticize – quickly, the privatizers had to assent to an unequal initial distribution of the country's resources (see Boycko *et al.* 1995).

On the other hand, large-scale privatization has been delayed in Poland. The reformers have been less willing to make the concessions to insiders that would have overcome the opposition of potential blocking coalitions relatively easily, and privatization has proceeded with impressive despatch.

13. There are many strands to the debate over the relative merits of these broad reform strategies. To help put the argument for gradualism that follows into perspective, it might be helpful to note two other arguments for gradualism:

    (1) *Aggregate uncertainty.* Dewatripont and Roland (1995) have shown that in the presence of uncertainty about the outcomes of reforms, and costs associated with reversing reforms, it might be optimal to choose a partial reform strategy even when reforms are complementary.
    (2) *Negative spillovers.* When private and social adjustment costs are the same, then immediate and complete reform is optimal (Mussa, 1986). However, when one person's adjustment has an adverse impact on others – for example, through the fiscal strain of paying unemployment benefits (see Aghion and Blanchard, 1994) – then a gradual reform may be superior to rapid reform in terms of efficiency.
14. It is also possible that Ω^E contracts with time. Early in this transition, the various stakeholders and potential owners could have a difficult time mounting an effective opposition. This is essentially the 'window of opportunity' argument: reformers can take advantage of the disorganization and momentum for reform in the early post-communist phase to push through reforms that would be more difficult, or even impossible, later on (see Sachs, 1993).

What is the optimal time-frame for privatization? To make this question meaningful, I assume that there is some cost to delay. An obvious example of such a cost is that delaying privatization also delays restructuring. This cost, $g(t)$, is assumed to be an increasing function of the delay, t. To bring out the basic trade-off, I assume that the social welfare-maximization problem takes the quasi-additively separable form:[15]

$$\max_{\omega \in \Omega(t)} S = f\{u_1[x^*_1(\omega)], \ldots, u_1[x^*_1(\omega)]\} - g'(t), \quad \text{where } g'(.), g''(.)>0 \qquad (2)$$

If allowing more time for privatization allows for a higher value of $f\{.\}$, (that is, $f_*\{t_2\}>f_*\{t_1\}$, where $t_2>t_1$ and $f_*\{t\}$ is the optimal value of $f\{.\}$ given t), but at a diminishing marginal rate (that is, $f_*'\{t\} > 0$, $f_*''\{t\} < 0$), then we can represent the optimal privatization time-frame, t^*, as in Figure 3.2.[16]

This admittedly rather rough-and-ready treatment of the optimal speed of reform provides, I believe, an important general lesson about transition strategy. Sachs (1994) makes a useful distinction between the core institutions of capitalism[17] - which are assumed to be common to all successful capitalist economies - and the details of these institutions, which differ markedly from country to country, and will depend on a country's history and cultural traditions. The policy message is taken to be that the core should be put in place as quickly as possible, letting the details that will give each country its distinctive flair develop over time. This strategy has a lot to recommend it when it comes to most reform tasks. Yet it seems inappropriate when deciding on how to privatize. Following the privatization path of least resistance will probably lead to an unequal division of initial property rights, with the well-connected

15. For simplicity, I am side-stepping any problems raised by time-discounting.
16. This argument for gradualism is distinct from the two arguments mentioned in note 13 above. There is no uncertainty about the outcome of the reforms, and delaying reform (in this case privatization) is *not* efficient. The reason for privatizing slowly is related to distribution rather than efficiency. Privatizing quickly - although efficient - forces the privatizers to assent to a distribution of property that is relatively unattractive socially.
17. The list of such core institutions includes competitive markets; a stable-valued internal and external medium of exchange; predominant private ownership; the corporate form for large enterprises; well-protected private property rights; openness to international trade in goods and capital; and a social safety net.

Figure 3.2 Optimal privatization time-frame

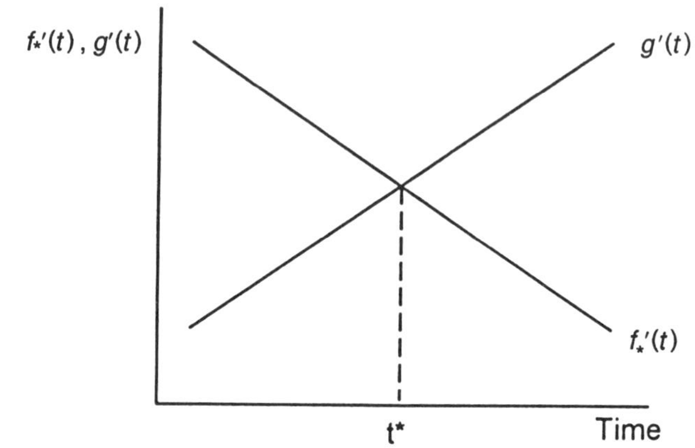

Delaying privatization has an efficiency cost (which is increasing in the delay) but it also expands the set of enforceable ownership distributions. At the optimal delay, t^*, the costs exactly equal the benefits of further delay.

and otherwise well-endowed best placed to gain from the privatization process. The resulting distribution of income may be far from optimal in social welfare terms. Certainly, the direct effect of the initial distribution of property rights will diminish with time; nevertheless, it is also true that those best placed to accumulate capital are those who have significant capital to begin with. And once the initial distribution of property rights has been made, it is difficult to rectify mistakes given the above-mentioned limitations on redistributing property rights in a private-ownership economy. Thus the speed with which (and more generally the method by which) the core is put in place will have a long-lasting impact on these economies.

Privatization and the Equity–Efficiency Trade-off

I have noted above the limitations on the practical applicability of the SFT in an established private-ownership economy. But the inability to make lump-sum redistributions does not usually mean an end to efforts aimed at securing distributional goals. It does, however, mean that, given the distribution of property rights, the government must use distortive instruments to meet these goals. The two main types of redistributive policy are distortive taxation - that is, taxation based on observed economic activity such as the income tax - and distortive transfers - that is, transfers based on observed income or wealth (which are largely determined by current or past economic activity).[18] In this section, I briefly consider the possibility that privatization can be a substitute for distorting taxes and transfers, and the possibility that there is also therefore an efficiency rationale for using privatization to pursue a more equal distribution of welfare.

3.1. A SIMPLE FRAMEWORK

In social welfare terms, the rationale for redistribution through the tax and transfer system is that marginal social welfare cost (or MSC) from taking a rouble from a richer person is less than the marginal social welfare benefit (or MSB) of transferring that rouble to a poorer person. In Figure 3.3 I present graphically the MSC and MSB curves for the cases where the redistribution is non-distortive and also where it is distortive. The MSC curve is assumed to be upward sloping even in the non-distortionary case because the social welfare function is a concave function of individuals' incomes. This also explains the downward slope of the MSB curve.[19] The slopes of both curves becomes steeper when we include the added social costs and reduced social benefits caused by the distortions. In other words, the distortions raise the additional social welfare cost of an additional rouble raised as tax revenue, and lower the additional social welfare benefit of an additional rouble transferred to someone by the government.

To see how privatization and redistribution through the tax and transfer system could be substitutes, assume that the privatization agency randomly chooses a distribution of initial property rights. To improve on this plan it has two options: (i) it can adjust the plan by

18. The distortions created by such redistributive instruments have been well documented. For example, if when you work extra hours you also pay more taxes, your incentive to work is reduced. Or if your state pension is lower when your income and wealth after retirement age are higher, your incentives to work after retirement age and to save before retirement are diminished.
19. The concavity does not necessarily imply a social preference for equity in well-being, but may simply be a reflection of diminishing marginal utility from income in the individual utility functions.

Figure 3.3 Social welfare redistribution

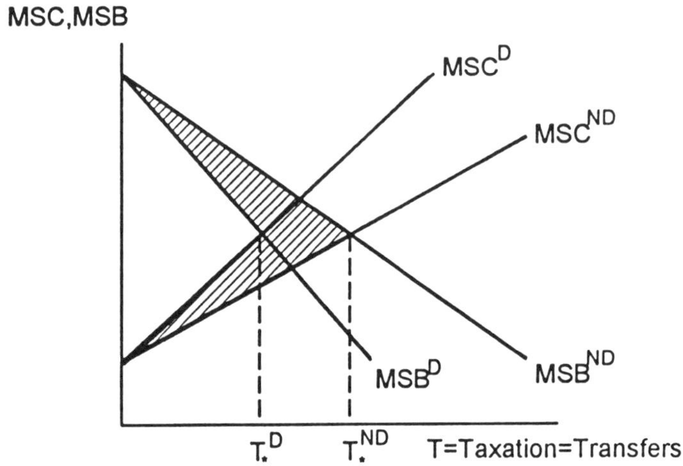

The non-distortionary and distortionary cases are labelled ND and D respectively. The shaded region represents the loss of social welfare from the absence of non-distorting redistributive instruments.

optimally transferring would-be property rights between individuals[20] (this is the non-distortive option, where it is implicitly assumed that the distribution of ownership does not affect efficiency[21]); or (ii) it can implement the plan, and then try to improve the outcome afterwards using distorting taxes and transfers. Figure 3.3 shows the social welfare implications of both the non-distorting and the distorting options. Both the amount of redistribution and total social welfare are large under the optimal privatization plan.

3.2. PRINCIPLES OF OPTIMAL TAXES AND TRANSFERS

This analysis of the distortive case might not even capture the worse-case scenario. It could be that, for political reasons, the amount of

20. We can think of the taking of property from someone as a tax equal to the value of that property, and the giving of that property to someone else as a transfer.
21. This is obviously a very strong assumption, and I will relax it in Section 4, below.

redistribution that takes place is greater than T_*^D, the efficient level of redistribution when the redistributive instruments are distortive. In other words, the political process might produce more than the social welfare-maximizing amount of redistribution. This violates a principle of optimal tax and transfer design: make transfers until the MSC of the additional tax is equal to the MSB of the additional transfer. Indeed, often implicit in economists' recommendations to reduce the size of government in established market economies is a belief that government spending and taxation reduce social welfare at the margin. Given the size of government obligations and expectations inherited from communism, the level of this 'excess' spending could be large in a transition economy.

In transition economies, it is almost certain that the second principle of optimal taxation is also violated: for any given target for total spending, raise the revenues in the least distortionary way. Since the loss of social welfare typically increases more than linearly with a tax, the principle recommends a broad tax base (in other words, tax many markets or individuals a little, rather than a few markets or individuals a lot). Unfortunately, taxation systems based on market activity are undeveloped early in a transition. Often, the treasury has to rely on a limited number of easily identifiable targets for taxation, leading to a high level of distortion for any given amount of total taxation.[22] In terms of Figure 3.3 this shows up as a large increase in social cost for any given increase in the target for total taxation. Consequently, the MSC curve is high to the left, and the optimal size of government, T_*^D, is small.

Of course, not all government spending is financed by raising taxes. Other methods of financing include borrowing, printing money and entering into arrears to government suppliers and workers. For any level of spending, there will be some optimal combination of financing instruments that minimizes the social-welfare cost of financing it. However, when there are great difficulties in raising tax revenue, the government might over-use an option such as printing money because of its comparative ease of availability. The result, as in many countries of the former Soviet Union, can be very high – and greatly distorting – inflation.

22. See Tanzi (1994).

4.1. WHY THE OWNERSHIP STRUCTURE MATTERS FOR EFFICIENCY

In Section 3, I argued that the alternative of trying to achieve distribution goals through the tax and transfer system forces the reforming government to face a severe trade-off of equity against efficiency. In this section, I admit that the reformers will also face this trade-off when choosing between privatization options.[23]

When I accepted the first fundamental theorem in Section 2, I accepted too quickly the efficiency of the market mechanism. The conditions required for a market equilibrium to be efficiency are quite demanding. One important condition required for efficiency is that there are no externalities in consumption or production. In other words, social benefits are identical with private benefits and social costs are identical with private costs. None the less, we should not be too eager to count the market out. Coase's celebrated article of 1960 on 'The Problem of Social Cost' showed the potential for the market to overcome such inefficiencies. The Coase Theorem, as interpreted by Stigler, states that, in a world of zero transaction costs, private and social costs and benefits are equal (see Coase, 1988). Even in the presence of externalities the relevant parties can transact amongst themselves to reach the efficient outcome. Most importantly in the present context, the initial distribution of ownership over assets does not affect the outcome, allowing us to separate concerns of distribution from those of efficiency.

Coase described what he had in mind by transaction costs as follows: 'In order to carry out a market transaction it is necessary to discover

23. A number of economists have argued that the value of existing assets at the end of communism is not high enough to justify too much fighting over. Kornai (1995 [1992]) extends this to argue that the scope for achieving egalitarian goals through an equal division of property is limited because of initial inequities in material wealth and human capital. Thus privatization should be geared to other goals such as the 'embourgeoisement' of society and efficient enterprise governance. He recommends (p.85) that 'Sincere advocates of a more equal distribution of income and wealth should campaign in the fields of fiscal policy, welfare policy, and education, health and housing policy, where the scope for furthering their objectives is greater.' Two points are worth noting, however. First, the analysis of this section shows that, when taxes and transfers are distorting, the optimal size of government is small, and the social welfare loss (for that size of government) is large. Second, in principle at least, the initial distribution of assets does not have to be equal: it could be chosen, for example, to compensate for low human capital.

who it is that one wishes to deal with, to inform people that one wishes to deal and on what terms, to conduct negotiations leading up to a bargain, to draw up a contract, to undertake the inspection needed to make sure that the terms of the contract are being observed, and so on' (Coase, 1988, p.6). Needless to say, such transaction costs will be very high in a transition economy. This is important because with transaction costs the distribution of ownership will normally matter. Distribution and efficiency cannot be separated, and the two-part reform strategy based on the fundamental theorems is less compelling. In the remainder of this section I will review how inefficiency results when the party that controls the asset does not receive the net social benefits from the use of that asset; that is, when private and social net benefits are not aligned.[24]

The typical large firm in a market economy faces the problem of separated ownership and control. Such firms are usually too large to be owned by one person; and even where there is one owner, that person is often unable or unwilling to manage the firm actively. This leads to a principal-and-agent problem, where the principal (namely, the owners) must hire an agent (that is, the manager) to run the firm: it is a problem because the owners and the manager have different goals (the owners want to maximize the value of the firm, while the manager wants to maximize his utility), and the manager has better information than the owners about his actions and the firm's opportunities.

There are a number of ways to align better the goals and information of the owners and the manager: monitoring through a board of directors, legally-enforced fiduciary responsibility on the part of the manager, incentive pay (such as profit-sharing, efficiency wages, or stock options) and so forth. Even given these control instruments, however, there are still better and worse owners, where the quality of the owner is judged by how oriented to long-run profit maximization they can force the firm to be. The conclusion is that the ownership structure does matter for efficiency. And if the way that privatization is done affects the ownership structure, then privatization cannot be separated from efficiency.

24. This is only one of the reasons why the ownership structure matters for efficiency, however. For example, recent research has emphasized how efficient investment can depend on the ownership structure. This can happen when an asset's value depends on its joint use with some other asset, and complete contracting is impossible (see Hart, 1995, and Williamson, 1985).

In a world of zero-transaction costs, if the initial distribution of asset ownership does not yield the most efficient ownership structure there are opportunities for mutually advantageous trade in ownership rights. The most efficient ownership structure would quickly evolve regardless of how the rights were initially allocated. This is not true, however, when the transfer of ownership rights is costly to accomplish. The actual distribution of ownership will then be sensitive to the initial distribution, and so privatization does matter for efficiency.[25]

4.2. EQUITY-EFFICIENCY TRADE-OFFS AND PRIVATIZATION

The difficulty of the problem facing a privatizing reformer seeking to maximize social welfare has become apparent as this chapter has developed. The simple two-part strategy outlined at the beginning is undermined by limitations on information and enforceability, and also by the imperfection of markets (which undermines the reformer's ability to separate privatization from concerns about efficiency). I now attempt to bring some of the previous arguments together using a diagrammatic analysis of a two-household economy.

Figure 3.4 reproduces the UPF for a two-household economy with access to a perfectly competitive market mechanism. Given the initial total endowments, ω, the curve shows the maximum utility of household 2 for any given utility of household 1. In Section 4.1, I allowed for the possibility that the economy is not perfectly competitive. In particular, I assumed that principal-and-agent problems make efficiency dependent on ownership. Given this market imperfection, I assume that point E is the only point on the UPF that is achievable, and that this point depends on a particular initial distribution of previously state-owned property. The broken curve is the constrained-utility-possibility curve (or CUPF).[26] This curve, sometimes called the *second best UPF*,

25. The importance of establishing good owners from the outset was stressed early on by Kornai (1995 [1992]) and by Frydman and Rapaczynski (1994). The importance of making ownership rights freely tradable following the initial distribution of such rights has been more recently stressed by Boycko *et al.* (1995), Gray (1996), and World Bank (1996).
26. Given the market imperfection, I assume that there are no possibilities for efficiency-enhancing government interventions.

Figure 3.4 Welfare maximizing

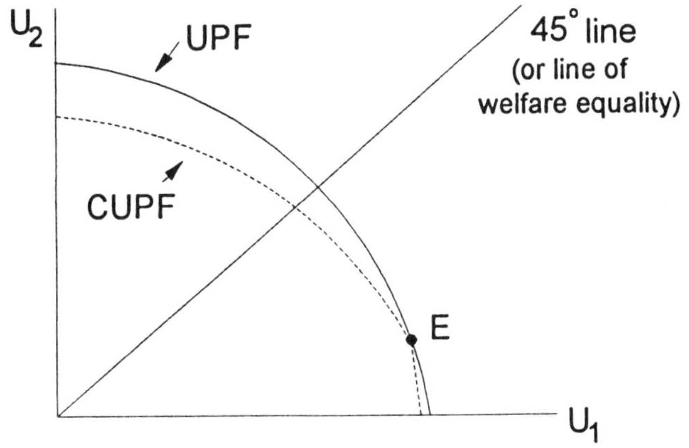

delineates the utility possibilities given the market imperfections. It lies inside the UPF except at point E, at which point the curves are tangent. Each initial distribution of endowments is assumed to lead to a particular point on the CUPF, that is, a particular distribution of welfare. Since there is an unequal distribution of welfare at E, the reformer faces a trade-off between equity (that is, a more equal distribution of welfare) and efficiency.

In Section 3, I argued that the reformer also faces this trade-off when using distortive taxes and transfers to pursue distribution goals. Given the efficient initial distribution of property, the reformer could use the distortive instruments to change the distribution of welfare from E. But again, the reformer will face a CUPF that lies inside the UPF, except at point E.

Therefore, the reformer has two options for achieving distribution goals: (1) choose the initial distribution of property, trading off efficiency for equity as she moves up along the CUPF from E; and (2) choose the efficient distributional of property, and then use distortionary taxes and transfers to trade off efficiency for equity (again moving in a north-west direct from E). Figure 3.5 shows the case where option 1 dominates option 2. In other words, the CUPF for option 1 (labelled $CUPF^1$) lies outside the CUPF for option 2 (labelled $CUPF^2$) except at

Figure 3.5 Equity–efficiency trade-offs

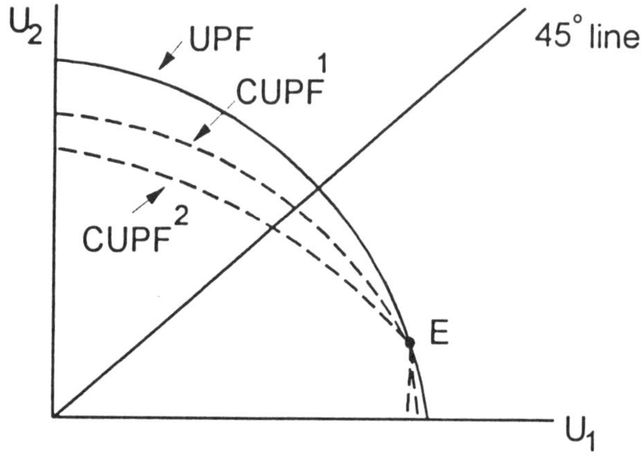

point E. Of course, it is also possible that option 2 dominates option 1. In that case, the concentration of the efficiency of privatization options is justified, since it is always better to choose the efficient ownership structure, and then redistribute income using taxes and transfers, that to choose an inefficient ownership structure to begin with. A third possibility is that the CUPFs cross. The best way of pursuing distribution goals will then depend on the shape of the social indifference curves, and thus on the form of the social welfare function.

Contrary to our finding in the idealized market environment of Section 2 that the privatizing reformer should focus on distribution goals – that is, on picking the point on the UPF – we now find that, given market imperfections, it is theoretically possible that this reformer should focus only on efficiency. The optimal policy depends on the empirical comparison of the efficiency–equity trade-offs faced when using alternative redistributive instruments.

In Section 3, I argued that the trade-off is likely to be very severe when using taxes and transfers in a transition setting. How severe is the trade-off between equity and efficiency in the choice of the initial ownership structure? It is heartening that there are indications that it need not be too severe. Gray (1996), writing from the perspective of the need to create efficient ownership, points to the success of voucher privatization methods (especially in the Czech and Slovak republics).

When designed well, these privatizations allow for a reasonably fast transfer of ownership, a concentration of ownership through investment funds, and a reasonably equal distribution of initial ownership rights.[27]

5. CONCLUDING COMMENTS

I have argued that post-communist reformers, and the economists who advise them, should weight distributional goals when evaluating options for privatization. The argument has not been based on the value judgement that an equitable distribution is desirable.[28] Rather it is based on one of the most practical of economic ideas: the division of labour. I have described how the central results in normative economics – the fundamental theorems of welfare economics – recommend a division of the attention of the reformer according to the subject-matter of the policy choice at hand. When the subject-matter is the micro-workings of the market system, the economist should probably focus mainly on efficiency. The Chairman of President Carter's Council of

27. Other privatization methods that appear to be at odds with equity also need not be if well designed. For example, the distribution implications of direct sales to core investors depends on what use is made of the revenues raised. If these revenues are used to lower top marginal tax rates then the beneficiaries will be better off, whereas if the revenues are used to fund poverty relief that would otherwise not be forthcoming, then the beneficiaries are less well-off. There are reasons to be concerned about sales of assets as the method of privatization, however. If liquidity constraints are widespread, the assets may be sold at deep discounts to those fortunate enough to have access to the necessary funds. If these people are members of the old *nomenklatura* that benefited under communism, then the fairness of such privatizations is highly questionable. Also, if the bidding for the firms is restricted to the well-connected (as seems to have been the case with the privatization of Russia's natural-resource-based industries), the distribution of the benefits of the privatizations will be skewed.

    Insider-based privatization can also lead to inequitable results, especially when the benefits go to managers rather than workers. Furthermore, a large fraction of the population does not work in state firms, and the value of firms varies widely (Sachs, 1993). In Sections 2.3 and 2.4, I noted that insiders can sometimes buy their support by giving them ownership shares on concessional terms. While the constraints placed on privatization by such enforceability limitations must be appreciated, it is important to weigh the distribution implications of this buying of support against the efficiency gains from early privatization.

28. The social welfare maximization formulation that I use is not completely free of value judgements, however. For instance, with its focus on utility outcomes, it provides no room for valuing aspects of the processes by which those outcomes are brought about, such as non-coercion.

Economic Advisors, Charles Schultze, has made the case for the economist as advocate of efficiency thus:

> A mainstream economist cannot fail to place major emphasis on the long-run efficacy of the price system to promote the national income and welfare. ... The economist has been trained to understand the complex ways in which the market system works to generate beneficial results and to recognize the roots of market failure when it occurs. ...
>
> For this reason, I strongly believe that economists in government have a particular role to play in the area of micro policy, not merely as disinterested purveyors of technical advice, but as advocates. I am not merely offering the pious statement that the economist ought to favour efficiency. What I am saying is that in matters of specific micro policy, and within reasonable bounds his role is to be the partisan advocate for efficiency *even when the result is significant income losses for particular groups – which it almost always is.* (Schultze, 1982, p.62; original emphasis)

But Schultze went on to clarify that this advocacy role was appropriate only when 'grand matters of progressive taxation, welfare reform and the distribution of income by income class' are not at stake. Surely, this admonition is even more appropriate when the subject matter is the 'time zero' distribution of ownership rights. Since the opportunity for making such a choice does not come along very often, it is perhaps not surprising that economists have fallen into the habit of seeing their role as advocates of efficiency in all economic policy decisions. This could explain why the economic analysis of privatization options has been overwhelmingly done from the perspective of efficiency. Although I have admitted that distribution cannot be separated from efficiency when markets are imperfect, I hope that I have still been reasonably convincing with my main contention: when the subject-matter of the policy decision is the initial distribution of private property rights, distribution implications should not be ignored.

BIBLIOGRAPHY

Aghion, P. and O. Blanchard (1994). 'On the Speed of Transition in Central Europe', *The NBER Macroeconomics Annual.*

Boycko, M., A. Shleifer and R. Vishny (1995). *Privatizing Russia* (Cambridge, MA: MIT Press).

—— (1996). 'A Theory of Privatization', *Economic Journal*, vol.106, pp.309–19.

Coase, R.H. (1988). *The Firm, the Market, and the Law* (Chicago: University of Chicago Press).

Dewatripont, M. and G. Roland (1995). 'The Design of Reform Packages Under Uncertainty', *American Economic Review*, vol.95, no.5, pp.1207–33.

EBRD (1993). *EBRD Review: Annual Economic Outlook*, September (London: European Bank for Reconstruction and Development).

—— (1994). *Transition Report*, October (London: European Bank for Reconstruction and Development).

—— (1995). *Transition Report: Investment and Enterprise Development* (London: European Bank for Reconstruction and Development).

Frydman, R. and A. Rapaczynski (1994). *Privatization in Eastern Europe: Is the State Withering Away?* (Budapest: CEU Press).

Gray, C.W. (1996). 'In Search of Owners: Privatization and Corporate Governance in Transition Economies', *The World Bank Research Observer*, vol.11, no.2.

Hart, O. (1995). *Firms, Contracts and Financial Structure* (Oxford: Clarendon Press).

Kornai, J. (1990). *The Road to a Free Economy: Shifting From a Socialist System – The Example of Hungary* (New York: Norton)

—— (1995). *Highways and Byways* (Cambridge, MA: MIT Press); first published as 'The Principles of Privatization in Eastern Europe', *Economist*, vol.140, no.2 (1992), pp.153–76.

Lieberman, I. and S. Rahuja (1995). 'An Overview of Privatization in Russia', in I. Lieberman, J. Nellis, E. Karlova, J. Mukherjee and S. Rahuja (eds), *Russia: Creating Private Enterprises and Efficient Markets* (Washington, DC: World Bank).

Mas-Colell, A., M.D. Whinston and J.R. Green (1995). *Microeconomic Theory* (Oxford: Oxford University Press).

Musgrave, R.A. (1959). *The Theory of Public Finance* (New York: McGraw-Hill).

Mussa, M. (1986). 'The Adjustment Process and the Timing of Trade Liberalization', in A. Choksi and D. Papageorgiou (eds), *Economic Reform in Developing Countries* (Oxford: Basil Blackwell), pp.68–124.

Nozick, R. (1974). *Anarchy, State, and Utopia* (New York: Basic Books).

Okun, A.M. (1975). *Equality and Efficiency: The Big Tradeoff* (Washington, DC: Brookings).

Sachs, J. (1993). *Poland's Jump to the Market Economy* (Cambridge, MA: MIT Press).

—— (1994). 'Understanding "Shock Therapy"', manuscript (Cambridge, MA: Harvard University).

Schultze, C. (1982). 'The Role and Responsibilities of the Economist in Government', *American Economic Review*, vol.72, no.2

Sen, A. (1983). 'The Profit Motive', *Lloyd's Bank Review*, no.147, pp.1–20; reprinted in A.K. Sen, *Resources, Values and Development* (Cambridge, MA: Harvard University Press, 1984), ch.3.

—— (1987). *On Ethics and Economics* (Oxford: Basil Blackwell).

Shleifer, A. and R. Vishny (1994). 'Politicians and Firms', *Quarterly Journal of Economics*, November.

Stiglitz, J. (1994). *Whither Socialism?* (Cambridge, MA: MIT Press).

Tanzi, V. (1994). 'Reforming Public Finances in Economies in Transition', *International Tax and Public Finance*, vol.1, no.2, pp.149–63.

Williamson, O. (1985). *The Economic Institutions of Capitalism* (New York: Free Press).

World Bank (1996). *From Plan to Market: World Development Report 1996* (Oxford: Oxford University Press).

4. A Comparative Analysis of Privatization: A Chinese Way and a Polish Way

Ken Morita and Kazuo Zaiki

INTRODUCTION

Since the post-communist countries began to transform their economies to market-oriented ones, one of the most serious targets for their transformation has been undoubtedly privatization, a topic discussed in depth in Chapter 3, above. However, most privatization processes in the post-communist countries have been delayed and have never been fully successful. The purpose of this chapter is to investigate the current situations and problems encounter in the privatization experience, focusing our attention upon Poland, and, on the basis of that experience, to project a future route for another interesting privatization case, namely that of China.

1. SOME POLISH EXPERIENCES OF PRIVATIZATION

1.1. The Current Situation of Privatization in Poland

The Polish method of privatization[1] may be classified into three types: (1) capital privatization, (2) direct privatization; and (3) liquidation. We call capital privatization a method whereby state-owned companies are

1. This section is based upon the following two excellent works on privatization: Bednarski (1995) and Karpińska-Mizielińska and Smuga (1996).

first transformed into companies wholly owned by the state Treasury, and then the Treasury sells the shares in these companies to investors. Direct privatization is, as the name indicates, a process of directly privatizing the company's ownership by (i) mainly leasing the company's assets, (ii) selling the whole company or a part of the company's assets, or (iii) using the company's assets to create other companies. Liquidation is a very unpopular way because the procedure requires a state-owned company to be wound up.

Normally we could expect to find all the above three types: large state-owned companies in a sound financial situation will be dealt with through capital privatization; small and medium-sized companies whose financial situation is sound will be disposed of through direct privatization; and small and medium-sized companies in a poor financial condition are likely to be placed in liquidation. However, as far as the domestic economy is concerned, there are no major differences among the three types: most concentrate on the industrial sector (see Table 4.1).

Table 4.1 Ownership transformation in 1990–95 by section of national economy and privatization method (per cent)

	Capital Privatization	*Direct Privatization*	*Liquidation*	*Total*
Industry	94.6	67.1	57.3	70.8
Agriculture	0.6	6.3	20.6	10.3
Services	4.8	26.6	22.1	18.9

Sources: Ministry of Privatization (Warsaw) (1996), *Dinamika Przekształceń Własnościowych*; Karpińska-Mizielińska and Smuga (1996), 'Ownership Transformation Process in Poland'.

As is often mentioned, the second type of privatization, particularly leasing, has been almost saturated because that type of privatization is the least disruptive way for workers. In the 6 years 1990–95, altogether 1,610 companies were completely privatized in Poland, among which 10 per cent were disposed of by capital privatization, 65 per cent by direct privatization and 25 per cent by liquidation.

The mass privatization programme in Poland was very much delayed in comparison with the original plans. More than five years after the reform, the National Investment Funds scheme was inaugurated in 1995. This scheme has 15 national investment funds and 512 companies - about the same number as mentioned by Lipton and Sachs: 'If most of the top 500 firms can be privatized, then an important part of the industrial sector, measured by employment, sale, and net income, will have been privatized' (see Sachs, 1993, pp.301–2). However, it is difficult to say that the Polish mass privatization programme has enjoyed a sound performance. We believe that it is too early to evaluate this method as policy, but several reasons are sometimes advanced criticizing the programme: (1) late implementation; (2) excessive detail; (3) centralization and red tape; (4) inclusion in the programme enterprises which so far have failed to adjust to the changing environment; (5) lack of interest shown by foreign capital, and so on (see Karpińska-Mizielińska and Smuga, 1996, p.161).

1.2. Some Problems of the Polish Privatization

Not only for Poland but also for all the transition economies, the main goals of privatization would be the following two: (1) at the micro-level, to identify entrepreneurs and to let them manage companies (needless to say, in order fully to implement the managerial roles it is necessary to develop a capital market - for direct finance - and to have efficient banks - for indirect finance); (2) at the macro-level, to dismantle a distorted production structure in favour of a more efficient one.

It goes without saying that the distorted production structure means an overblown industrial sector and an underdeveloped service branch. As Winiecki has correctly observed (1988, ch.3), the distorted structure was the result of over-substitution of imports and the autarkic bias in favour of centrally-directed companies (both of these features are the legacy of the Soviet-type economy). Statistically speaking, we could easily find evidence of the distortion. Table 4.2 shows the excessive growth of industry in Poland compared with Greece, Portugal and Spain. To reform the economy for greater efficiency, therefore, there is a need to dismantle the overgrown industry and to foster the service sector.

Table 4.2 Distribution of output by sector, 1987 (per cent)

	Poland	*Greece*	*Portugal*	*Spain*
Industry	61	30	40	37
Agriculture	13	13	9	5
Services	26	57	51	58

Source: Sachs (1993), *Poland's Jump to the Market Economy.*

If we now evaluate the results of privatization in Poland, two main problems should be identified. There has been, as Balcerowicz noted (1995, p.332), 'a declining share of industry (including construction) from 52.3 per cent of the GDP in 1988 to 46.6 per cent in 1991'. However, since 1992 industry's share of GDP has been growing by 8.8 per cent, although agriculture was declining by 0.8 per cent and services declining by 8.0 per cent. Since 1992, industry has grown rather than being reduced as far as the structure of GDP is concerned.

The second problem concerns the micro-level, and is shown in Tables 4.3 and 4.4. Table 4.3 indicates that the ratios of total costs to total revenues, and in 1991–94 the cost input in percentages, in the private sector were greater than in the public sector (that is, the public sector was more efficient than the private sector). Table 4.4 shows the ratio of gross profit to total costs, and indicates that, except in 1992, the ratio of profit to costs in the public sector were higher than in the private sector (in other words, the public sector was more profitable than the private sector).

Table 4.3 Cost input (per cent)

	1991	*1992*	*1993*	*1994*
All economic entities	94.0	96.8	96.1	95.7
Public sector	*93.7*	96.0	94.9	94.7
Private sector	*97.8*	99.9	98.5	97.4

Sources: Central Statistical Office (Warsaw), *Rocznik Statystychny*, annual.

Table 4.4 Profitability (per cent)

	1991	*1992*	*1993*	*1994*
All economic entities	4.8	2.2	2.9	4.2
Public sector	–	3.6	3.9	5.5
Private sector	–	6.0	1.1	2.1

Sources: Central Statistical Office (Warsaw), *Rocznik Statystychny*, annual.

Given the above statistics concerning the excessive growth of the industrial sector and the greater efficiency of the public sector, it is difficult to assert that up to 1994–95 the Polish privatization policy had achieved a good result.

1.3. What Should Be Next for Privatization?

Privatization is a policy tool which aims to raise economic efficiency through dismantling an inefficient structure. According to a study investigating the reasons for privatized companies' good performance (see Karpińska-Mizielińska and Smuga, 1996), these are (1) the quality of managerial staff; (2) a low rate of conflict in the enterprise; (3) good adjustability to changing external conditions and so on; it suggests, moreover, that privatization does not appear to have a critical effect upon a company's performance. In other words, whether it is state-owned or not, good management makes companies improve.

On the basis of Polish experience, the following could be understood as the important factors. First, a newly established company, particularly in the tertiary sector, needs support; second, as was mentioned above, private companies are less efficient than public. Among several factors accounting for the inefficiency of the private sector one of the most serious is a lack of capital, which makes companies' scale too small and renders efficient management difficult. Although, as is often suggested, the low profitability of private companies occurs partly because they do not want to report their true profits, it is hard to confirm this scientifically. The factor of capital shortage is still critical. Third, as will be indicated below, one goal of privatization is to free a government from the burden of relieving inefficient state-owned companies. Generally, a soft-budget arrangement for granting sufficient capital would not constitute a sound policy. Instead of a soft-budget scheme, an 'infant industry' approach should be adopted, which needs some criteria for selecting which industries are to be favoured. According to Karpińska-Mizielińska and Smuga (1966, p.167), 'Capital privatization is to cover the following branches: the manufacture of tobacco, chemicals, pharmaceuticals, foodstuffs and beverages, machinery and equipment, building material; trade and the banking sector.' The criteria seem to be the price of shares and terms of payment, the export-oriented nature of investment and so on. Apart from the above criteria adopted by the Polish government, from the viewpoint of the excessive growth of the industrial sector, appropriate industries for capital privatization would be the industries that enjoy a comparative advantage, such as foodstuffs and beverages, machinery and equipment, and the trade sector.[2]

Referring to the Polish experience for privatization, therefore, we would stress that the necessary conditions for successful privatization are more active governmental support towards the establishment of new private companies and improving the potential of industries that possess a comparative advantage.

2. WHAT IS A CHINESE WAY?

In this section we first define the term 'privatization'. In our understanding, privatization has two different dimensions: (1) 'ownership' and (2) 'management'. Here we use the term 'privatization' to indicate the dimension of management, which means that privatization is a process of forming entrepreneurs who manage firms independently of central planning.

Economic reform experiments in Eastern Europe and China share both the crucial elements of 'capitalization' and 'marketization'. As far as a process of reform towards a market economy is concerned, there are two necessities: (1) a 'market' - that is, a framework for

2. Polish car manufacturers are not privatized at the moment. However, the majority of FSO and FSM could be taken over by such foreign companies as Daewoo, FIAT and GM, as has been planned. After they would start producing the whole auto-making process in Poland, Poland would have more efficient production structure regardless of ownership

marketization; and (2) an 'enterprise' that works well within that framework. The latter is, in other words, a privatized company.

In this presentation, in focusing upon the Chinese case we investigate how China is planning to create enterprises for a market-oriented economy and elaborate on two principal questions: alternative ways of privatization and the difficulty of reforming state-owned firms. We also consider what the specific Chinese feature is compared with East European experiences.

2.1. Two Ways in Privatization

As regards ways to create market-oriented actors, the East European way of privatizing the existing state-owned enterprises is not the only approach. Another way is to let entrepreneurs and investors establish new firms. It may be possible to argue that establishing new firms might be more effective than privatizing the existing state-owned enterprises. In our view, the privatization experience of Eastern Europe gives us grounds for such an assertion.

For example, the East European experience reveals some problems associated with attempts to convert the existing state-owned firms into joint-stock companies. First, in the East European approach, a majority of the stock is preferentially allocated to managers and workers of the firms concerned. This automatically means that the management decisions are left to managers and workers who have no experience of a market-oriented economy. Most state-owned firms have unprofitable sections and workers, and in order for these inefficient firms to survive in a market-oriented system, managers have to take the initiative in rationalizing their organization. Managers and workers generally resist the rationalization of their business and organization since that leads to unemployment. At an early stage, therefore, all the workers and organizations would need to be transferred to a new firm. Second, the new firm would take over the existing equipment and machines, and utilize them for a while. In the former socialist countries, since there was no competition among firms, most state-owned firms used fairly old-fashioned equipment and machinery. Needless to say, with such outdated equipment it was very difficult to produce high quality products efficiently. Factories also were ancient and inefficient. Even if these firms were privatized, the situation would remain unchanged. It is to be expected, therefore, that privatization would be less than successful. Third, there are grounds to suspect that the former state-owned firms discharge polluted air and water, so a privatized firm taking over a state-owned firm would become responsible for the pollution. Naturally, these pollution-producing firms are not attractive to foreign investors. Let us consider another case, in which private investors create totally new firms. In this case, needless to say, an owner of the firm has no need to take over the existing workers and organizations: instead, all workers can be newly employed. The new owner does not have to take over old-fashioned equipment and machinery, neither is he responsible for pollution.

As mentioned above, it would be too simple to expect that the privatization of the existing state-owned firms automatically produces efficient market-oriented private enterprises. A more efficient way towards a market-oriented economy, therefore, would be for inefficient state-owned firms that have no good prospects to be declared bankrupt by the government. It would also be necessary for the government to allow private investors and businessmen to establish new firms.

2.2. Difficulty of Reforming State-Owned Firms

As a matter of fact, it is not an easy matter for a government to declare state-owned firms bankrupt, mainly because with the bankruptcy many workers lose their jobs, and it would be too optimistic to assume that newly established firms could absorb the unemployed workers. If the problem of unemployment became very serious, it might make a society unstable, and such instability would be more serious for a socialist government than for a capitalist one.

Responsibility for managing a state-owned firm is taken in the final count by the government. This means, therefore, that the debt of a state-owned firm should be financed by the government, and in the socialist era, the East European governments undertook a huge amount of expenditure to finance the debt. New governments in Eastern Europe have tried to end the soft budget policy - indeed, that has been a principal purpose of the privatization policy since the East European reform started.

East European governments hope that a kind of natural selection operates through a market mechanism (in place of government regulation) to bankrupt inefficient firms. Unemployed workers who lost their jobs through government regulations would be deeply critical of the government's policy. If a market mechanism purges inefficient firms and workers, however, they cannot directly criticize government policy. Thus, natural selection as a means of purging inefficiency is a reasonable function of the market economy.

As mentioned above, it is not always a sound policy to privatize existing state-owned firms in order to create competitive private enterprises. In Eastern Europe, however, in order to purge unprofitable state-owned firms it was necessary for the governments to privatize state-owned firms first of all.

Unlike Eastern Europe, China has possessed a socialist system, and the goal for China is to establish a 'socialist market economy'. In the Chinese economy today there are two different economic sectors: one is a 'planning sector' and the other is a 'free-market sector'. The former consists mainly of state-owned firms and the latter of foreign companies and local firms. It is undoubtedly the case that the latter has been a principal driving force for high-speed economic growth in China. The problem of the economy lies in the state-owned firms, one-third of which are assumed to be in deficit. As far as state-owned firms are concerned, China is planning to separate ownership from management and to privatize management activities. We believe that the Chinese way has something in common with the reform attempted by former socialist governments in Eastern Europe. The future will answer the question of whether the Chinese reform will succeed in overcoming the East European failure or will follow the same unsuccessful way as the East European countries.

CONCLUSION

Let us conclude with the following assessment of the current situation in Poland and China:

1. As far as the statistics on privatized companies' performance in Poland since 1990 are concerned, it is difficult to agree that Polish privatization has been successful.
2. It is also hard to see a new and more efficient production structure emerging from the dismantling of a distorted production structure.

3. The main reason for these failures is the lack of newly established private companies which was originally due to a lack of capital and technology, and to the political battle which delayed the implementation of privatization.
4. In the management privatization in the Chinese manner, therefore, the key factors would be capital and technology.
5. Finally, above all, privatization is a long-term effort and more than a decade is necessary for a definitive evaluation of the process.

REFERENCES

Balcerowicz, Leszek (1995). *Socialism, Capitalism, Transformation* (Budapest: Central European University Press).

Bednarski, Marek (1995). 'Outcome and Effects of Ownership Reforms', in IPISS, *Social Policy in 1993–94: Main Problems in the Transition Period* (Warsaw).

GUS (Central Statistical Office), *Rocznik Statystyczny* (Statistical Annual).

Karpińska-Mizielińska, Wanda and Tadeusz Smuga, (1996). 'Ownership Transformation Process in Poland', in IRISS, *Transforming the Polish Economy 1995* (Warsaw).

Lipton, David and Jeffrey Sachs (1992). 'Privatization in Eastern Europe: The Case of Poland', Brookings Papers on Economic Activity, 2.

Ministry of Privatization (1996). *Dynamika Przekształceń Własnościowych* (Dynamics of Ownership Change) (Warsaw).

Sachs, Jeffrey (1993). *Poland's Jump to the Market Economy* (Cambridge, MA: MIT Press).

Winiecki, Jan (1988). *The Distorted World of Soviet-Type Economies* (London: Routledge).

5. Integration Compatibility of the Hungarian Economy

Karoly Foldes

1. INTEGRATION COMPATIBILITY AND SYSTEMIC CHANGES

The recent integration drive of Hungary is a logical corollary of systemic changes begun back in 1989. Through this transition the nation has begun to acquire an integration compatibility with its Euro-Atlantic environment. There are two levels of integration compatibility: the first comprises steps that should be introduced from the viewpoint of general economic rationality; the second contains measures pertaining more specifically to EU regulations. Hungary has passed through the first level, while the country's steps to membership of the European Union assume a drive for EU enlargement that has recently been on the agenda of the Inter-governmental Conference.[1] A sober and definitely reformist attitude both to deepening and to widening the community has been adopted. It is recognized that enlargement will involve costs and benefits both for the EU and for its new members. The forthcoming fifth expansion deals with a zone of small or medium-sized countries with less advanced economies than the EU average. Previous expansions also included some similar nations (such as Greece and Portugal), but this one is the first to deal with several former Eastern-bloc states. Because of its scope and its diversity, this expansion has to be preceded by more important changes than the previous ones. In addition to and in connection with the deepening of the Union at different speeds, the EU will have to address the

1. Commission Opinion, *Reinforcing Political Union and Preparing for Enlargement* (Brussels, 1996).

implications of the increased number of members. Still greater flexibility is needed so as to give enough time to the new member states to attain integration conditions gradually. The actual accession may take place only in a sequence. Treatment of countries as a bloc is excluded, even in respect of the Visegrad cooperating countries. Three nations of this group have a chance to be among the first to gain full membership: Hungary, Poland and the Czech Republic.

It is appropriate therefore, to review some similarities and a few particulars of their background and the process of social transformation. Economic conditions are the main concern from the viewpoint of both their transformation and their integration compatibility. At the beginning of changes, in 1990, the GDP per capita indicator, compared to the Austrian level, was 30.4 for Poland, 37.8 for Hungary, and 50.4 for the Czech (and Slovak) Republic,[2] which also provides evidence of differences between them. This gap remains in relation to Austria, but industrial restructuring, evolving services and rising productivity are salient indicators of change. Growth is rapid in Poland and the Czech Republic and has been renewed in Hungary. De-nationalization of most assets has been an essential element of the economic transformation, and millions of small entrepreneurs have emerged to become the most important accelerating factor of the development. Large companies, allowing for some negative consequences, contributed greatly to capital imports and economic growth.

The Euro-Atlantic and global implications of changes are emphasized by, *inter alia*, the operation of non-European multinationals in the sub-region, OECD membership of the Czech Republic, Hungary and Poland and positive efforts on the part of these countries to adhere to the North Atlantic defence community.

There are also transformation (not transition-specific) correlative links and similarities of this area with the rest of Europe: for example, the evolving digitalization of life and a degree of dismantling of welfare systems. The same is true concerning the fight against drug abuse, terrorism, money laundering, nuclear trade, and so on.

2. *Comparaison internationale des produits intérieurs bruts en Europe 1990* (New York and Geneva: United Nations, 1995), p.5.

2. SOME HUNGARIAN PARTICULARS

The particulars of Hungary on the way from association with the EU (ratified in 1994) to accession will be discussed throughout this chapter. From the beginning it has to be noted that this country borders on the territory of the tumultuous southern Slavic area. Hungary's accession to the EU will consolidate the realm of stability to the north of this territory. Moreover, the future expansion of stability and the adoption of community norms on minority rights would also improve the conditions of millions of Hungarians living in several neighbouring states.

A further distinct feature of Hungary is a model of society that is historically different from the Soviet model of Communism having been steadily reformed, particularly following the introduction of a new economic mechanism in 1968. The ambivalence of the system stemmed from the fact that it was established as the antithesis of the 1956 revolution, even though it later incorporated a good deal of the latter's legacy. In its own interest it acquired a degree of adaptability to domestic needs and the norms of the international community. Even if the reforms were partly reversed and failed to reach a critical level of change in the 1970s and 1980s, they none the less helped to modernize and open up the economy and extended personal freedom, thereby appealing to the other peoples of the Eastern bloc and meeting a rather hostile reception on the part of their conservative leaders. Hungary made a start in breaking the ossified social structure in practical business. In the 1980s the reforms were already unable to mitigate the decline in economic performance, but they contributed to the recruitment of some pragmatically-minded people into the ruling elite, and increasingly even into part of the governing bodies. Finally, in a unique move, this group took power from the old-style party bosses, began to demolish the old order and consented to free elections: that is, were willing to be voted out of power. In doing so they secured not only the euthanasia of the system but also economic survival for themselves. The end of the regime was thus much better than its start.

Both a negative and a positive peculiarity of Hungary stemmed from its early openness: high indebtedness and high foreign investments. The Czech Republic, boasting of the best indicators of the sub-region, was much less indebted. Poland had more debt. However, the per capita indebtedness was at its highest in Hungary. Nevertheless, the country managed to avoid rescheduling of its debt repayments, while the debt itself made substantial privatization a necessity. Privatization and a sound business environment have been the main factors due to which Hungary attracted a fairly generous share of capital imports, the highest per capital in the sub-region.

The following sections will discuss some integration and transition steps taken by the country in the economic field. Preparing for full membership of the EU goes hand in hand with profound economic and social change - a process which is in the short and medium term jeopardizing stability. Hungary, as a prospective EU member may count on receiving some financial transfers from the Community. As an associate it has already received PHARE benefits. Stand-by loans from the IMF, benefits from the World Bank and EBRD investments also play a major role and help defray a part of the costs of transition. Coordinated with EU assistance they can make a substantial contribution to the preparation of conditions for integration. In spite of this, the country itself is to bear the main burden of changes. Accordingly, our problem-setting should revolve around internal efforts to apply a matrix of integration measures to concrete circumstances in the field of economic performance, policy, regulation and institutions.

Before a detailed assessment of the recent situation a short general account of the 1990s is appropriate. The macroeconomic situation has been by no means favourable during the decade, as the GDP decreased for five years. The transition was complicated not only by the debt service: ill-conceived programmes, unwise and ill-administered economic measures and abuses have greatly contributed to the worsening of the situation, at least in the fields of agriculture, public finances and indebtedness that continued to grow up to 1996. In another complicating development the country lost overnight about two-thirds of its East-European trading partners and markets for its products, which could not be sold elsewhere. The supply of commodities and raw materials from these markets has dried up equally. The impact of war in former Yugoslavia was anything but beneficial.

In the light of these events, which exerted a more or less similar impact on the three nations, a degree of versatility in the potential of their economic culture was demonstrated by a shift (in fact, a reorientation) of foreign trade to Western Europe, which now accounts for about two-thirds to three-quarters of Hungarian exports. The export boom did not last for long and the terms of trade worsened, but an actual orientation of trade to Europe was completed in two years.

3. THE FIRST YEARS: 1990–92

As early as 1990 major moves to liberalize trade were made in conformity with the World Trade Organization (then known as GATT) rules on the abolition of non-tariff restrictions. A newly introduced set of laws was aimed at harmonizing the Hungarian system with EU standards. Acts of economic legislation appear to be the most important of these. Since 1990 the Hungarian government has been controlling the prices of only about 10 per cent of goods and services. This concerns mainly public enterprises providing the postal service, electricity supply, and so on. New legislative acts (such as laws on investment funds, accounting, the Central Bank, financial institutions, bankruptcy, and so forth) were conceived so as to ensure a safe and sound climate for foreign involvement: investments were and are guaranteed against nationalization; foreign companies may repatriate their profits in convertible currencies; a value-added tax and a business profit tax were introduced as the two key taxes on business activity; depending on the type of economic activity, tax exemptions were offered. This legislative direction was continued through the decade.[3] In 1991–92 the Hungarian macro-policy could boast of some improvement in stability and the nation was indeed doing relatively well in comparison with some of its neighbours. It was during this period that the bulk of foreign trade shifted to Western Europe.[4] International current payments were balanced, and the inflow of foreign capital was continuous. It slowed down afterwards for some time, but the nation gained a fairly good share of all investments in East–Central Europe.

As far as bad news is concerned, negative growth must be mentioned. GDP decreased by 20 per cent from 1989 to 1992, industrial output decreased by about a quarter, and the rate of unemployment reached about 13 per cent.[5] In 1991 inflation and interest rates reached more

3. *Hungarian Rules of Law in Force* (*HRLF*), 1992–96.
4. *Statisztikai Havi Közlemények* (Monthly Bulletin of Statistics) (Budapest: Központi Statisztikai Hivatal), 1992, no.7.
5. National Bank of Hungary, *Monthly Report*, March 1992.

than 35 per cent, and the maximum tax rate on personal income was 50 per cent. In connection with a slower rise of consumer prices (at about 23 per cent) in 1992 the tax ceiling was reduced to 40 per cent. The nominal interest rates were also lowered. But the state budget deficit was the highest ever recorded in Hungary: depending on the method of calculation, it was estimated at 6–8 per cent of GDP.[6]

The recession was no Keynesian one where aggregate demand should be increased so as to reduce incompletely utilized capacity and manpower reserves. In Hungary the employment level had been maintained in an artificial way. Nor did the excess money supply give enough grounds to identify the inflation as a classical Friedmanite one. As reported by the Central Bank, while all economic indicators of output worsened, the money supply increased in 1992 by 25 per cent.[7] The Hungarian macroeconomic policy might be seen as one that embraced both an abused monetarism and an inflationary bias. As shown by statistical data the extremes were distributed unequally: while the money was supplied to the government, access of the business sphere to credits was restricted.[8] In this way, the inflation generated partly by deficit financing was complemented by a recession generated partly by credit scarcity.

Commodity structure, and the technical, marketing and organizational level expressed in competitiveness and international performance, remained the core weaknesses of the Hungarian economy. Central and local bureaucracy was likewise a major hindrance to doing efficient business.

At least four more factors created the environment for macroeconomic policy. One was state redistribution of income. In Hungary more than 63 per cent of GDP was concentrated in various funds of the central government, state social security and municipal authorities.[9] The government failed to begin reforms in this field, and for five more years this indicator remained unchanged. Another factor was the mounting pressure on the government to compensate for the diminishing real purchasing power of final consumers by indexation. While the government was siphoning inflated money into the budget the recipients of indexed benefits tended to siphon the same amount of real

6. *Statisztikai Havi Közlemények*, 1992, no.12.
7. National Bank of Hungary, *Monthly Report*, March 1992.
8. Ibid.
9. Minister of Finances, *Report to Parliament*, 27 August 1991.

value away from the budget as previously. Abolishing indexation at the existing speed of inflation, however, would have meant impoverishment for hundreds of thousands of the population. Slowing down inflation should have been a main priority for the economic policy, but, along with welfare reform, it was not.

The third factor was the speed of liberalization, which was somewhat exaggerated in view of the actual level of development of the country, while the depreciation of the Hungarian currency was insufficient.

Some paradoxical phenomena could be discerned over this period: (1) output was declining, yet exports were growing because other demand factors such as investments (constantly) and consumption (in 1991) decreased at a higher rate than the GDP; (2) the currency was appreciating, yet export share was increasing because production outlays were being covered by export earnings; (3) in spite of negative real interest rates, savings were accelerating during a period of two-digit inflation, which may be explained partly by the appeal of an overvalued currency and partly by the fact that for small businesses it was safer to keep liquid assets in the form of personal savings; (4) low real lending rates did not stimulate investments because other conditions offset their impact: undeveloped capital markets and expectations of recession; (5) money supply was excessive, while effective demand was contracting as a result of discrimination in money supply and interest rates for private against public borrowers and also because of high taxes; (6) the price level and unemployment rates were increasing together owing to the inflationary recession.

4. DEVELOPMENTS IN 1993 AND 1994

There were some signs of economic recovery in 1993. There were fewer registered unemployed (which did not, however, signify an increasing employment rate) and the rate of inflation did not accelerate. Investment expansion began. The contraction of markets to the east also stopped thereby opening some rather restricted potential for growth.

In 1993 the growth in the influx of Western foreign investments was continuing, but at a decreasing speed. For some time, Hungary lost its preferred position in the East European region as a destination for foreign investment. The stock of foreign investments amounted to 7 billion dollars accumulated in the years 1990–93. The balance of payments drastically deteriorated in 1993 to reach a deficit of about 3.5 billion dollars, which was partly a result of decreasing agricultural production and exports. There remained also serious imbalances in the state budget.[10] Inflation was checked at 22.5 per cent compared with the previous year's 23 per cent. The minimum reserve requirements for banks were raised in order to ensure the safety of the banking system, and a major programme of bank and debtor consolidation began. These measures were necessary, but the way in which they were implemented after a while released the money supply. Further indicators of the economy on 31 December 1993 are shown below.[11]

(a) Data on (1992=200): *Industrial output:* 104; *Exports:* 86.9; *Imports:* 113.5; *Investments at current prices:* 117.5.
(b) Banking interest rates: Lending rates on loans maturing within a year, weighted average: 25.6 per cent; Deposit rates, same maturity: 16.6 per cent.
(c) Deficit of the state budget: 199.66 billion HUF.

Along with transition processes a profound deterioration in living standards was under way. That fact itself was tolerated conditionally by the public within a perspective of economic growth in the not too distant future. A danger of potential social unrest was also inherent in the continuing decrease in the level of individual consumption up to 1993. Nor could a minor increase in the total consumption change the picture by very much.

A change of administration took place about the middle of 1994. Data for the first half of 1994 show continuing growth and continuing disequilibrium.[12] For the first five months, on the basis of the same period of 1993, the volume of industrial output reached 108, and of investments, 150. Gross international debt was increasing and so was state budget deficit, and these imbalances did not stop under the new government. Disequilibrium reached a peak at the end of 1994, when

10. National Bank of Hungary, *Monthly Report*, April 1994.
11. Ibid.
12. MTI Press releases (MTI Hirek), 26 April and 11 May 1994.

the balance of payments deficit amounted to about four billion US dollars and the deficit of the state budget reached 349 billion forints (about 3 billion US dollars).

The same trends continued in the first quarter of 1995. They were stopped as a result of sweeping austerity measures and a sharp turn in the economic policy of the government: this will be presented in the next section.[13]

5. STABILIZATION IN 1995

The stabilization targets included a cut in the balance of payments deficit to 2.5 billion US dollars (by 1.5 billion HUF), a cut in the state budget deficit to 200 billion forints (by 140 billion forints), a reduction in the number of state employees by 15 per cent, and a target rate of inflation of 27 per cent.[14]

Stabilization entailed the following measures:

1. A depreciation plan begun on 13 March 1995: 13 March (first move): 9 per cent; 16 March–30 June: 0.41 per cent per week, 1.9 per cent per month; 1 July–31 December: 0.29 per cent per week, 1.3 per cent per month (adjusted to 1.2 per cent);
2. A temporary import tariff supplement: (March 1995–June 1997): 8 per cent; a car consumer tax increase: 10 per cent;[15]
3. A raising of the reserve requirements for banks from 14 to 15 per cent; interest rates on foreign reserves: from 12 to 14 per cent; on foreign currency reserves: from 24 to 29 per cent. Refinancing operations of the Central Bank were limited.[16]
4. A limitation on credit demand of the whole public sector at 350 billion forints, which could be covered mostly by household savings. Credit demand in the business sector was expected to reach 300 billion forints (approximately 2.5 billion US dollars), equal to the targeted balance of payments deficit.

13. Government decree 1023/1995, *Magyar Közlöny*, 22 March 1995.
14. *Népszabadság*, 16 March 1995.
15. Ibid.
16. *Napi Gazdaság*, 16 March 1995.

The above plan, introduced with some modifications, greatly contributed to stabilization and the turning of Hungary to the path of sustainable growth that is shown by comparative data for 1994 and 1995.[17] Thus, whereas in 1994 export sales reach 83 per cent of the 1985 level, in 1995 they reach 99.3 per cent, that is, they practically equalled the 1985 figure. The volume of retail trade stood at 91.1 and 81 per cent respectively, in accordance with the shrinking consumer demand. Investments rose from 842.7 billion forints in 1994 to 1070.1 billion in the following year.

Employment went on shrinking. Taking 1990 as a base, from 1994 to 1995 industrial prices changed from 176.2 to 224.3, and consumer prices from 241.6 to 309.7. The state deficit was reduced by about 40 per cent in 1995. A major foreign capital influx in December 1995 amounted to approximately 3 billion US dollars. This was due mainly to privatization. Altogether in 1995 this influx reached some 4.5 billion US dollars.

The consolidation borrowing position of the government is reflected in the indicators of net external debt instead of gross debt, and debt of the state instead of the whole indebtedness of the country. Net external debt at the end of 1995 amounted to 16.8 billion US dollars of which the state debt was 11 billion US dollars.[18]

Towards the end of 1995 the use of privatization income became a controversial issue. In the end, all such income earned above previously estimated amounts was to be applied to the repayment of debt, with the aim of moderating debt-service costs in the future.

In 1995 reducing the general government budget deficit was given high priority in the government's economic strategy. An actual reduction in real wages of approximately 12 per cent was asserted by the government to have contributed to the reallocation of income to savings and to an improvement in the competitiveness of Hungarian products. (In my judgement that was not the case: the reduction of real wages was overdone, and it hindered growth and the collection of more state revenues.) Finally, the debt-service ratio was reduced.

The *Financial Times* has remarked that a combination of high state debt (the largest per capita in the region), high interest rates and inflation, and high taxes has depressed economic growth despite the

17. *Statisztikai Havi Közlemények*, 1996, no.1.
18. *Népszabadság*, 22 March 1996.

country's impressive privatization record and its leading position in attracting investment. GDP rose in real terms at 1.5 per cent in 1995, well below the 5–7 per cent attained in Poland and the Czech Republic. Inflation was at slightly over 20 per cent in Poland and below 10 per cent in the Czech Republic, whereas the Hungarian rate was 28.3 per cent.[19] It may be added, that a major decline in the public sector deficit has up to recently been hampered by the growing interest payment liabilities of the budget.

Hungarian steps to EU membership were discussed in a rather descriptive manner in the previous sections. The rest of this chapter will present a normative analysis of selected tasks in the field of economic convergence criteria.

6. FURTHER CONDITIONS OF FULL EU MEMBERSHIP

1. Economic growth can be sustained, only by means of further strong stabilization measures accompanied by a coordinated income, fiscal and monetary policy aimed at accelerating capital formation. On the assumption that these requirements are lived up to, economic growth would gradually accelerate also and reach the annual average of EU countries in 2–3 years and a higher level afterwards in order to attain a catching-up speed.
2. The aim of raising the share of capital investments requires a whole system of measures consisting of a reduction of the public debt as a percentage of GDP, increasing savings incentives, improving the balance of payments, decreasing external debt and reducing inflation. These are expected to give greater opportunities on the supply side to introduce and accelerate favourable structural changes.
3. Full EU membership requires the adoption of further harmonization changes in addition to those implemented already. Particular attention should be paid to the environmental conditions of the country, which are unsatisfactory.
4. There is a need for a substantial lowering of state transfer payments. As the *Financial Times* wrote,[20] while Hungary's GDP per capita is a

19. *Financial Times*, 12 March 1996.
20. Ibid.

fifth of the OECD average, the share of GDP it spends on welfare is 1.4 times higher. Around a third of state spending is channelled through the countrywide pension and health funds and central government must finance their deficits.[21] Some narrowing of their authority has been on the legislative agenda recently.

5. In accordance with EU targets the consolidated government deficit should fall below 4 per cent of GDP and then stabilize at still lower levels.
6. Assuming that the change of productivity and corporate income exceeds that of wages, by 1997 inflation should drop from the current 20 per cent and more to below 15 per cent, and by 1998 to below 10 per cent. This might exceed the EU threshold.
7. Hungary, during the period as an Associate Member ought to try to negotiate an extension of the preferences in accession to the EU agricultural market. As a precondition the sector has to develop in order to conform to EU requirements in animal and plant health, and state subsidies should be regulated in compliance with the Association Agreement.
8. With a new Foreign Exchange Act passed by the parliament, convertibility on the current account is essentially complete. Convertibility on the capital account must be completed within a few years in order to achieve full liberalization of capital movements.
9. In order to facilitate integration into the money and capital market of the EU it is necessary to privatize the banks as soon as possible and regulatory functions should be used to oblige the banks to engage in prudent lending activities.
10. Monetary stability must be sustained.

Summing up the past, present and future efforts of Hungary to live up to the requirements of its accession to the EU, it has to be recognized that integration is intended not only to provide new prospects but also to require different patterns of behaviour from all business and public actors. A gradual advance from low competitiveness and poor international performance to a developed market economy compatible with the EU is under way in the country.

The Hungarian disadvantages in this respect stem from the previous years when changes were achieved at the expense of negative growth,

21. OECD, *Social and Labour Market Policies in Hungary* (1995).

increasing unemployment and monetary disequilibria. The reorganization of the social security system was delayed. Present economic indicators also fall far behind EU requirements on inflation, the monetary system and the budget deficit. On the other hand, there are important pluses, namely achievements in restructuring, growth renewal, privatization and marketization. The economy is business-friendly, the currency is convertible and foreign capital is pouring into the country. Economic policy improved fundamentally in 1995, and this contributed to the steady inflow of foreign resources and substantially improved the macroeconomic situation. The optimistic scenario foresees that the economic conditions for full membership will be accomplished by the end of this century.

Part III

International Organizations and the Transitional Economies in Eastern Europe

6. Economic Conditions of Accession of the East European Transforming Economies to the European Union: A Policy Proposal

Lucjan T. Orlowski

1. INTRODUCTION

Following the discussion on Hungary in the previous chapter, I would like to suggest that, from a political and a historical perspective, it is inevitable that most of the transforming economies of Central Europe (CE) will be admitted to the European Union in the early years of the twenty-first century. Their accession is, after all, consistent with the vision of the founding fathers of the united Europe to have all nations of the 'old continent' united in the political and economic senses.

This chapter identifies economic problems and desirable policies for the future accession of Central European countries to the European Union (EU). It is not aimed at providing an assessment of the costs of the eastern enlargement of the EU. Satisfactory cost estimates are at this juncture implausible since the Central European economies are still undergoing deep structural changes and adjustments of relative prices, and the future of the EU Common Agricultural Policy (CAP) and structural funds (SF) is still to be determined upon a conclusion of the EU inter-governmental conference (IGC). Thus, specifically, cost estimates for the future inclusion of their agricultural sectors to the framework of the existing CAP based on current relative prices are misleading. The literature evaluating the possible impact of the EU eastern enlargement on the Union budget is extensive (Baldwin, 1994; De Crombrugghe, Minton-Beddoes and Sachs, 1995; Breuss and Schebeck 1996;

Lavigne, 1996; Gagrisch, 1996). In the framework of this study, more important than the problem of costs of the eastern enlargement is the identification of desirable economic policies that will bring Central European countries closer to the economic laws and structures of the EU at some point in the future.

A central assumption of this analysis is that the eastern enlargement is essentially a political and a historical problem and the economic concerns and future policies will have to be identified and designed to facilitate this process. This assumption is consistent with the viewpoint presented by the special survey of the problem in *The Economist* (18–24 November 1995) and shared by the majority of studies addressing the problem of the EU eastern enlargement. *The Economist* survey further states that the first phase of the eastern enlargement should include five countries (CE-5): Poland, the Czech Republic, Slovakia, Hungary and Slovenia. This choice is determined both by historical factors (they were a part of the former Habsburg empire) and by political interests (extending the EU eastern border closer to the former Soviet Union's boundaries).

In the most optimistic scenario, a feasible time of accession of CE-5 will lag by two years behind the targeted year of 2000 promised to Poland by the German Chancellor Helmut Kohl. Negotiations with these countries could start approximately six months after the expected conclusion of the IGC in the late summer 1997. An additional two years for accession talks and a further two years for approval by the European Parliament and by the candidate countries will set the year 2002 as a feasible time for accession. This scenario is consistent with the strategic compromise between an 'empty' membership (or a long transition period without derogations favouring the candidates countries and with derogations favouring the EU) and immediate full membership (Richter, 1995). The second option is strongly advocated by De Crombrugghe, Minton-Beddoes and Sachs (1995).

If the five Central European countries are to be admitted to the EU within the next several years, they must undergo significant adjustments of their economic systems. This study attempts to identify desirable directions of these adjustments and to recognize possible shortcomings of a fast reorientation of their economic policies. The discussion introduces an expected conflict between short-term costs and long-term benefits of the accession to the candidate countries that may significantly erode public endorsement of European unification. The general hypothesis is that the programme of accession to the EU is an extraordinary opportunity for Central European transforming economies to further their long-term market-oriented economic reforms and to resist pressures from selected interest groups willing to return to a more centralized and regulated economic system. The programme of preparations for accession will constitute a core of the second phase of the economic transformation, somewhat different from the solutions of reform programmes of the early 1990s which were based on price liberalization, deregulation of commodity, financial and labour markets and a partial currency convertibility. More specifically, the second phase will require an increasing reorientation of monetary policy towards the stabilization of exchange rates (rather than policy based on the money supply). Trade policies, fiscal policies, tax laws and social welfare policies will all have to be coordinated with EU laws. This study identifies desirable directions for these policies: it strongly emphasizes the role of fiscal consolidation in preparations for accession of CE-5 countries to the EU. A comprehensive policy of disinflation applied by these countries is also stressed.

Section 2 examines general economic conditions for the accession of these countries to the EU, followed by an analysis of recent economic changes and a proposal of specific convergence criteria in Section 3. Monetary policy adjustments in Central European countries in the context of accession to the EU are discussed in Section 4 and fiscal policy in Section 5. The conflict between short-term costs and long-term benefits of the accession is examined in Section 6. The concluding Section 7 identifies further tasks and possible obstacles in the future implementation of these policies. Since the presented analysis emphasizes desirable changes in future economic policies, it adopts mainly a normative approach. In the future process of preparation by Central European transforming economies for accession to the EU it will be necessary to monitor and to assess empirically a degree of adherence of actual adjustments to the fundamentals of the integration programme. It will be further noted that the eastern enlargement will be essentially a very different task from the experiences of accession of Nordic and southern states to the Union, because of the simultaneous continuing economic transformation to a market-based economy in eastern countries. Therefore, their accession programme will emphasize not only monetary and fiscal convergence but also significant structural and institutional reforms.

2. GENERAL ECONOMIC CONDITIONS FOR THE EASTERN ENLARGEMENT

The EU eastern enlargement ought to be fully consistent with the concept of a larger Europe without barriers, stemming from the vision of Jean Monet, Konrad Adenauer, Jacques Delors, and the authors of the Treaty of Rome and the Maastricht Treaty. Undeniably, the eastern enlargement means accession of considerably poorer countries to the Union than the existing members in terms of the GDP per capita. In addition, the Central European candidate countries are still battling with the remnants of central planning and they are trying to change inadequate and obsolete economic structures created by the Soviet-dominated system. Their immediate and full accession would have to be accompanied by considerable income transfers from the West in the form of direct transfers supporting the extension of the CAP and in the form of indirect transfers collected by Central European countries as exporters to the West of many products priced below competitive market prices in industrial nations. The costs of the eastern enlargement can be very significant, although estimates presented by Baldwin (1994) are exaggerated and simply unrealistic. Baldwin estimates the costs of extending the CAP to Central Europe on the basis of relative prices prevailing in the period before the price liberalization of the early 1990s in Central Europe. In a study that takes into account the 1992 MacSharry Agricultural Reform, the Uruguay Round Final Act provisions, and partial reforms of structural policies, Breuss and Schebeck (1996) conclude that the net transfers related to SF and CAP to all Central European countries would reach 30 billion ECU, or 0.4–0.5 per cent of the EU GDP by the year 2000. Transfers to Poland, Hungary, the Czech Republic and Slovakia would amount to 17 billion ECU. This is still less than the burden of the Marshall Plan after the Second World War of approximately 1 per cent of the United States GDP. A more convincing cost estimate is presented by the European Commission which claims that the costs of the EU eastern enlargement related only to CAP subsidies would amount to 9 billion ECU in the first year of the CE-5 accession programme, rising to 12 billion ECU in the tenth year (*The Economist*, 3 August 1996, p.42). In spite of numerous predictions of costs to the EU, the discussion on the expected distribution of macroeconomics costs and burdens on the candidate countries has been very limited (Gabrisch, 1996). The real costs of the EU eastern enlargement remain highly uncertain since future formulas of CAP and SF are still being debated within the framework of the IGC and projected transfers to CE-5 countries are highly negotiable. De Crombrugghe, Minton-Beddoes and Sachs (1995) recommend considerable concessions by the candidate countries in terms of CAP and SF transfers in exchange for a speedy accession. Indeed, since the CE-5 countries GDP per capita is approximately a third of the EU average, well below the current benchmark for SF entitlements of 75 per cent, the current income equalization scheme of the Union countries would be extremely expensive and essentially unaffordable if applied to the eastern candidates.

It is also doubtful that Western consumers will immediately start buying Central European products simply because they are less expensive once trade barriers are lifted. Many of these products are inferior, and they do not satisfy the demands of high-income consumers, especially during economic recovery. Nevertheless, competition policy and the removal of barriers to trade should be a focal point of the economics of the eastern enlargement, as is strongly emphasized by the Commission of the European Communities White Paper of 3 May 1995 when addressing conditions for accession of Central European candidates to the EU (Commission of the European Communities, 1995, paras 2.27–2.29 and 4.22). An environment of competitive markets is fully consistent with the desirable directions of the Central European economic transformation. It is a basis for the evolution of internationally competitive economic structures. It provides incentives for economic profits, technological progress and product development in these countries. To generate gains from free trade, CE-5 countries must diminish the dominance of state monopolies that, with the removal of impediments to trade with the West, would be tempted to exercise restrictive agreements and to engage in market sharing. The integration programme emphasizing active competition provides an opportunity to further disseminate monopoly structures in Central European industries which have been inherited from the command economy system.

The economic criteria of the future accession of CE-5 countries to the EU ought to be based on desirable targets of monetary and fiscal convergence (disinflation and a low budget deficit:GDP ratio). Moreover, since the programme involves economies in transition from a command system to a competitive market, the accession criteria should strongly emphasize institutional and structural changes as well. These changes are essential to make the candidate countries' economic legislation compatible with that of the existing EU members. In this sense, the eastern enlargement differs from the experiences of the Nordic states and South European countries upon admission to the Union. Although the role of the public sector in some of these countries was significant before they joined the EU, specifically in Sweden and Spain, the tasks of privatization and of the development of new private businesses are far greater among the Central European candidates.[1]

In essence, what really matters in the programme of accession of CE-5 countries to the EU is the introduction of fair trade, market access and competition policy. These conditions can be adopted in a short time period, as an extension to the existing association agreements of the EU with these countries. Trade liberalization will not cause a severe decline in the incomes of incumbent members of the Union owing to rather price-inelastic demand for Central European exports. On the contrary, it may contribute to income growth among the current members since the growing economies of Central Europe are expected to increase demand significantly for superior quality western products.[2] Therefore, estimates of possible income losses stemming from a greater market access do not make sense. The CAP certainly remains a problem here. It may be true that immediate accession by the Visegrad Group countries (Poland, Hungary and the Czech and the Slovak Republics) would bankrupt the CAP (Baldwin, 1994), but in the future, relative prices in Central Europe are likely to become gradually aligned with those in the EU, and the expenses of the CAP, which already constitute more than a half of the EU budget, are expected to be gradually reduced. These subsidies in their present form are simply unsustainable for the Union.

Concerns related to equalization of GDP per capita levels will not really matter in the accession programme, again owing to predominantly inelastic demand for generally inferior Central European

1. The experiences of Spain with economic deregulation and the introduction of a competitive policy in the course of preparations for integration with the European Community are discussed by Misala (1992).
2. The European Union can draw lessons from NAFTA (North American Free Trade Agreement) in this issue. Liberalization of trade between the United States, Canada and Mexico has resulted in 1994 and in 1995 in a very strong Mexican demand for US and Canadian goods, which contributed to the real appreciation of the peso pegged in 1994 to the US Dollar and to the deterioration of the Mexican trade deficit.

products. As stated above, rising incomes in the east may contribute to the growth of eastern demand for superior EU goods, so the alleged costs of income equalization may not occur. Moreover, liberalization of trade and capital flows may induce many multinational corporations to re-examine the locations of their direct investment. Many of them are presently interested in expanding to CE-5 countries in order to by-pass eastern trade barriers and to take advantage of considerably lower labour costs. But the future elimination of trade and capital restrictions may induce them to allocate direct investment in the West to take advantage of a better infrastructure, high labour productivity and location in affluent markets with strong currencies.

Fears of a massive migration of workers from CE-5 countries to the West with the elimination of barriers to labour mobility are highly exaggerated. Europe has and will have in the future a high discrepancy in come per capita among various regions, as does the United States. However, Europe has a much higher degree of immobility of labour than the US. Cultural and linguistic barriers to mobility are more significant in Europe, although institutional barriers may be now comparable between the EU and the US. Yet, workers do not massively migrate in the US to the wealthiest states. Adversely, the experiences of the 1990s show a net outflow of businesses and workers from most affluent areas where costs of operations and of living are becoming prohibitive. Similarly, massive migration of labour to the West from CE-5 countries is unlikely to happen to the degree feared by some officials in Brussels. Central European workers may be willing to sacrifice higher remuneration in return for the social and cultural benefits of living in their native areas, especially when the EU labour markets are plagued by high unemployment and attractive jobs are hard to find. For those unemployed for structural reasons, whose skills do not match the labour market demand, unemployment benefits granted in Poland or in Hungary may be already as generous as in the West (Orlowski, 1995a). There might be, however, a 'brain drain' type of labour migration of highly qualified, multilingual workers from the East, which is always beneficial to host countries in any case.

Fiscal and monetary convergence should matter in the programme of accession and will have to be emphasized even more in the future when the CE-5 countries prepare to join the European Monetary Union (EMU). Excessive inflation in a single country within an integrated economic system and, more importantly, in a common currency area results in an 'inflation tax' situation, whereby the country gains seignorage (revenues from money emission) by generating a much higher supply of money than other members. It is essential that candidates for accession to the EU currently experiencing excessive inflation (Hungary and Poland) institutionalize long-term policies to combat inflation.

It is also important to establish requirements for consistency in economic policy in the programme of accession to the EU. The dangers of policy inconsistency understood in the framework of the model advanced by Kydland and Prescott (1977) seem to be serious in CE-5 countries. In 1995, voters in Poland and Hungary, burdened by tight fiscal and monetary policies, chose left-wing governments favouring a slower, more gradual approach to transformation. Policy reversals in the direction of higher government spending and subsidization of state-owned enterprises (SOEs), coupled with a heavy taxation of the private sector are very dangerous for the programme of accession to the EU. They impede structural and institutional adjustments, slow down the alignment of relative prices and generate excessive budget deficits normally financed by money creation. High spending and non-restrictive money policies may consequently contribute to chronic, persistent inflation.

The fiscal policy of the candidate countries should be fairly autonomous. It is advisable that the inclusion of the eastern candidates to the EU is accompanied by separate tax treatment of the new members: it should not be based on the fiscal system of tax sharing. CE-5 fiscal budgets should be separated from the EU overall budget with the exception of structural funds aimed at balancing incomes among member countries. Structural funds currently account for a third of the total EU budget. The tax separation arrangement will be beneficial for both the existing EU members and the CE-5 countries. For the candidate countries, this solution will allow them the establishment of prudent fiscal policies. It may be noted that in this respect the eastern enlargement of the EU will be considerably different from the problems of German unification, where eastern provinces were instantly included in the federal system of tax sharing that entitled them to huge, automatic fiscal transfers.

In addition to fiscal and monetary targets, the accession criteria should include structural and institutional tasks that can be generalized by aiming for a high share of GDP contributed by the private sector.

Because of the emphasis on structural and institutional adjustments, the programme of preparations for accession to the EU ought to have a different time horizon from the first phase of the economic transformation in Central Europe. The initial phase was based on deregulation and price liberalization, and on monetary and fiscal tightening that could be accomplished in a 'shock therapy' manner. Such fast-track changes have been applied in all CE-5 countries except Hungary, where reforms have been more gradual. At some point the second phase of transformation, based on the programme of preparations for accession to the EU, will have to emphasize longer-term structural tasks, including privatization, social welfare reforms and the establishment of a better institutional and legal framework for developing business.

In sum, the economic criteria of accession of CE-5 countries to the EU ought to include at minimum the following general elements:

- deregulation
- price stability
- fiscal reform and stability
- evolution of modern financial markets
- favourable conditions for direct investment
- a growing share of the private sector in the national economy
- a modern legal environment for business

Since the implementation of these tasks requires a long time horizon, a speedy integration of the eastern candidates with the EU economic system is not advisable.

In addition to the problems of speed and scope, general economic solutions of matter of the eastern enlargement should address the issue of whether the five Central European candidates ought to be admitted in a bloc or separately, at different times. A complex combination of political and economic factors examined by the *Economist* survey (18–24 November, 1995) favours their simultaneous accession to the EU in one bloc. Specifically, Poland may be a poorer country than the Czech Republic in per capita income terms, but its economic growth in 1995–96 outperformed that of other countries in the region and it has an important strategic location of the eastern boundary of the future EU. Moreover, Hungary may have the highest inflation among the five countries, but its trade and capital ties to the West are the strongest – it has attracted the highest value of foreign direct investment, as discussed in Chapter 5. The EU's comprehensive admission policy will have a non-discriminatory character, so it may be less susceptible to criticism on grounds of political favouritism. A uniform policy on admission will be relatively easier to monitor than a diverse one.

The future accession criteria should be built upon the existing association agreements with the CE-5 countries which happen to be also CEFTA members, as is advised by the 1995 European Commission White Paper. Although these agreements have been negotiated on a bilateral basis, they should be followed by a unilateral programme of accession for the reasons stated above. Some analysts have also proposed to treat the CEFTA as an interim step towards integration with the EU (Bakos, 1993; Kawecka-Wyrzykowska, 1995). However, the economic convergence with the EU goes far beyond coordination of trade policies, therefore CEFTA may be a helpful but not an essential interim tool of integration.

3. ECONOMIC CONDITIONS FOR ACCESSION: RECENT EVIDENCE AND A PROPOSAL OF ACCESSION CRITERIA

The economic transformation among the five candidate countries has so far shown a different degree of success. Problems with economic convergence and with structural reforms encountered by these countries are quite diversified. The recent record of economic stability indicators is presented in Table 6.1.

The candidate countries of Central Europe are at present experiencing fast-track economic growth which outperforms the average real GDP growth rate of the existing EU members. Hungary had the slowest rate of the GDP growth in 1995 among the CE-5 countries, but it was expected to show a better income performance in 1996. Growth in the Czech Republic accelerated in 1995 and the economic growth of Poland, Slovakia and Slovenia remains strong and it is expected to continue in the immediate future. Since the examined countries' GDP growth rates outperform the average real income growth in the EU, they are expected to narrow the income gap with the Union members although the candidate countries' per capita GDP is still roughly a third of the EU level. Nevertheless, it is unrealistic to expect an alignment of

Table 6.1 Selected economic convergence and growth indicators in Central Europe

	*Consolidated Government Budget**		*CPI Inflation Rate*		*Real GDP Growth Rate*		*Open Unemployment Rate*		*Current Account**	*Public Debt**
	1995	*1996*	*1995*	*1996*	*1995*	*1996*	*1995*	*1996*	*1995*	*1995*
Czech Republic	+0.4	+0.3f	9.1	9.6	+4.8	+4.0f	3.0	3.1	-3.8	20.1
Hungary	-2.4	-1.0f	28.3	22.9	+1.5	+3.5f	10.4	11.0	-5.5	83.3
Poland	-2.6	-2.8f	21.6	20.5	+7.0	+4.0f	14.9	14.8	-1.0	56.2
Slovakia	+0.1	-1.3f	7.2	6.0	+7.4	+5.0f	12.1	12.5	+4.4	26.0
Slovenia	+0.3	0.0f	8.6	11.3	+3.5	+2.6f	14.4	13.5	-0.2	13.1
EU average	-5.0	-4.2f	2.9	2.3	+2.7	+1.5f	11.1	11.0	-1.8	71.2

* = percentage of GDP   f = forecast

1996 inflation and unemployment rates are actual rates as of the third quarter.

Sources: OECD, Eurostat, Datastream and PlanEcon.

CE-5 countries' per capita GDP with the poorest of the present members of the EU by the end of this decade, perhaps with the exception of the Czech Republic.

The existing course of monetary and fiscal convergence shows mixed results. The countries under review have significantly improved control over government budgets. Fiscal deficits as a share of GDP in these countries are smaller than the EU average and would even satisfy the 3 per cent benchmark consistent with the Maastricht criteria of eligibility for inclusion in the EMU. Slovenia and the Czech Republic lead the score of the five countries with a practically balanced budget. The budgets of Hungary, Poland and Slovakia are burdened by heavy allocations for state pensions, income security and wage increases in public enterprises (Orlowski, 1995a). These high income transfers result mainly from rapidly ageing populations in these countries and from the dominant role of state pension funds and state enterprises in the system. In addition, Poland still maintains the highest (although steadily declining) level of unemployment, since it provides quite generous benefits and applies lax eligibility criteria that ought to be tightened. Hungary's excessive inflation is still burdened by large budget deficits that prevailed until 1994: in that year, the fiscal deficit reached 7.0 per cent of GDP, and this, combined with the large current account deficit equal to 10 per cent of GDP, resulted in the deterioration of saving and added to inflationary pressures.

The level of inflation in Hungary is extremely disappointing. The high CPI-based inflation reflects the pervasive indexation of prices and wages and the fiscal and current account deficits. An improvement in the political climate and a stronger commitment to economic deregulation, privatization and structural adjustments are essential for a reversal of unfavourable convergence indicators in Hungary. The developments of 1995/96 are promising, at any rate. The government budget deficit fell considerably in 1995 and in the first quarter of 1996 the country generated a large fiscal surplus. The reduction of fiscal and current account deficits is critical to promoting saving and to alleviating pressures on excessive real interest rates that restrain domestic investment. Hungary, and Slovenia as well, may gain from a possible improvement in the political climate in the rest of the former Yugoslavia by reinstating exports to the nations battered by the political turmoil. Hungary's structural adjustment tasks are very extensive. The country has the highest share of agricultural production in the GDP (about 7 per cent in

1994) among the five economies under scrutiny, so it is likely to become a large net recipient of CAP subsidies once admitted to the EU.

Inflation trends in the remaining CE-5 countries are more favourable. This includes Poland which was plagued by the highest inflation (indeed, hyperinflation) in the early 1990s. However, 1995 inflation rates ranging from 9.1 per cent in the Czech Republic to 21.6 per cent in Poland are still excessive. Their reduction should be a top priority of national economic strategies. The reasons for persistently high inflation rates are complex. Wage and price indexation, insufficient internal competition, strong net capital inflows and fiscal deficits can be identified as the most critical factors stimulating inflation. Furthermore, the existing 'crawling band' exchange rate system in Poland and Hungary is based upon predetermined crawling devaluations (at present in both countries, daily devaluations at a monthly rate of 1 per cent in terms of a basket of currencies) that by themselves are a source of high inflation expectations and the automatic indexation of prices and wages (Orlowski, 1996b and 1997). Net capital inflows pose a serious problem for their anti-inflation efforts. The increase in foreign currency reserves of the Czech Republic reached an unprecedented level of 18.0 per cent of GDP, against 7.7 per cent in Poland, and 3.7 per cent in Hungary in 1995 (Orlowski, 1997). The impact of fiscal deficits on inflation should not be understated. For instance, a comparison of deficits and inflation rates in Slovenia and in Slovakia indicates that Slovenia has been more successful in reducing inflation, having succeeded in balancing the government budget, while the growing deficit in Slovakia has obstructed the reduction of inflation.

Some of the most urgent tasks for Poland should include a departure from the pervasive indexation of wages, social security and state pensions. Privatization efforts must be accelerated in order to promote internal competition and structural adjustment. The most critical task for the Slovak Republic is a restoration of privatization which was virtually halted at the end of 1994, and adopting a faster pace of structural reforms. Although the convergence indicators for the Czech Republic are the best among the five countries, structural adjustment in that country has been rather slow. Moreover, balance sheets of newly privatized enterprises are still fragile and the mechanism of corporate governance ought to be considerably improved (Banerjee *et al.*, 1995).

The examination presented above of the general record of economic convergence and recognition of the needs of the candidate countries in terms of structural and institutional reforms allows us to propose a set of criteria essential for the programme of accession of these countries to the EU. As previously suggested, since the structural and institutional reforms require a longer time horizon, the optimal time for accession could be set for the year 2002. Consequently, by the end of 2001 the five candidate countries ought to achieve the following characteristics:

- a ratio of the general government budget deficit-to-GDP not exceeding 2.5 per cent;
- a targeted rate of annual inflation not exceeding 5 per cent;
- a requirement of at least two-thirds of the GDP to be generated by the private sector;
- an exchange rate system that would ensure stable rates of their currencies against the Euro and allow them to enter the EMU at some subsequent date.

The call for stable exchange rates against the Euro is consistent with the requirement of the elimination of crawling devaluations in Poland and in Hungary. Poland needs to change the basket of currencies which is the basis for the present crawling band system from the dominant weight assigned to the US dollar into stronger weights to the DM and the ECU. Specific interest rate margins customized for the CE-5 countries above the corresponding EU (mostly German) interest rates should be designated as intermediate monetary policy targets to ensure the relative stability of their currencies in terms of the EU currencies, and after 1999, in terms of the Euro.

The fiscal convergence criterion is somewhat more rigorous than the Maastricht requirement. Yet it pertains to countries willing to decentralize and to deregulate their economies and to strengthen the role of internal competition and private businesses. Perhaps paradoxically, the fiscal convergence requirement will be the easiest to achieve. The 5 per cent benchmark for inflation (on the CPI basis) seems feasible, although difficult to achieve by Hungary and Poland. The Czech Republic should have no problems reaching this target. Realization of this task requires a comprehensive anti-inflation policy that should not be restricted to monetary tightening. This target should be a central pillar of a comprehensive anti-inflation policy. It should be reached by annual intermediate targets reflecting a diminishing rate of inflation from the current level to 5 per cent in 2001. The intermediate targets ought to follow a linear pattern. Non-linear reductions, implying an excessively optimistic plan for disinflation in the first two years of the pre-accession strategy, may fail and undermine the credibility of the entire accession programme if it is not backed by dramatic corrections of inflationary factors. Fiscal and current account balances and proper management of capital inflows, along with real efforts towards the creation of competitive commodity, labour and capital markets, must all be included in a comprehensive strategy to eliminate inflation.

The inclusion of the third requirement is very critical for the tasks facing the economies in transition. Currently, more than a half of the GDP of Poland, the Czech Republic and Slovenia is generated by the private sector. The task of reaching two-thirds of GDP contributed by the private sector - or restriction of the public sector role to a third of GDP - will motivate the candidate countries to pursue active structural and institutional reforms aimed at strengthening internal competition and at improving the overall economic efficiency.

4. REQUIRED CONDITIONS FOR MONETARY CONVERGENCE

The economic programme of accession of the CE-5 countries to the EU ought to be centred upon stabilizing inflation. Specific targets and methods applied for the purpose of accomplishing price stability depend on a thorough investigation of the factors that contribute to persistent inflation at the present stage of economic transformation.

At the beginning of transformation, expectations of inflation in the economies of Central Europe played a relatively small role. Citizens and businesses were accustomed to central price fixing, usually at levels far below equilibrium prices, and such fixed prices contributed to widespread shortages of goods and services. At the same time, rising wages of workers generated a considerable monetary overhang (excess money supply) (Bruno, 1992). Liberalization of prices in the period 1989–91 in the transforming economies resulted in the rapid elimination of the monetary overhang and in the shock of immediate and steep inflation. Hungary was an exception, since price deregulation there was more gradual. There, the initial shock was followed by several smaller, secondary shocks, resulting from discretionary changes in the course of monetary and fiscal policies and from adjustments of administratively controlled prices of energy, transport and several other 'strategic' goods and services (Orłowski, 1994).

Inflation during the early stages of the economic transformation was rather short-lived and it had generally a self-correcting character: it did not need to be corrected by a tightening monetary policy. The initial near-hyperinflationary shocks that follow price liberalization are generally self-correcting, and hence easy to overcome. It is usually sufficient to announce to the public a course of tight fiscal policy and a clear programme of budget deficit-reduction measures in order to suppress inflationary expectations in these circumstances.

As the transformation evolves, the inflationary process assumes a very different character. If stabilization policies are unable to reduce inflation, backward-looking or adaptive expectations concerning inflation may persist, and these may result in wage indexation and automatic adjustments of wholesale and retail prices by the margin extrapolated from the established inflationary trend. This process will show symptoms of 'moderate' or 'chronic' inflation.[3] Such an inflationary process is usually self-propelled by automatic wage and price indexation, and the resulting inflation inertia becomes gradually more difficult to cure, since wage and pension contracts are based on the mechanism of indexation. Financial contracts incorporate the established inflation inertia as well, contributing to very high nominal interest rates and, with uncertain expected inflation, to unstable real interest rates. Their unforeseeable path diminishes incentives to save and to invest.

The inflation inertia is triggered in many economies by persistent budget deficits stemming from indexation of major components of government spending, including wages in public enterprises, subsidies, state pension funds, and so on. Given only a limited ability to finance through public debt creation, budget deficits in transforming economies are increasingly financed by money creation, thereby contributing further to inflationary pressures. Central banks augment government revenues by generating seigniorage (government income from money emission).

The problem of inflation inertia has become increasingly pervasive in Hungary, Poland and even in Slovakia, although it is still less

3. Various reasons for moderate or persistent inflation are thoroughly examined by Dornbusch and Fischer (1993).

persistent than in Latin American economies in the 1980s. Indexation of wages, pensions and the design of financial contracts generate excessive inflation in these countries. Hungary further contributed to inflationary pressures by expanding the budget deficit and by generating a relatively high seignorage, or inflation tax, until 1994. Measured by the ratio of the change in the monetary base relative to GDP, seigniorage in Hungary amounted to 3.5 per cent of GDP in 1994, while in Poland and in Slovakia it was considerably lower (1 per cent of the GDP in both cases) (IMF, 1995, p.62). The Hungarian situation in 1995 and in 1996 was reversed as a result of a successful fiscal consolidation.

The programme of accession of CE-5 countries to the EU provides an extraordinary opportunity to design policies aimed at reducing inflation inertia in their economic systems. Economic policy makers know today that the policy of eliminating inflation in the presence of high inertia requires quite decisive fiscal adjustments and explicit institutional reforms aimed at enhancing the credibility of financial policies. Therefore, the task of lowering fiscal deficits to the proposed targeted level of 2.5 per cent of GDP is critical for successful disinflation. Equally essential for price stability is the construction of modern, effective financial markets and a competitive, well-capitalized banking system. At the same time, it is critical in these economies to increase the role of bank credit, which until now was very low in comparison with the EU. As reported by the EBRD 1995 Transition Report, the ratio of outstanding bank credit to GDP in Poland was 33 per cent in 1994. It was higher for Hungary and Slovakia (63 per cent in both cases) and the highest in the Czech Republic (95 per cent). By comparison, the same ratio reached 149 per cent in Germany and 118 per cent in the United Kingdom in 1994. Moreover, the candidate countries' central banks should enjoy a considerable degree of autonomy and pursue a relatively tight, long-term-oriented monetary policy conducted in a non-discretionary fashion in order to enhance the credibility of policy. Establishing such credibility is essential for the task of eliminating indexation and inflation inertia.

It becomes apparent that in order to achieve policy credibility and low inflation central banks of transforming economies ought to establish a solid record of a steady and autonomous monetary policy. Only in extreme cases, when the credibility record of autonomous central banks is very poor, is the only tool of disinflation a pegging of the currency. Currency boards should be avoided. Fixing the exchange rate of domestic currency to a key international currency allows monetary authorities to 'borrow' credibility from a foreign central bank at the expense of losing monetary policy autonomy. This extreme solution is not advisable at the present time for monetary authorities of the economies in transition that are generally doing well in establishing credible policies. In order to enhance credibility central banks have to pursue a course of tight money supply. This task is difficult to accomplish when the monetary authorities are expected to inject sufficient domestic credit to facilitate structural changes in transforming economies. Consequently, for the next few years central banks of those economies should be given a relatively high degree of autonomy for the purpose of strengthening their policy track record. A higher degree of monetary autonomy is consistent with an expansion in the flexibility of exchange rates. When active preparations for accession are implemented, the candidate countries will gradually have to peg their currencies to the Euro. However, for the time being before the initiation of a pre-accession programme, CE-5 countries should expand the band of permitted fluctuations of their currencies, preferably to plus or minus 15 per cent against a basket that emphasizes the DM and the ECU (Orlowski, 1997). For the time being, they should gear monetary policy to targeting the money supply, since this choice (as opposed to targeting interest rates) is more effective in reducing inflation. Furthermore, targeting the money supply helps to institute a less discretionary monetary policy based on predetermined rules, and such a policy is more effective for enhancing the credibility of monetary authorities.

The process of integration with the EU brings up a policy dilemma of what to target.[4] On the one hand, targeting money supply is favourable for reducing inflation and establishing monetary stability. But on the other hand, a closer integration of CE-5 countries with the EU will require increasing coordination of domestic monetary policies with the leading EU central banks, or in the future with the European Central Bank. This means that the candidate countries' central banks will ultimately have to target the stability of exchange rates rather than domestic money supply, gradually surrendering autonomy in the policy field. Moreover, if the Bundesbank or other leading EU central banks

4. See Orlowski (1995b) for a comprehensive examination of monetary policy choices, targeting and instrumentalization in the process of preparations for accession of CE-5 to the EU.

pursue a tight monetary policy course in the future, the candidate countries will have to apply even tighter monetary policies which may impede the supply of credit necessary to facilitate structural adjustments (Orlowski, 1995b).

Consequently, a rapid accession of CE-5 countries to the EU may be detrimental for the establishment of sound monetary policies in these transforming economies. They need time to establish a credible policy record and they need room to provide sufficient credit for structural adjustments. It should be understood that this credit may add to inflation, therefore it seems reasonable and realistic that the future inflation target, suggested at 5 per cent, should not be too stringent. The target will have to be tightened in the future when these countries prepare to join the EMU.

5. FISCAL CONVERGENCE: CONSTRAINTS AND CRITERIA

A critical factor for economic stability and for the successful evolution of the economic transformation in Central Europe is the ability to reduce government budget deficits. Lessons from episodes of hyperinflation in the world economy indicate that in the majority of cases very high inflation is preceded by a loss of government control over spending and tax revenues, resulting in surging fiscal deficits.

As shown in Table 6.1, large deficits do not appear to be a severe problem in Central European countries. However, there are still many problems with the structure of government spending and tax revenues that ought to be addressed during the next stage of the economic transformation and in the programme of accession to the EU. One of them is a high proportion of government expenditures (for example, income transfers) in total spending. These expenditures do not directly contribute to the growth of GDP and they do not stimulate any improvement in labour productivity. Pressures on high levels of income transfers in CE-5 countries are related to a variety of factors (Orlowski, 1995a). In the first place is the historical guarantee of a minimum standard of living to all members of the society, which existed in the former command economy system. People whose skills are not suitable for a new, competitive economic environment are still seeking welfare, unemployment and pension transfers even today. The second apparent reason for high transfer payments is the accelerated ageing of Central European societies (as in Western Europe). Dependency ratios of pensioners to total employed are very high, ranging in 1992 from 57 per cent for Poland to 67 per cent for the Slovak Republic. Finally, a strong demand for transfer payments stems from mounting unemployment and expanding poverty. High jobless rates in Central Europe, with the exception of the Czech Republic, result in a strong demand for unemployment benefits which are high at some point in the region (Orlowski, 1995a). Consequently, government income transfers reach very high levels in these countries: their share in the GDP ranged in 1992 from 22 per cent in Poland to 33 per cent in Hungary.

Pressures on budget deficits result also from insufficient privatization and from the sluggish pace of institutional reforms. State-owned enterprises (SOEs) protected by the government patronage still dominate the industrial structures in the region, and they generally do not produce goods suitable for competitive world economy conditions (Gros, 1997). Moreover, governments find it difficult to privatize many SOEs since their market value is very low. At the beginning of the economic transformation the economic authorities cut subsidies to SOEs considerably. In the four Visegrad countries subsidies fell from 15–25 per cent of GDP in the period preceding liberalization to 3–5 per cent after liberalization (IMF, 1995, p.69). Despite such efforts to impose 'hard budget constraints' on SOEs, government transfers to them are still being continued in a somewhat different form. They have recently reappeared in the form of tax arrears (Schaffer, 1995), which were estimated in 1993 to have reached a high level of 5–10 per cent of GDP among the Visegrad countries.

The conversion of former subsidies into tax arrears proves how difficult it is to discontinue direct fiscal transfers to SOEs. Their drainage of government budgets would be effectively halted only if these enterprises were forced into bankruptcy. It becomes apparent that the programme of accession to the EU should stress the formulation and enforcement of bankruptcy laws and procedures for SOEs that are unable to survive competitive open economy conditions.

Further pressures on budget deficits in transition economies come from practices of transfer pricing by multinational corporations that have acquired local companies or established new subsidiaries in these countries. The scope of this problem needs to be thoroughly investigated and attested with evidence, although it seems paradoxical that Hungary, which until 1994 has acquired the largest share of foreign direct investment among the five countries under examination, experienced simultaneously the most severe budget deficit.[5] In addition, on several occasions the Polish government has expressed concerns about extensive transfer pricing practices of multinational corporations. To reduce incentives for transfer pricing, fiscal authorities should consider lowering rates of profit-tax, capital gains tax and other taxes that affect business profitability. Central European taxes seem at present to be excessive by international standards. They have been imposed with the alleged belief in their capacity to bolster revenues and to balance government budgets. Comprehensive cuts in tax rates would very likely enhance tax revenues by triggering growth of taxable income and by reducing incentives to transfer pricing, tax deferrals and tax evasion. Furthermore, tax revenues are likely to be improved when inflation expectations are subdued. According to the Olivera–Tanzi effect, conditions of high inflation provide incentives for tax deferrals and thereby reduce real tax revenues. Consequently, a clear anti-inflation programme would be helpful for strengthening government incomes.

The future programme of accession to the EU should emphasize means of gaining credibility on the part of fiscal authorities. This task is essential for the purpose of improving economic stability among candidate countries for the EU eastern enlargement. As Tanzi (1994) argues, fiscal credibility can be retained even under conditions of policy tightening if the authorities clearly explain to their societies the reasons for the policy change and if they are perceived to be sincere, competent and capable of choosing and consequently implementing policy directions. Citizens and businesses are likely to endorse restrictive fiscal policies and bear their costs and sacrifices if the needs and the burdens of fiscal adjustments are honestly and thoroughly explained to them by policy makers. It is essential that the programme of accession emphasizes the need for an open dialogue between governments and citizens of the candidate countries addressing fiscal policy preferences (Orlowski, 1996a).

5. The analysis of the record and policies of foreign direct investment in transition economies can be found in Meyer (1995).

Fiscal consolidation is essential for the programme of bringing the transforming economies of Central Europe closer to the EU, but it will not be successful without simultaneous institutional reforms aimed at educating honest taxpayers and legitimate recipients of government funds. The sound fiscal process will be more effectively facilitated by well-developed financial markets. CE-5 candidate countries should further strengthen their tax laws so as to bring their fiscal legislation closer to EU regulations. As discussed above, bankruptcy laws should be extended and effectively implemented. Reliable commercial courts and efficient financial systems still need to be developed. All these important tasks ought to be incorporated in the programme of accession to the EU.

6. THE CONFLICT BETWEEN SHORT-TERM COSTS AND LONG-TERM BENEFITS OF ACCESSION

Preparations for the accession of Central European candidate countries to the EU will involve not only monetary costs to the existing Union members, but considerable economic and social costs to the candidates as well. The pre-accession strategy will entail structural and institutional adjustments in the candidate countries on a greater scale than the required institutional preparations of the EU for the eastern enlargement. The CE-5 economies are much smaller than those of the EU member states, so they will have to undergo deep structural changes aimed at finding a proper niche of specialization within the integrated pan-European trading bloc. Such a transition exacts considerable economic and social costs.

A prolonged period of high unemployment in Central Europe will be the most apparent effect of structural adjustments to the integrated European economic system. This unemployment not only stems from the integration process itself, but it is the cost of the continuing economic transformation and reintegration with the world economy as well. The economic system of Central European countries still maintains remnants of central planning and it is plagued by excessive government regulation. The former system promoted growth of heavy industries that supported the military sector of the Soviet bloc. In the course of the first stage of the economic transformation, the protection of heavy industries has been partially eliminated and their output has been reoriented into consumer durable goods. As a result, these sectors are now facing more rigorous efficiency requirements and they have already laid off large numbers of workers. Preparations for accession with the EU will require further structural changes in these sectors, facilitated by large-scale investments in both factor and human capital.

A mainly well-trained, skilled and competitive labour force will be demanded by companies operating in the internally-opened system of the EU. A large part of the Central European unskilled labour will either remain unemployed or seek early retirement. These people demand considerable public assistance and social protection, making it difficult to cut government spending and to balance fiscal budgets. Programmes for retraining the Central European labour force and developing entrepreneurial skills will have to be financed by a combination of public and private funds. These direct costs to the Central European economies can be alleviated by the assistance from the EU through the PHARE–ACE and other programmes identified in the European Commission 1995 White Paper on preparations of the Central European candidates for accession to the EU. It is a better policy for the EU to finance retraining of the Central European labour force than to provide direct fiscal transfers in the future to governments that are running deep fiscal deficits induced by unemployment and welfare payments. In any case, it needs to be stressed that without the appropriate EU assistance the entire strategy of eastern enlargement will fail.

Unemployment compensation, funds for labour-force retraining, and financing the modernization of the largely obsolete Central European capital stock are among the predictable costs related to the integration into the EU that will have to be incurred during active preparations for accession to the Union. These are necessary expenses that will burden the candidate countries' budgets in the presence of the fundamental fiscal consolidation and the increasingly tight monetary policy. The availability of public funds will be limited by the need to achieve the desirable level of fiscal convergence and by the adjustments of monetary policy aimed at stability of exchange rates. In the presence of tight credit and relatively high real interest rates only the most efficient investment will take place. Thus, infrastructural investments or the financing of labour force retraining programmes yield predominantly long-term benefits, but they do not necessarily guarantee a high rate of return in a short-to-medium-term perspective. Consequently, low interest rates in the EU, and correspondingly in the candidate countries, would help to reduce the costs of structural adjustments in Central Europe.

In addition to measurable or explicit costs of the accession to the candidate countries, there will be also a broad range of implicit costs. Among them is a risk of loss of political sovereignty, which is at the present time being disregarded in the discussion on the EU eastern enlargement (Bofinger, 1995). But the problem of diminished sovereignty does not have only a political dimension. In the economic sphere, a lower degree of autonomy on the part of policy-making institutions will be apparent once the pre-accession programme is actively implemented. In particular, the central banks of the candidate countries will have to face gradually diminishing policy autonomy with the reorientation of monetary policy towards exchange rate stability (Orlowski, 1995b).

While most of the costs related to integration with the EU will have to be incurred immediately, during the implementation of the pre-accession strategy, the economic benefits of the integration will take time to materialize. By contrast, political benefits, such as a guaranteed military and political support from the EU and NATO, will emerge almost instantaneously, while the economic gains will mostly result from the long-term income growth derived from the accession. Perhaps the most apparent gain to the new eastern members of the Union will be a net creation of trade resulting from the integration. However, in order to generate income from growing duty-free exports to the Union, the candidate countries must restructure their economies and complete direct investment projects in the areas consistent with their comparative advantage and specialization within the integrated bloc. The wider market access to the EU system will generate economies of scale or gains from an expanded size of output for Central European firms. The larger optimum size of output will allow them to reduce average costs of production and improve their profitability. Nevertheless, these are net effects of long-term adjustments that may take at least several years to materialize.

In sum, the accession process is likely to be accompanied by a conflict between short-term economic and social costs and long-term benefits. This conflict and the perceived initial sacrifices on the part of societies of the candidate countries pose a risk in Central Europe of erosion of public endorsement of integration into the EU. Therefore, it is important to identify and to formulate means of cushioning the net costs of preparations for accession to the Union for Central European societies and businesses. Among the factors diminishing short-term social and economic costs of the accession are:

- direct CAP and SF transfers to the new member states;
- PHARE-ACE assistance to prepare the Central European labour force and institutions for effective functioning with the integrated bloc;
- an open and exhaustive dialogue between policy makers in charge of the integration process and political and civil society organizations and citizens of the candidate countries.

Among these three factors, a thorough explanation of costs and sacrifices of the preparation for accession and the long-term nature of the benefits of integration to the central European societies and business organizations is most critical. It will become particularly indispensable if the EU fails to provide CAP subsidies and SF transfers to the new eastern members on the basis of current rules and entitlements.

7. CONCLUDING REMARKS: IMPLEMENTATION OF ACCESSION CRITERIA

The analysis of conditions of monetary and fiscal convergence and the need to undergo structural and institutional reforms in the candidate countries of Central Europe prior to accession to the EU suggest that preparations for integration will require some time. The programme designing these preparations should be extended over the period of several years so as to allow the desirable changes in Central European economies to take place. Specifically, central banks must establish a solid record of pursuing a credible monetary policy, and they need a considerable degree of autonomy in order to do so. Monetary authorities need to choose money supply targets in order to set a foundation for disinflation and, at the same time, to release sufficient credit for structural adjustments. The close integration of CE-5 countries into the EU will require an increasing orientation of monetary policy towards targeting the exchange rate, which in the presence of credit tightening in the EU would imply very restrictive monetary policies among the candidate countries.

Fiscal consolidation and institutional reforms also require a longer time horizon. Governments must prove a firm commitment to balancing their budgets in order to diminish the needs for public debt creation or the monetization of deficits. Although most CE-5 authorities have adopted solutions bringing their taxation system closer to the EU laws, such as the introduction of value-added taxes, their system of government revenues generally needs further reform. Among the remaining changes, they should consider cutting high profits taxes so as to diminish tendencies toward tax deferrals, transfer pricing and tax evasion. Financial institutions and markets should be further strengthened in order to facilitate investments and effective capital transactions.

All five countries examined by this study should be admitted in one bloc and at the same time in a non-discriminatory fashion. Their accession should be conditional upon a uniform, possibly specific, pre-accession strategy, and, once adopted, the accession criteria must be firm and not subject to renegotiation or revision. The European Commission will face the task of establishing monitoring policies and procedures and, as stated in the Commission's 1995 White Paper, it will make structural funds, PHARE and other programmes available for economic adjustments in the candidate countries. Once granted, the membership of these countries in the EU must be full, not partial, with the exception of the membership in the future EMU. Yet, even an option of joining the EMU must be available, since some countries, most notably the Czech Republic, are likely to qualify for entering the system.

Efforts towards the preparations of CE-5 countries for accession to the EU shall also consider the possible costs of non-enlargement, addressed by several analysts (Welfens, 1993; Kawecka-Wyrzykowska, 1995). These costs include stagnation of real wage differentials and strong incentives for Central European labour to migrate to the West.

In sum, the programme of preparations for accession to the EU will create opportunities to design the solutions and tasks of the second stage of the economic transformation of former centrally-planned economies. The adoption of such a programme will serve as a political tool defending the course of market-oriented reforms against currently increasing internal pressures to reverse these reforms, emanating from the groups that enjoyed special political and economic privileges in the past.

BIBLIOGRAPHY

Bakos, Gabor (1993). 'After COMECON: A Free Trade Area in Central Europe?', *Europe–Asia Studies*, Vol.45, No.6, pp.1025–44.

Baldwin, Richard E. (1994) 'Towards an Integrated Europe' (London: Centre for Economic Policy Research).

Banerjee, Biswajit, Vincent Koen, Thomas Krueger, Mark S. Lutz, Michael Marrese and Tapio O. Saavalainen (1995). 'Road Maps of the Transition: The Baltics, the Czech Republic, Hungary and Russia, International Monetary Fund: Occasional Paper No. 127 Washington, DC: (September).

Bofinger, Peter (1995). 'The Political Economy of the Eastern Enlargement of the EU', London: Centre for Economic Policy Research: discussion Paper No. 1234.

Breuss, Fritz and Fritz Schebeck (1996). 'Ostöffnung und Osterweiterung der EU' (Eastern Opening and Eastern Enlargement of the EU) (Vienna: WIFO Monatsberichte, no.2), pp.139–52.

Bruno, Michael (1992). 'Stabilization and Reform in Eastern Europe: A Preliminary Evaluation', Working Paper no. WP/92/30 (Washington, DC: International Monetary Fund) (May).

Commission of the European Communities (1995). 'White Paper: Preparation of the Associated Countries of Central and Eastern Europe for Integration into the Internal Market of the Union', COM (95)163 (Brussels) (3 May).

De Crombrugghe, Alain, Zanny Minton-Beddoes and Jeffrey D. Sachs (1995), 'EU Membership for Central Europe: Commitments, Speed and Conditionality' (Cambridge, MA: Harvard Institute for International Development); mimeo.

Dornbusch, Rudiger and Stanley Fischer (1993). 'Moderate Inflation', *The World Bank Economic Review*, vol.7, no.1, pp.1–44.

Economist, The (1995). 'A Survey of Central Europe', 18 November.

—— (1996). 'Arguments for Enlargement', 3 August.

Gabrisch, Hubert (1996). 'An Eastern Enlargement of the EU: Macroeconomic Effects in New Member States', paper presented to the conference of the European Association for Comparative Economic Studies, Grenoble, 12–14 September.

Gros, Daniel (1997). 'Conditions for the Accession of Transforming Economies of Central Europe to the European Union', in Lucjan T. Orlowski and Dominick Salvatore (eds), *Trade and Payments in Central and Eastern Europe's Transforming Economies* (Westport, CT: Greenwood Press).

International Monetary Fund (1995). 'World Economic Outlook' (October).

Kawecka-Wyrzykowska, Elzbieta (1995). 'Stowarzyszenie Polski ze Wspólnotami Europejskimi: czy bliżej do członkówstwa?' (The Association Agreement of Poland with the European Union: Is It Closer to Membership?), in *Polska–Unia Europejska: od stowarzyszenia do członkówstwa* (Poland–European Union: From Association to Membership) (Warsaw: Szkoła Główna Handlowa) (October).

Kydland, Finn E. and Edward C. Prescott (1977). 'Rules Rather than Discretion: The Inconsistency of Optimal Plans', *Journal of Political Economy*, vol.85, pp.473-92.

Lavigne, Marie (1996). 'The European Union and the Central and Eastern European Countries: The Pre-Accession Process', paper presented to the annual meeting of the International Studies Association, San Diego, CA, 16–18 April.

Meyer, Klaus E. (1995). 'Foreign Direct Investment in the Early Years of Economic Transition: A Survey', *Economics of Transition*, vol.3. no.3, pp.301–20.

Misala, Jozef (1992). 'Ireland, Greece, Portugal and Spain as Members of the European Communities: What Can We Learn from Their Experience?', PISM conference paper, Warsaw, 7 November.

Orlowski, Lucjan T. (1994). 'Problems of Corrective Inflation in Transformation from Central Planning to a Market Economy: The Experience of Poland', in John L. Campbell and Stanisław Owsiak (eds), *Fiscal Reforms in Post-Communist Countries* (Cracow: Cracow Academy of Economics), pp.273-306.

—— (1995a). 'Social Safety Nets in Central Europe: Preparation for Accession to the European Union?', *Comparative Economic Studies*, vol.37, no.2, pp.29–48.

—— (1995b). 'Preparations of the Visegrad Group Countries for Admission to the European Union: Monetary Policy Aspects', *Economics of Transition*, vol.3, no.3, pp. 333–53.

—— (1996a). 'Fiscal Consolidation in Central Europe in Preparation for Accession to the European Union' (Warsaw: Center for Social and Economic Research: Studies and Analyses), no.77.

—— (1996b). 'The Path of Exchange Rates in the Polish Economic Transformation' (Warsaw: Center for Social and Economic Research: Studies and Analyses).

—— (1997). 'Exchange Rate Policies in Transforming Economies of Central Europe', in Lucjan T. Orlowski and Dominick Salvatore (eds), *Trade and Payments in Central and Eastern Europe's Transforming Economies* (Westport, CT: Greenwood Press).

Richter, Sandor (1995). 'Advantages, Disadvantages and Dilemmas: Considerations on the Accession of the Central and Eastern European Countries to the European Union', *Acta Oeconomica*, vol.47, no.3–4, pp.343–56.

Schaffer, Mark E. (1995). 'Government Subsidies to Enterprises in Central and Eastern Europe: Budgetary Subsidies and Tax Arrears', in David M. Newburry (ed.), *Tax and Benefit Reform in Central and Eastern Europe* (London: Centre for Economic Policy Research).

Tanzi, Vito (1994). 'The Political Economy of Fiscal Deficit Reduction', in William Easterly, Carlos Alfredo Rodriguez and Klaus Schmidt-Hebbel (eds), *Public Sector Deficits and Macroeconomic Performance* (a World Bank publication) (Oxford: Oxford University Press), pp.513–24.

Welfens, Paul J. (1993). 'Osterweiterung der EG: Anpassungserfordernisse, Konwergenzprobleme und ordnungspolitischer Reformbedarf in Europa', in H. Groner and A. Schüller (eds), *Die europäische Integration als ordnungspolitische Aufgabe* (Stuttgart, Jena and New York: Gustav Fischer Verlag).

7. Eastern Europe and the World Trade Organization: The Present Position and Prospects of Accession

Jozef M. van Brabant[1]

With the inauguration of the transitions in the eastern part of Europe, beginning in 1989, two overarching purposes have dominated policy making: moving towards political democracy and anchoring this latter by building a functioning market economy. To utilize the latter both as an instrument for moving towards market-based competition and as a goal in itself, virtually all transition economies[2] have stressed the need to 'integrate into the world economy'. That claim has various meanings, but at least it calls for putting into place a fairly open trade regime as but one component of broader liberalization, and joining various multilateral economic institutions while subscribing to their underlying regimes. Among the latter (see Brabant 1991) is featured the postwar international trading system (ITS) as embodied in the General Agreement on Tariffs and Trade or GATT[3] and since 1995 in the World Trade Organization (WTO).

1. Staff member of the Department for International Economic and Social Information and Policy Analysis of the United Nations Secretariat in New York. The views expressed here are the author's and do not necessarily reflect those of the United Nations Secretariat.
2. I shall deal chiefly with the European countries that were dominated by a Communist Party and subject to some kind of administrative planning. There are 27 such countries (counting all the successor states). Occasionally I refer also to China, Cuba, Mongolia and Vietnam.
3. This terminology, referring to the General Agreement as the underlying legal instrument as well as the secretariat entrusted with safeguarding that instrument, was always confusing. Until the end of 1994, that secretariat was officially known as the Interim Commission of the International Trade Organization (ICITO), even though the project of establishing the ITO itself was for all practical purposes

The 'internationalist' clamour by managers of the transitions has various origins. One certainly is as a reaction against the peculiar relationship maintained with the GATT and the ITS under state socialism.[4] I examine this first, if only because it has implications for present and potential members[5] that are not yet committed to far-reaching liberalization. This was perhaps more pronounced for those countries that were 'Contracting Parties' of the GATT, or that had sought such a status towards the end of state socialism (notably Bulgaria, China and the Soviet Union) as detailed below, but it also manifested itself rather quickly in the other transition economies. In order to understand this, a brief elucidation of the role of rule-bound international regimes is necessary, which I provide thereafter in conjunction with the discussion of problems of reconciling state socialism with the GATT's fundamentals. Examination of the GATT's functions, together with the broader purview of the WTO, follows. Why WTO membership may be a critical component of the broader strategy of merging the transition economy into the world economy deserves a fuller description, and this is presented in the following section. I then look at the status of WTO membership, if only because it may be a precondition for joining other regional organizations. I conclude by considering a few salient aspects of 'opening up'.

1. ORGANIZING WORLD TRADE AND STATE SOCIALISM

The GATT was essentially conceived for mature market economies. Paradoxical as it may seem, several state socialist countries participated in it almost from its inception in 1948; the qualifying 'almost' is important, for none was involved in the negotiation of the General Agreement and none of the founding members had such an economic system in

abandoned by December 1950 at the latest (see Brabant, 1991, pp.49ff).

4. Because there is such confusion about communism, socialism, real socialism, modified socialism and so on, I shall use the notion 'state socialism' as a shorthand to describe the economic and political regimes in the eastern part of Europe prior to the events of 1989.
5. At times I use this informal designation in preference to the official Contracting Parties, when reference is to *all* GATT members; otherwise I refer to a 'Contracting Party' (Long, 1985, p.6).

place when that ITS was inaugurated. By the end of state socialism, however, six of these countries had benefited to some degree from being a Contracting Party at one point or another (Cuba, Czechoslovakia, Hungary, Poland, Romania and Yugoslavia). Furthermore, two (Bulgaria and China) participated in the ITS as observers because in 1986 they both requested that machinery be set in motion to become a full Contracting Party; in the case of China, that really meant readmission (Hartland-Thunberg, 1987; Herzstein, 1986). Moreover, at least two such countries (the Soviet Union and Vietnam) had by 1989 been expected soon to submit a request for 'regular' accession. The Soviet Union became an observer in early 1990 and was succeeded by Russia. Vietnam obtained that status only in 1994. If these requests had been considered favourably, the state socialist countries outside the GATT would probably have revamped their traditional stance, too (Brabant 1988, 1989, 1991), and those already inside would have been keen on upgrading their participation and renegotiating the odder instruments of accession.

There never was any doubt that central planning is incompatible with the market-type trading rules that, admittedly deep down, form the backbone of the General Agreement (Brabant, 1991, pp.192ff; Kostecki, 1979, 1984; Matejka, 1990). In its original conception, the ITS was anchored to two fundamental principles: the complete and immediate abolition of non-tariff barriers (NTBs) and the gradual reduction of all tariffs on the basis of reciprocity. Both goals were to be fostered with the framework of a comprehensive code governing world trade. It was envisaged that such codification in international law would ultimately constrain severely the right of individual governments to interfere with the free flow of private trade. Because governments were expected to be strictly law-abiding, the main tasks of the international body would have been to interpret the convention, investigate complaints, settle differences among members, and if need be enforce the code (Gardner, 1969, p.104). That is to say, the ITS with the ITO as its institutional format would have functioned very much like an international trade court. The institution's role in persuading governments to resort to more responsible trade policies, in providing a framework for the accommodation of divergent viewpoints and in setting up the machinery for the mediation of commercial disputes would have been secondary.

Would state socialist countries ever have been able to truly belong in the framework sketched above? To answer that question it should be recalled that, when the groundwork for the ITS was being laid during and after the Second World War, its architects were ambitious and envisaged a broadly based, nearly universal set of trade regulations and enforcement mechanisms (Brabant, 1991; Culbert, 1987). They saw the ITS as one node of the network of international economic organizations (IEOs) to deal with money, finance and trade. This was expected to prevent any re-emergence of the critical factors that contributed to and aggravated the global economic crises of the 1930s, ultimately setting the stage for the Second World War. Near-universal membership was in itself sought as a guarantee for reversing the sharp rise in the degree of intervention of the state in economic affairs since the 1930s. Against that backdrop, compromises had in principle been entertained to accommodate countries with 'another economic system,' if only because it was believed that participation in the global order would persuade those countries in time to bring their system into closer harmony with those of mainstream market economies.

There is no need to recount the details of these negotiations and the way in which the Soviet Union in the end either abstained from the negotiations or ceased to participate. One consequence was, however, that several members of the IEOs when they turned to state socialism in the late 1940s were forced either to withdraw or to restrict their participation sharply. Others that attempted to join later on were either inhibited from doing so, largely at the USSR's behest, or were accommodated or rejected by the members of the ITS in particular on political grounds. For that reason, 'state-trading countries' occupied a special place in the ITS as 'state trading' provisions (under Article XVII of the GATT, dealing with state monopolies in market economies) provided the only modality by which these economies could be accommodated, however awkwardly (Brabant, 1991, pp.192ff).

When it became clear that the ITO would not come into being, the only ITS instrument left was the General Agreement negotiated in 1947. This preserved the fundamental principles of removing NTBs and reducing tariffs, but largely for manufactured products. Agriculture remained outside the framework. So did all other international transactions (such as services, intellectual property and capital flows) that have since assumed such importance in the globalizing economy. It also initially confined the membership to like-minded market economies, although in time a serious effort was made to incorporate many developing countries and to some degree state socialist economies.

The consequence of the extremely scanty provisions in the General Agreement for anything that even remotely resembled the situation of state socialist administration was considerable difficulty in using the GATT as a framework for the integration of such countries into the ITS. Not only was the GATT deprived of a universal status, it was unable to perform any significant role in fostering East–West trade. As a result, the latter remained within the purview of the broader foreign policy of key market economies, notably the European Union[6] (and the United States, at least until the events of 1989.

2. STATE SOCIALIST COUNTRIES AND THE GATT

The fundamental problems of integrating state socialist countries into the ITS were on the agenda of GATT debates at various times for different reasons. A first case occurred after Czechoslovakia, a founding Contracting Party, embraced state socialism in early 1948, following shortly upon the GATT's coming into effect. The United States, in particular, contended that Czechoslovakia should no longer benefit from GATT membership, that is, chiefly most-favoured nation (MFN) status. But this petition was rejected because other major Contracting Parties found it to be politically motivated. As a result, Czechoslovakia and the United States suspended MFN treatment on a reciprocal basis with the concurrence of the GATT. Other Contracting Parties largely ignored this mutation. Because Czechoslovakia did not insist on reciprocity and the other Contracting Parties preferred direct control of imports from state socialist countries, Czechoslovakia never participated actively in GATT affairs prior to 1990. Much the same status has applied to Cuba since 1962, although there has never been an official sanction of such a policy.

Second, the successive requests for accession first as observer,[7] in

6. I use the term 'European Union' as shorthand for the postwar integration efforts in western Europe, excepting the European Free Trade Association (EFTA).
7. Literally the authority to sit in on some meetings. This status is usually granted upon request.

some cases an associate member,[8] and later as full member by Yugoslavia (actually attained in 1950, 1959 and 1966 respectively[9]), Poland (actually attained in 1957, 1959,[10] and 1967, respectively) Romania (in 1957, no association and 1971, respectively), Bulgaria (an observer since 1967 and applied in 1986 for full accession), Hungary (in 1966,[11] no associate status and 1973, respectively), Bulgaria and China (observers since 1986), and the Soviet Union (as observer since early 1990) reopened the myriad theoretical and practical questions. The answers provided at the time were thoroughly pragmatic. For Poland and Romania, reciprocity was based on the granting of MFN by Contracting Parties, but with some restrictions chiefly on the part of the United States, in exchange for a commitment by the other party to increase its imports from the signatory countries by a given quantitative target – a very special 'entrance fee' in lieu of tariff concessions. Given these special provisions, other GATT members arrogated the right to protect their economies from any damage that might result from trading with such 'state-trading countries'. These conditions applied also to Czechoslovakia, and continue to apply to Cuba, as a matter of policy rather than through a negotiated agreement.

The accession of Hungary was handled very differently, chiefly because Hungary claimed, as Yugoslavia had in the early 1960s, that its economic reform first introduced in 1968 included multi-tier tariffs and domestic prices would be adjusted to world prices. Bulgaria (prior to 1990) and China[12] built their case for accession along the same lines by appealing to MFN-like features of their contemplated economic reforms; the Soviet Union did so by invoking, rather feebly and disingenuously, the far-reaching ambitions of *perestroika*. The other state

8. Associate status implies that commercial relations between Contracting Parties and 'state trading countries' can be conducted in conformity with GATT rules to the extent that state socialism permits. It also enables the country to participate in various organizational bodies of the GATT, including the multilateral trade negotiation (MTN) Rounds (Kostecki, 1979, p.25).
9. It acceded provisionally in 1962 and became a full Contracting Party in 1966, following rather tortuous negotiations with the Contracting Parties because the country did not really possess private firms.
10. In fact, Poland became an associate together with Yugoslavia on the basis of a special, limited status by means of declarations (Dam, 1970, p.320).
11. Its first application for observer status lodged in 1958 had to be withdrawn under political pressure from key industrial countries, especially the United States.
12. One of the major stumbling-blocks in its GATT/WTO negotiations has been China's insistence on being treated as a developing country (Yang, 1996).

socialist countries prior to 1990 could have been expected to submit their case for accession on similar grounds.

In other words, fusing the interests of selected state socialist countries and the GATT occasioned much improvisation. But there never was a comprehensive attempt to negotiate an agreement in order to accommodate such economies more flexibly. Invariably the country-by-country route was chosen, largely for political reasons. The one attempt made (GATT, 1960) to work out a comprehensive agreement failed to garner support for the same reasons (Brabant, 1991, pp.205ff). This aversion toward formulating a systemic solution certainly stemmed in part from the considerable differences in the trade systems of the countries concerned. But the country-specific approach also enabled some Contracting Parties to uphold double standards during the negotiations. Indeed it was part and parcel of the foreign-policy precepts of leading developed economies to deal separately with the state socialist countries.

3. UNIVERSALISM AND SYSTEM DIFFERENCES

Whereas during the Second World War and in the ensuing two decades many foreign-policy analysts, and even economists, looked positively at the possibilities of 'global economic management', that enthusiasm has since waned considerably. The reasons for this are legion. They include vastly exaggerated hopes of what can reasonably be accomplished in the context of essentially an intergovernmental body. There are two sides to this. One is divergence of views among the members on what precisely they wish the IEO to undertake. And there are evidently issues related to how this assignment is translated into the operational activities of the IEOs. But scepticism about global cooperation since the early 1970s also derives from equally mistaken views that IEOs are not particularly useful; indeed, some claim that they cause more harm than good.

I do not subscribe to either extreme view of what IEOs can accomplish. I simply assert that I consider the existence of IEOs, in which many countries participate and air their own interests as well as their perceptions of more global issues, to be an essential ingredient of a 'normal' state of affairs in an interdependent global economy in which the various actors have their own interests that diverge and even conflict and this may call for transitional regimes (see Brabant, 1991, pp.215ff.; Drábek, 1996). Without labouring this point, it is useful to state more generally what is meant by an international regime or system[13] and why countries may wish to take part in organized international relations and submit to the regime's rules.

An international economic regime, such as the ITS, can best be thought of as a set of gradually accepted rules and conventions regarding how countries are expected to conduct their economic policies that have significant external repercussions. Without endowing this order with fully-fledged organizations and institutions through which the agreed rules and conventions can be enforced in a predictable manner, an international economic order is likely to fragment quickly into a state of affairs characterized by, at best, weak rules and easy breaches of those rules as countries adopt entirely at their own discretion policies that have pronounced international repercussions. As such, a regime consists of 'explicit or implicit principles, norms, rules and decision making procedures around which actors' expectations converge' (Krasner, 1982, p.186) on a given component of the international economic order and which may help to coordinate their behaviour. *Principles* are essentially beliefs of fact, causation and propriety or rectitude. In contrast, *norms* are standards of behaviour set in terms of general rights and obligations. These two terms constitute the fundamental traits of a regime and are consistent with a variety of rules and *decision-making procedures*. *Rules* are specific prescriptions or proscriptions regarding behaviour. Finally, *decision-making procedures* are practices that exist for making collective choices and implementing them. Because changes in rules or decision making procedures do not fundamentally alter the regime as such, they are usually treated as within-regime transformations. In any case, a regime is by its nature distinct from a temporary arrangement that can mutate or that is modified with every shift in power or interest. It cannot be based purely on short-term or even unilateral calculation of interest of one or a few actors.

A regime's usefulness derives from the fact that it motivates

13. This is standard terminology in the literature even though the international regimes have really neither been global nor have they brought 'order' in global economic affairs (Brabant, 1991, pp.11ff.).

individual states to engage in cooperative behaviour. Because it may satisfy the realization of a common purpose beyond what individual actors can attain by themselves, a regime is essentially a vehicle to maximize the benefits derived from a public good according to some acceptable understanding on the sharing of benefits and costs. The importance of the externalities that affect the welfare of individual actors or well-defined élite groups is likely to grow when the degree of interdependence in the world is inexorably rising.

Membership of IEOs entails costs. Since economies in transition encounter chronic fiscal problems, one may well ask why they should be bent on joining IEOs. The costs consist of a variety of direct and indirect outlays: contributions to the organization's regular budget, participation in meetings, maintenance of some representative office attached to each IEO, and submission to explicit or implicit constraints on the behaviour of the state in international relations. To justify such costs, the country seeking membership must perceive palpable advantages and, depending on its political organization, may have to justify them. Benefits can take the form of an enhanced status in global affairs or opportunities for policy makers and civil servants to travel abroad and establish 'contacts' that they deem useful for themselves, their interest group, or their perception of national needs. Second, a country's view on some set of problems cannot at times attain the desired visibility without an affirmative presence in the appropriate international forum. Third, being an insider may yield valuable intelligence and other information that supplements and, from an individual country's perspective, complements the information available in the public and no-so-public domains. Often it is faster than awaiting it to be aired in the usual media, and thus permits timely reaction if necessary. This includes advance information on what actions nations and international secretariats are proposing; forming judgements about the merits and strengths of such proposed actions well before they can be implemented and assessing the likelihood that they will be carried out, and when, on the basis of 'adequate' information; and gaining access to a plethora of political, economic, administrative, scientific or technological background papers and documents prepared to facilitate deliberations about the proposal in question and perhaps even technical assistance and financial resources. Fourth, membership may confer tangible economic, strategic and other gains. Finally, some desirable actions cannot be undertaken by any one country in isolation. Note that adherence to a particular regime may yield benefits and costs that are quite visible. There may also be future costs; but these, I submit, are rather small. Much more significant are the benefits that accrue only indirectly and are, therefore, not readily identified as such, or that materialize only through a roundabout evolution.

In this connection, it bears recognition too, that the existing regimes are essentially public goods, and thus by definition indivisible. Yet, one critical aspect of maintaining a regime is to ensure the fair distribution of costs and gains in the presence of considerable potential for free-riding. This means that the benefits cannot be apportioned to members who contribute to maintaining the public good; it may even be impossible to limit them to the group (Keohane, 1986, p.12). In that case, there may be an argument for ushering many countries into the regime. There cannot be perfect symmetry in sharing costs and gains, however, let alone in tying the latter to the former. Medium-sized and smaller countries benefit proportionately more from a public good, such as that provided by the ITS, than do large countries. Yet the effective operation of the GATT, now the WTO, and its ability to function properly can be ensured only if major trading partners - the United States, Japan and the EU - provide continued support and positive participation.

But there are other reasons for drawing all major actors of the world economy into a coherent, common framework for examining and devising acceptable solutions for problems besetting international economic interdependence. One certainly is that international economic relations are not a zero-sum game; that is, international behaviour cannot be steered by one single country. Another derives from the proposition that a well-organized regime is likely to curb the power of big members by transferring some decision making to forums governed not by the will and in the interest of one state, but by a multilateral complex of interests, checks and balances (Sakbani, 1985, p.173). As the past has amply demonstrated, the greatest danger to international stability often arises from those actors whose real power is inadequately reflected in both the relevant parts of international arrangements and symbols of status therein. That is not to say that stability is predicated on universal organizations with equal or even proportional representation in all cases adjudicated within a given regime. Yet, imaginative mechanisms for balancing universalism with the need for operationality of the regimes deserve to be devised. For all these reasons I deem it useful to try to draw all major actors of the world economy into a coherent, common framework for examining and discussing problem areas that inhibit the smooth conduct of trade with a view to devising all-around acceptable solutions.

One must recognize that there is an inevitable conflict between universalism and efficiency in managing the regime. But meaningful, intelligent solutions may be found pragmatically. The argument can be phrased in two different ways. One depends essentially on the advantages of multilateralism. A firm commitment to multilateralism is an essential ingredient in maintaining peace, stability, predictability, security and reliability in international affairs. Participation in one or more mutual security organs ought to be fostered to the extent that it does not compromise either the basic principles upon which these institutions act or the functional degree of cooperation that can be ensured by expanding membership. In addition to the adjustments that potential applicants may have to engage in, universalization may require some modification on the part of the present membership and perhaps even in the particular focus of the activities of these organizations. This does not mean, however, that there would be no room for smaller steering groups exerting representatives governance when it proves to be too unwieldy to manage decisions through universal organs.

4. FUNCTIONS OF THE GATT AND WTO

From its inception, the GATT discharged essentially five functions (Stone, 1984, pp.23–24). First, it provided a permanent framework, however loose in view of its weak constitution, for international consultations on developments and concerns surrounding global trade policy in general and trading practices of individual Contracting Parties in particular. Second, together with supplementary codes and agreements, the General Agreement embodied a set of rules for trade conduct that constrain and discipline the trade policies and practices of individual countries. Third, it set an environment for the further liberalization of world trade basically through tariff negotiations, commitments not to raise tariffs save in exceptional circumstances and the application of rules that prohibit or restrain the use of NTBs.

Fourth, GATT offered facilities and agreed procedures to resolve trade disputes among the countries that abide by the General

Agreement. Finally, it provided the infrastructure for collecting and disseminating information about developments in world trade, trade policies and individual actions of Contracting Parties, and relatively independent research on and analyses of trade-related policy and legal issues.

The foundations of the General Agreement rest on reciprocity, transparency, non-discrimination and safeguards. Trade protection was to be based as far as politically feasible on tariffs with a view to restricting divergences between domestic and trade prices to normal factors of time and place. NTBs were to be replaced by tariffs and the latter gradually reduced through tariff negotiations. In other words, GATT's non-discrimination among all actors in the global economy was preconditioned on the assumption that trade is conducted primarily by private firms whose actions are guided by commercial, particularly profit, motives. In such an environment, it was taken for granted that prices result solely from commercial, not necessarily competitive, decisions. Note that these objectives may accord with the requirements of mature market economies, but they are ill-suited to be transposed to countries that cling to substantial macroeconomic control through direct commands, including commands over trade, that do not possess fully integrated domestic markets (Brabant, 1991; Hartland-Thunberg, 1987; Ryan, 1994), or that are in the process of society-wide transformation (Drábek, 1996).

Although non-discrimination was the principal creed of the General Agreement, the GATT approach was always pragmatic. From the ITS's inception various kinds of waivers and exceptions on that principle were embodied and several others were incorporated in one form or another over the past four decades. The most important were: (1) to permit the continuation of existing tariff preferences especially to accommodate the UK's Imperial Preference and the French colonial arrangements, but the Contracting Parties committed themselves not to raise the discriminatory duties; (2) customs unions of one kind or another that conform to conditions specified in detail, including free movement of the vast majority of goods and services and external tariffs not exceeding the average of the pre-union tariff; (3) quantitative restrictions (QRs) for balance-of-payments reasons; (4) waivers to permit developed countries to extend non-reciprocal tariff preferences to developing countries – hence not subject to MFN – and the latter countries among themselves; (5) a limited number of waivers to permit individual countries to give preferential tariff treatment to particular target imports from specified countries as in the automobile trade agreement between the United States and Canada); (6) QRs. on imports of textile products on a discriminatory basis; and (7) conditional MFN treatment upon supplementary codes and arrangements concluded during the Tokyo Round.

With reference to the regime's principles, the ITS was based on the belief that reciprocal trade liberalization helps to sustain the level of economic activity and contributes broadly to better relations among countries, not just in economic exchanges. The purpose, then, was to ensure that the basis for export expansion of all countries was provided without unduly impairing one single party. For that, the Contracting Parties adopted a host of substantive and procedural norms (Finlayson and Zacher, 1981), the most important of which are non-discrimination, trade liberalization through tariff reductions and removal of NTBs, reciprocity, safeguards, and, since the mid-1960s, special treatment for developing countries (Patterson, 1986); as noted, a similar modification to accommodate state socialist administration never materialized. Rules as prescriptions and proscriptions are anchored to the commitment not to raise the level of protection beyond so-called 'bound' margins, that is, levels negotiated within the ITS framework or brought into it through provisional accession. Regarding decision-making procedures, the ITS provides for ways to arrange Ministerial Meetings, to lower trade barriers through rounds of multinational negotiations (MTN Rounds), to facilitate the accession of Contracting Parties to the machinery for dispute settlement through Working Parties and Panels, and decisions by the executive organ possibly made by voting, although that occurred infrequently.

Even when well disposed to the ITS in place, commentators over the years frequently complained that the rules of the General Agreement were weakly enforced, easily circumvented and widely abused, thereby contributing significantly to the weakening of multilateralism. Beginning with the late 1960s, the ITS became less and less universal and multilateral (Keohane, 1984), a victim of the 'balkanization of international trade policy' (Gadbaw, 1984, p.38), or derogations from the General Agreement. These 'mini-GATTs' emerged because some Contracting Parties failed to settle their differences under the General Agreement, and so resolved to draft nearly independent agreements, each of which had somewhat different decision-making and enforcement mechanisms. Seen in the legal context of the General Agreement, the process of enforcement was always complex. The GATT was not a policing organization, neither had it enforcement powers of its own. In view of its antecedents in reciprocal tariff and other commercial-policy concessions, the General Agreement was anchored to the precepts of nearly balanced exchange of import concessions and export benefits among the Contracting Parties. Reneging on such an arrangement by one partner was, as a result, an act tantamount to withdrawing equivalent concessions, or an offer of acceptable compensation for the injury sustained by other Contracting Parties. Furthermore, this injury must be 'declared' by the Contracting Parties, as the GATT itself had no powers to initiate such proceedings.

Many of the problems derived from the ITS's nature as a public good; hence, the need to come to grips with free-riding (Artis and Ostry, 1986, p.75). Furthermore, the ITS was in need of being adapted to changes in the global economic and political environment, something that could hardly be accomplished in a transient instrument. These changes include the expanding role of developing countries, the accommodation of state trading, the rise of newly industrializing developing countries (Ryan, 1994), rules deciding how best to foster structural adjustment, the competitive export of unemployment and agricultural protectionism.

The many derogations of the General Agreement enacted over the years justified a comprehensive reassessment of the functions of the ITS in a world quite different from that for which it had first been negotiated. A concerted effort to improve the institutional mechanism for decision making, rule development, dispute settlement, enforcement and the coordination of national policies affecting trade became a prerequisite for restoring parts of the multilateralism at the global level lost since the late 1960s. At least a first step in this direction was set with the Uruguay Round agreement and the commitments made at Marrakech in April 1994 to initiate further trade negotiations later in the decade, as taken up as a first step in Singapore in mid-December 1996 (WTO, 1996d).

Many, but far from all, of these concerns about the weak foundations of the ITS via the General Agreement have been met as a result of the Marrakech agreements. However, whereas the WTO is the successor of the GATT, the one is not a simple extension of the other. Indeed, the WTO completely replaces its predecessor[14] and has a very different character. Five such differences should be borne in mind (WTO, 1996b). First, the GATT was simply the General Agreement with no institutional foundation, a 'temporary' secretariat of modest dimensions, and otherwise expected to be superseded by the ITO. The WTO is a permanent institution with its own secretariat serving its membership, and thus able to act, albeit within limits, without constantly resorting to initiatives of Contracting Parties. Second, the General Agreement was applied on a 'provisional basis' pending the ITO's establishment, although that lasted for nearly fifty years! The WTO commitments are full and permanent. Third, the GATT rules applied to trade in merchandise goods with several derogations for agriculture and textiles and clothing in particular; but even less transparent interferences were enacted, beginning in the 1970s. The WTO covers not only merchandise trade but also services and trade-related aspects of intellectual property; and increasingly other instances of international interaction. Fourth, while the General Agreement was a multilateral instrument, by the early 1980s many new agreements had been added of a 'plurilateral', and therefore selective, nature. The agreements of which the WTO is the custodian are almost all multilateral and thus involve commitments for the entire membership.[15] Finally, the WTO's dispute-settlement system is faster, more automatic, and thus much less susceptible to blockades, than the General Agreement's. Also, the implementation of dispute findings will be more easily assured. If utilized judiciously to chart new law concerning international exchanges, this may be a particularly valuable instrument for small and medium-sized countries.

14. Note that the General Agreement continued to exist until the end of 1995, thus allowing all GATT members to accede to the WTO and permitting an overlap of activity in areas such as dispute settlement. Of course, the General Agreement, updated during the Uruguay Round as endorsed on 15 April 1994 in Marrakech (for details see WTO, 1994), forms an integral part of the WTO Agreement and thus continues to provide the key disciplines affecting international trade in goods (WTO, 1996b).
15. Again this should not be exaggerated. One of the major achievements of Marrakech – the General Agreement on Trade in Services (GATS) – has not been endorsed by the full membership.

5. THE BENEFITS AND DRAWBACKS OF THE GATT APPROACH

Although there is a wide range of appraisals about the effectiveness of the GATT and the significance of the General Agreement for the postwar expansion of global trade, there is little dissent about treating the ITS as one of the more successful efforts in postwar near-global economic cooperation. Aside from obtaining MFN status, and allowing the less-developed to benefit from special preferences, the GATT offered a multilateral framework for settling trade disputes. Inasmuch as catch-up development is possible only by measurably expanding exports of manufactures, often goods subject to special treatment (including foodstuffs, textiles and apparel, chemicals, steel, automobiles and others), dispute-settlement machinery is valuable even to large countries. Adhering to an international code might also strengthen the hands of policy makers bent on forging ahead with a market-oriented reform in spite of domestic opposition.

From its inception, the ITS has yielded unique benefits for small and medium-sized countries in particular (Stone, 1984, p.26). It has enabled them to influence policy debates at the global level more effectively than they could have through simple bilateral relations. Since the ITS has facilitated commerce among sovereign states (Gardner, 1969, p.xxxv), the General Agreement exerted a valuable constraint on the trade policies and practices of larger countries and helped governments to stave off, or to withstand, pressures by domestic producer and labour interests to a larger degree than would otherwise have been the case. Also, multinationals in an environment where currencies are convertible afford small countries a better chance to capture larger markets than they could have otherwise. Finally, the dispute-settlement mechanism in principle affords countries the means to settle trade disputes with larger countries more equitably and more expeditiously than within the ITS. I mention this even though the dispute-settlement machinery lost much of its earlier lustre as the most important Contracting Parties resorted to bilateral and small-group arrangements (Lipson, 1982, p.436) prior to the recommitment in the Uruguay Round.

Positive appraisals of the GATT approach notwithstanding, I recognize that the General Agreement had its limitations as the role of merchandise in international exchange waned over time. The Uruguay

Round made a first stab at tackling these other areas. But much remains to be accomplished to reach a truly universal code governing such transactions. Also, in areas where previously Contracting Parties had nibbled away at the GATT's role in the above-cited areas, the Uruguay Round Agreements have set a first step in eliminating these discriminatory regimes. It is now important also to live up to the spirit of the new ITS, and ensure that the less transparent trade-restricting policies enacted since the mid-1970s to shield domestic products and labour against international competition are in fact reversed. And the need to promote domestic economic policies more generally while taking their global implications into account remains a goal yet to be achieved, particularly in the larger trading countries.

Finally, GATT's rules for economic unions, customs unions and free trade areas have not been very effective in preventing or controlling a number of arrangements - most notably in western Europe but also elsewhere - that are simple extensions of trade preferences. Inasmuch as they violate parts of the agreed code, they are discriminatory even in the rather permissive ITS (WTO, 1995, 1996c).

With the WTO, the prospect of universal membership has become more immediate, and so it is worthwhile highlighting the specific advantages that the transition economies can expect to reap, or already enjoy, from membership. It is useful to distinguish between the benefits that may eventually accrue from the given regime by forestalling the emergence of arrangements that prospectively narrow the area of fruitful interaction from the gains and losses directly following from belonging to the regime. Among the benefits that accrue from the General Agreement in the strict sense, it may be useful to stress six. First, members obtain most-favoured nation (MFN) treatment on a predictable and multilateral basis, rather than to having to negotiate for it periodically on a bilateral basis. Inasmuch as most trade of the European transition economies is now with the EU, where most already benefit from MFN, widening the scope to the global level may not seem such a great step. However, with catch-up growth the transition economies will in all likelihood avail themselves of the global economy, and hence will profit from global MFN treatment.

Second, the transition economies benefit from MTN rounds and can now help to shape them. Their importance will rise as further rounds focus on newer areas of international exchange. A non-member with MFN status can, of course, benefit from rounds to which it has not been a party (and which hence has not extended reciprocal concessions) because of the public-good character of the arrangement. Given the aspirations of most transition economies, however, they have a legitimate interest in influencing both the size and the distribution of the concessions tabled during the rounds. Third, inasmuch as transition economies are bent on becoming further integrated into the global economy, lower tariffs on their exports makes these countries more competitive, thereby promoting their market access for new products. Such an opportunity might well fail to materialize with free-riding. Fourth, small and medium-sized transition economies in particular (all but China and Russia, which could conceivably resolve their trade disputes bilaterally) can avail themselves of the multilateral machinery for settling disputes. This is not a negligible advantage, given the derogations from MFN that these countries have had to negotiate bilaterally even with the EU. Fifth, accession to some desirable regional organizations, including the Central European Free Trade Agreement (CEFTA) and the EU, is predicated on the potential member's sharing in the purposes and goals of these organizations and their underlying regime. Thus, further expansion of CEFTA (until 1996 consisting of the Czech Republic, Hungary, Poland and Slovakia; Slovenia acceded in 1996 and Bulgaria and Romania were expected to do so in the course of 1997) is contingent on WTO membership and having signed (but not necessarily ratified) a Europe Agreement (Brabant, 1996). Maintaining a close rapport with the EU would probably also be impossible without applying the fairly liberal ITS rules, though here the intention of pursuing WTO membership is probably more important than having reached that stage. In turn, a closer association with the EU will in all likelihood facilitate the negotiations for accession to the WTO. Finally, the transition economies with little experience in trade diplomacy, or in macroeconomic policy for that matter (and this certainly includes most newly independent countries), stand to gain information about trade regimes in the broad sense, including obtaining technical assistance, that might be very costly to compile by any one country in isolation.

The corresponding advantages to the Contracting Parties are, of course, less clear. Gaining access to useful economic intelligence and insights into the workings of the external sector in transition economies is undoubtedly a benefit, particularly for small Contracting Parties. Being able to press for more transparent forms of reciprocity is also a bonus, though that certainly should not be exaggerated. However, agitating for better and wider access to the markets of transition economies may yield positive export increments even for these countries.

Some benefits may eventually be reaped from the ITS by forestalling the emergence of arrangements that could in time narrow the arena for fruitful commerce for which the transition economies may in the future wish to compete. Helping to shape the future trading environment for manufactures is certainly not an important consideration for a country that has traditionally concentrated its exports on goods that still fall outside tariff rules (such as agricultural products) or for which tariffs are close to zero (such as most raw materials and fuels). However, if that country aspires to acquiring an export-led pattern of development paced by the dynamism of the manufacturing sector, the prospect of being able to graduate into a trading world subject to predictable rules should itself be counted as a goal worth pursuing. This should favour membership.

On the other hand, there are costs to joining the ITS framework. They consist essentially in the obligation to disclose information on trading arrangements and performance, submitting to negotiations when Contracting Parties request them, and sharing in the comparatively small operating budget of the WTO, as noted above. These drawbacks are, however, rather minor for a country that is truly bent on integrating itself into the global economy.

6. THE TRANSITION AND THE APPROACH TOWARDS GATT/WTO

Since the transition's inception, several changes have occurred in the relationship between these countries and the GATT, and now the WTO. It is important to bear in mind three types of approaches and their implications. The first has been regularization of the position of these countries in the GATT when they were already a Contracting Party. The transition economies that had previously not fully benefited from the provisions of the General Agreement (Hungary, Poland, Romania and Yugoslavia) or that had kept their membership dormant (Czechoslovakia) were keen on regularizing their position and thus being recognized on a 'normal' basis; presumably Cuba would want to do so too if it were to opt for the creation of a market economy. In the case of Poland and Romania this required the renegotiation of the entry provisions on reciprocity. For Hungary and Yugoslavia, it entailed the abolition of discriminatory quantitative restrictions under Article XIII of the General Agreement. With the exception of Yugoslavia, this was fairly swiftly accomplished; even the successor agreements for the Czech Republic and Slovakia were negotiated quickly. The Yugoslav case is special as the dissolution of the old federation has been viewed by all IEOs as a final break-up. As a result, the request of rump Yugoslavia (Montenegro and Serbia) to be treated as the successor to the old federation was rejected. The successor republics have had to approach the GATT as if they were new applicants almost *ab ovo*.

Note that the recognition of the above countries as 'market economies' for GATT/WTO purposes does not remove the residual need to come to grips with the discriminatory trade regimes of the transition economies not yet committed to opening up their economies on a fully competitive basis. Bulgaria's accession on 1 December 1996, for example, at a time of severe economic crisis with foreign sectors in appalling disarray, offers an extreme illustration of what would seem to be required by way of surveillance and guidance to ensure that the domestic transformation processes firm up, rather than loosen, market-based foundations. This applies as well, albeit perhaps to a lesser degree, to the transition economies bent on deepening their domestic markets in an open environment. This needs to be carefully monitored to ensure that trade liberalization and domestic structural change remain in harmony without harming the interests of other WTO members.

Second, the countries that were observers in the GATT one after another requested that the process of application for full accession be initiated fairly quickly. But as recent experience has shown, accession is a protracted process, particularly for countries undergoing radical shifts in economic structure and macroeconomic policies and institutions. Since the transition erupted, only two countries - Bulgaria and Slovenia - have been admitted.[16] There are then seven transition economies as full members as of early 1997: Bulgaria, the Czech

16. Mongolia's protocol of accession was adopted by the General Council in July 1996; but at the time of writing it has not yet been ratified by Mongolia's national legislature.

Republic, Hungary, Poland, Romania, Slovakia and Slovenia (WTO, 1996a).

Finally, the transition economies that were not associated with the GATT one after another requested, and were granted, observer status. Some have since submitted their request for full accession, and the various procedural steps to reach that stage have been put in train for a number of these countries. As of the end of 1996 (WTO, 1996a) accession for eighteen transition economies (Albania, Armenia, Belarus, China, Croatia, Estonia, Georgia, Kazakhstan, Kyrgyzstan, Latvia, Lithuania, Macedonia, Moldova, Mongolia, Russia, Ukraine, Uzbekistan and Vietnam) have been negotiated, and in time these countries will presumably be able to join the WTO. Finally, Azerbaijan, Tajikistan, Turkmenistan and following the end of the sanctions, rump Yugoslavia are observers. Since the latter has accepted the procedures for readmission into the Washington IEOs, it seems fairly certain that the same rule will soon be applied with respect to WTO.

Apart from delivering the kind of services for which GATT/WTO has been the custodian of the ITS, the secretariat has been providing technical assistance concerning the General Agreement and the successor ones of the Uruguay Round and the way in which these instruments are being administered, and also about the broader aspects of preparing an application for accession. Among the latter, the desirable features of trade and foreign-exchange regimes to function appropriately within the context of the ITS have also been clarified through various training seminars. The accent has been on trade policy (that is, essentially what reciprocity and MFN entail) as well as the institutional requirements for operating such an open trade regime and participate in the GATT/WTO.

CONCLUSIONS

Just like other regimes of the international economic order, by its nature the ITS straddles the border between economics and politics, and it may well have a heavier touch on the second of these than on the first. From an economic point of view, particularly for countries bent on pursuing an outward-looking economic policy, the benefits of belonging in the ITS generally outweigh the drawbacks, even though the ITS is rarely applied in the spirit in which the underlying agreements were drafted. This is reinforced for the political endorsement, credibility and reliability that membership conveys to the partners of the transition economies, and also to those managing the transformation as far as their own domestic support base is concerned. The transition economies are well on their way to eventual full membership in the WTO. But it will take more time for them to exploit fully the potential of functioning within an ITS for the most dynamic products in global economic exchanges. However, by committing themselves to strict rules, such as those of the GATT/WTO, the managers of the transition may be jeopardizing policy credibility. A transition regime for accession might therefore be useful (Drábek 1996), for much the same reasons that it would earlier have been (and perhaps is now) useful for other groups of countries, including those that maintain vestiges of state socialist administration (Brabant, 1991).

BIBLIOGRAPHY

Artis, Michael and Sylvia Ostry (1986). *International Economic Policy Coordination* (London: Routledge & Kegan Paul, for the Royal Institute of International Affairs).

Brabant, Jozef M. van (1988). 'Planned Economies in the GATT Framework: The Soviet Case', *Soviet Economy,* vol. 4, no.1, pp.3–35.

—— (1989), 'The Soviet Union in the GATT?: A Plea for Reform', *International Spectator*, vol.43, no.2, pp.72–93.

—— (1991). *The Planned Economies and International Economic Organizations* (Cambridge: Cambridge University Press).

—— (1996). *Integrating Europe: The Transition Economies at Stake* (Dordrecht, Boston, MA, and London: Kluwer Academic Publishers).

Culbert, Jay (1987). 'War-time Anglo-American Talks and the Making of the GATT', *The World Economy*, vol.10, no.4, pp.381–99.

Dam, Kenneth W. (1970). *The GATT: Law and International Economic Organization* (Chicago: University of Chicago Press).

Drábek, Zdeněk (1996),'The Stability of Trade Policy in the Countries in Transition and Their Integration into the Multilateral Trading System', *The World Economy*, vol.19, no.6, pp.721-45.

Economist, The (1996), 'World Trade - All Free Traders Now?', *The Economist*, 7-13 December, pp.21-3.

Finlayson, Jock A. and Mark W. Zacher (1981). 'The GATT and the Regulation of Trade Barriers: Regime Dynamics and Functions', *International Organization*, vol.35, no.4, pp.561-602.

Gadbaw, R. Michael (1984), 'The Outlook for GATT as an Institution', in Seymour J. Rubin and Thomas R. Graham (eds), *Managing Trade Relations in the 1980s: Issues Involved in the GATT Ministerial Meeting - 1982* (Totowa, NJ: Rowland & Allenheld), pp.33-49.

Gardner, Richard N. (1969). *Sterling-Dollar Diplomacy: The Origins and the Prospects of Our International Economic Order* (new expanded edition, New York: McGraw-Hill).

GATT (1960), 'Terms of Accession for a Country with a Centrally Planned Economy' (Geneva: General Agreement on Tariffs and Trade, document no. INT (60)20; mimeo).

Hartland-Thunberg, Penelope (1987), 'China's Modernization: A Challenge for the GATT', *The Washington Quarterly,* vol.10, no.1, pp.81-97.

Herzstein, Robert E. (1986). 'China and the GATT: Legal and Policy Issues Raised by China's Participation in the General Agreement on Tariffs and Trade', *Law and Policy in International Business*, no.2, pp.371-415.

Keohane, Robert O. (1984), *After Hegemony: Cooperation and Discord in the World Political Economy* (Princeton, NJ: Princeton University Press).

—— (1986) 'Reciprocity in International Relations', *International Organization,* vol.40, no.1, pp.1-27.

Kostecki, Maciej M. (1979). *East-West Trade and the GATT System* (London: Macmillan, for the Trade Policy Research Centre).

—— (1984). 'Can Tariff Be Effective Under Central Planning?', *Economia Internazionale*, vol.37, no.1/2, pp.94-107.

Krasner, Stephen D. (1982). 'Structural Causes and Regime Consequences: Regimes as Intervening Variables', *International Organization,* vol.36, no.2, pp.185-205.

Lipson, Charles (1982). 'The Transformation of Trade: The Sources and Effects of Regime Change', *International Organization*, vol.36, no.2, pp.417–55.

Long, Olivier (1985). *Law and its limitations in the GATT Multilateral Trade System* (Dordrecht: Martinus Nijhoff).

Matejka, Harriet (1990). 'Central Planning, Commercial Policies and How CPEs Fit Into the GATT Framework', *Journal of Development Planning*, No.20, pp.141-62.

Patterson, Eliza R. (1986). 'Improving GATT Rules for Nonmarket Economies', *Journal of World Trade Law*, vol.20, no.2, pp.185–205.

Ryan, Michael P. (1994). 'East Asian Political Economies and the GATT Regime', *Asian Survey*, vol.34, no.6, pp.556–71.

Sakbani, M. Michael (1985). 'The Crisis of the International Economic System: Proposals for Monetary and Financial Reforms', *Trade and Development*, no.6, pp.149–93.

Stone, Frank (1984). *Canada, the GATT and the International Trade System* (Ottawa: The Institute for Research on Public Policy L'Institut de Recherches Politiques).

WTO (1994). 'A Summary of the Final Act of the Uruguay Round' (Geneva: WTO Internet posting; probably late in the year).

—— (1995). 'Trade Policy Review of the European Union' (Geneva: WTO Internet posting; 18 July).

—— 1996a). 'Membership of the World Trade Organization' (Geneva: WTO Internet posting; 13 December).

—— (1996b). 'The Roots of the WTO' (Geneva: WTO Internet posting; probably early December).

—— 1996c). 'Regionalism and the Multilateral Trading System; (Geneva: WTO Internet posting; probably early December).

—— 1996d). 'Draft Singapore Ministerial Declaration' (Geneva: WTP Internet posting; 13 December).

Yang, Yongzheng (1996). 'China's WTO Membership: What's At Stake?', *The World Economy*, vol.19, no.6, pp.661–82.

Part IV

Selected Aspects and Perspectives

8. Industrial Policy: Does Eastern Europe Need One?

Iliana Zloch-Christy

> The ideas of economist and philosophers, both when they are right and when they are wrong are more powerful than is commonly understood. Indeed the world is ruled by little else.
>
> — John Maynard Keynes

> An economist who is nothing but an economist cannot be a good economist.
>
> — Friedrich von Hayek

INTRODUCTION

Scholars working on Eastern Europe, Russia and the former Soviet republics remain as convinced today as in 1989 that one of the most fascinating issues of contemporary politics are the post-1989 changes in this region. For economists, the region attracts great professional interest because the restructuring of the former centrally planned economies, as Lawrence Summers has put it, is the 'greatest reconstruction job in history'.[1] Many of us continue to deal in our papers, books, research projects and consultancy work with two fundamental questions of economic policy: the positive one of 'What can be done', and the normative one, based on value judgements, of 'What should be done'.

1. *The Transition*, The World Bank, August 1994, p.2.

For me as a scholar, two major topics have been of great professional interest since 1989: the East European Payments Union[2] and the industrial policy of the region. The first issue is obviously long forgotten by economists and politicians both in the East and in the West, and the issue of industrial policy is an unfashionable term, hardly seen in scholarly publications in the past five years and hardly heard in international conferences held either in the East or in the West.[3]

This chapter addresses the question of whether Eastern Europe needs to have an industrial policy. It also attempts to provide a preliminary basis for future research towards an analytical framework for assessing challenges and responses of the current transformation with a focus on industrial policy. The structure of the chapter is as follows: the first part addresses the question of what we have learnt from the transformational recession in Eastern Europe; the second part poses another question - whether the post-communist economies should approach the challenges of the 1990s with long-term thinking; the third part turns specifically to a discussion of industrial policy in Eastern Europe: definition (3.1), types (3.2) and the question what Eastern Europe can learn from the experience of Western Europe, Japan and the USA (3.3); the final part analyses briefly the issue of industrial policy in relation to two other important aspects of the economic and political transformation - privatization and foreign investments - in the context of the policies of the newly elected leftist governments (that is, renamed communists) in most of the countries in the region.

1. WHAT HAVE WE LEARNED FROM THE TRANSFORMATION DEPRESSION?

As an introduction to this part, I would like to make here a general observation concerning the challenges facing research on the post-communist economic transition.[4] The scholars working on the political

2. This interesting problem is discussed in my study, 'Some Issues on the Convertibility of the Eastern European Currencies', prepared for the United Nations Economic Commission for Europe, Geneva, March 1990.
3. The only exception in this regard has been the study of Jozef M. van Brabant, *Industrial Policy in Eastern Europe: Governing the Transition* (Dordrecht and Boston, MA: Kluwer Academic Publishers, 1993).
4. A discussion of the goals of transition and its man problems and challenges is

economy of transformation in Eastern Europe are confronted with the constraint of lack of a profound theoretical framework for assessment of the challenges and responses presented by the transformation. The same was true at some point (since we have the pioneering works of Peter Wiles, János Kornai, Alec Nove, Michael Kaser and others) when we wrote our studies in graduate school on the former centrally planned economies. Economic theory is in essence a collection of models: simplified representations of reality. Do we possess a model or models for the transformation? The answer is definitely 'no'. And how can one define the enormous quantity of publications on the economics of transition, drawing on the amusing classification of the American economist Paul Krugman (pointed out to me in a recent discussion as well as in his publications): namely 'Greek letters economics' (mathematical), 'up-and-down economics' (descriptive and prescriptive) and 'airport economics' (entertaining business studies)? The answer is obviously by reference to 'up-and-down economics'. And this style of economic analysis dominates the work of professional economists who, again using Krugman's classification, can be called policy entrepreneurs (advising East European governments),[5] rather than professors (who write for other professors). And these policy entrepreneurs offer unambiguous diagnoses and solutions even where the scholarly professors are uncertain. Very often they are insufficiently familiar with local circumstances in Eastern Europe, and they offer easy answers or are co-authors of *x*-day programmes for radical changes in the economies, even where the professors doubt whether any easy answer can be suggested. The arrogant incompetence of the old communists was replaced by the intellectual arrogance of policy entrepreneurs in Eastern Europe.

But let me turn to the question of what we have learnt from the transformational depression in Eastern Europe. Intellectual honesty requires us to admit that in 1989–90 many scholars, policy entrepreneurs and politicians in Eastern Europe believed that the beautiful simplicities of the market order would soon be established and the

presented in my paper, 'Eastern European Economic Transformation: Economic Sense and Non-Sense in the Time of Diminished Expectations', prepared for the V World Congress of Central and East European Studies, Warsaw, 5–12 August 1995.

5. Obviously not a difficult effort since, as Keynes once remarked, 'politicians have ears but no eyes': cited in Elisabeth Johnson, 'John Maynard Keynes: Scientist or Politician', in Joan Robinson (ed.), *After Keynes* (Oxford: Basil Blackwell, 1973), pp.12–25 (p.13).

problems of transition would be resolved by themselves. Five years later the Oxford political economist John Gray wrote that the prevailing economic reforms in post-communist Europe were 'not only intellectually indefensible', they were 'politically frivolous, and dangerous in the highest degree' (*Financial Times*, 24 February 1994, p.14).

What was wrong with our heightened expectations in 1989–90? What have we learnt from the transformational depression?

The American economist Ed Lazear pointed out to me in a discussion in July 1995 three main features associated with a successful market economy: free prices, privately-owned capital and a stable monetary system. In my 1991 study (Zloch-Christy, 1991, p.83; written in 1989–90), I stressed the importance of the following policies in the transition period from a centrally planned economy (characterized by the political monopoly of the communist party, a predominance of public ownership, a direct command managerial structure, economies of shortage, a negligible role of monetary policies, external imbalances) to a market economy: import liberalization, market-clearing prices, a unified exchange rate and currency convertibility (on the current account), elimination of direct and indirect state subsidies, and rapid privatization. I omitted to stress the importance of a competitive banking system subject to close supervision.

Have most of the post-communist countries (and particularly the Central and Southern European ones) fulfilled the above criteria? The superficial answer is: to the Lazear criteria 50:50; to my expectations, almost 80 per cent. But if we take for comparison the UK and the US economies, which briefly can be defined as 'share-based capitalism' (although they have a large governmental sector, which, according to the American economist Robert Barro, absorbs in the US 34 per cent of GDP and in the UK 41 per cent: *Financial Times*, 30 May 1995, p.13), or the continental European (German) 'bank-based capitalism', the present economies of post-communist Europe, according to *The Economist*, can be briefly described as 'non-share capitalism', with illiquid capital markets and chaotic banks (*The Economist*, 20–27 May 1995, p.27). And one can observe that the market risks to economic reform are replaced by political risks: at elections voters give their support to the old comrades who have turned chameleon-like into democratic socialists as the melancholic events of recent years showed in a number of countries, including Poland, Hungary and others. The only real achievement of transformation seems to be the abolition of the monopoly of the communist party. Intellectual honesty requires us to state clearly that all across Eastern Europe semi-chaos dominates, with unemployment, inflation (mainly price inflation, inflation of the government's budget and inflation of budget deficit, using Machlup's terms in specifying this important phenomenon) and poverty rapidly increasing after 1989. And, as Keynes put it, unemployment is stupid and poverty is ugly (cited in Robinson, 1973, p.9). And I should not forget to add to this picture the ugliness of the corruption and the mafia, as discussed in, for example, Lazear (1995, pp.340–66).

And what of the *economic costs* of transformation?

Few of the principal economic indicators included in the so-called 'misery index', using Robert Barro's term, illustrate the depression clearly. The misery index considers changes in four main indicators: inflation, unemployment, long-term interest rates (related to the long-term outlook for inflation), and real economic growth. The rate of aggregate domestic investment has fallen and is negative in all the East European countries. The gross national savings rates (gross investment minus capital imports) and the net savings rates (gross national savings minus capital depreciation) have fallen also and are negative. Inflation, as stressed above, is a major economic problem. Eastern Europe's labour force is trained, literate, industrious, but *not* disciplined. The (Keynesian) unemployment rates reached some 12–16 per cent in 1993–94; the only exception is the Czech Republic, although it seems to me that the low level of some 3 per cent unemployment in that country is due to 'statistical cosmetics' which hide real unemployment of more than 10 per cent. East European management is energetic, but it lacks experience of domestic and international competition and is not adjusted to the new rules of the market. The nationality conflicts in a number of countries in the region (for example, the CIS, Hungary, Romania and former Czechoslovakia) and the accumulated external debt and the collapse of the former CMEA system for multilateral trade and payments exacerbated the crisis of the domestic economies. The long-term interest rates are very high. Real economic growth in all these countries is negative with some signs of slow recovery in 1995. And I should add here briefly another point: the dismal picture in some of these countries also shows huge external debt (Hungary, Poland, Bulgaria, Russia). Another issue in, for example, Poland, Hungary and the Czech Republic, is that there is a potential danger that the flood of foreign capital will create tension in the domestic economy. As experience from developing countries has shown, a flood of foreign capital can destroy a developing economy (such as the post-communist economies) by creating a crippling current account deficit - the difference between what is received from exports and what is paid out for imports and interest on foreign debt. Foreign investors are also likely to pull their money out in a crisis, further destabilizing the economy (corporate investments in plants and equipment is not a problem). Foreign investments can also spur domestic price rises, and this leads to over-valuation of the national currency, which hurts domestic competitiveness in international trade and puts a squeeze on exports. All that points to the lack of (and the need for) capital controls, for example, setting limits on the amount that foreign banks may invest.[6]

What of *economic growth*? Although the statistics show some growth in some of these countries, including Poland, the Czech Republic, Slovenia and the Baltic states, which can give grounds for criticism that my assessment is inaccurate (and this criticism will mostly come from the policy entrepreneurs) we should not fail to observe the following: (1) the slow rise was associated mainly with the utilization of capacity (severely depressed in 1989–93), and not with rise in potential output or most importantly with productivity growth; (2) Disraeli's statement that there are three kinds of lies: lies, damned lies, and statistics, should also not be ignored in this regard. And I should stress here another point in connection with economic growth: it is observed that positive rates were recorded after socialist governments came to power; however, the credit for these developments should not be given to them, but to those who in 1989 in Poland and in 1990–92 in the other countries introduced the first steps towards reform. As business cycle economics teaches us, the fluctuations of the business cycle have very little to do with the economic policies of the administration in power. And it is not surprising that a certain recovery is evident in Eastern Europe, and it is evident precisely because there are so many unemployed resources available as a result of the depression. All that has nothing to do with the policies of the newly elected descendants of the old comrades.

6. It might be interesting to mention here a point made by Ludwig von Mises in a letter to Friedrich von Hayek of 28 March 1944 (and documented in the Hoover Archives at Stanford University): 'Even investment bankers, planning ample post-war credits to foreign nations, believe that it would be against natural law to restrict any debtor nation's power to take *ad libitum* recourse to foreign exchange controls.'

The most important task in the early 1990s and at the present time has been economic stabilization (requiring complex anti-inflationary macroeconomic policies). And if we ask the question, what is *economic success*? – for example, is stabilization a success and is it sustainable? – the answer is not clear. One of the lessons learnt in the past five years is that it is a nonsense to believe that if you unify exchange rates, eliminate import restrictions or introduce a currency board you are on the right track. But is it all so simple? Are those the only conditions to stabilize the economy? The answer is 'no'. They are not *sufficient* conditions. And experience from some developed, but mostly developing, countries bears witness that such stabilization policies become critically important and particularly dangerous in those cases in which domestic economies lack a long-term development programme, relevant state administrative capacities and a solid institutional base. The latter applies also to Eastern Europe. And precisely for these reasons the countries in the region are now at the stage of diminished expectations. To the above-mentioned lessons learnt from the transformational depression, I should add also the observation that the development of market coordination takes time, which might be shortened (by appropriate legal regulations and state initiatives in the form of legislative acts, supervisory agencies and state guarantees) or prolonged (if such policies are absent). And finally let us not overlook a long-forgotten and unfashionable issue for discussion, namely the multilateral payments union for Eastern Europe, which could have helped such market coordination to develop more smoothly and reduced the social costs of transition.[7]

2. CAN THE EAST EUROPEAN ECONOMIES FACE THE CHALLENGES OF THE 1990s WITHOUT LONG-TERM THINKING?

The discussion in the first section above raises the questions of what can be done and what should be done and whether post-communist Europe can face the challenges of the 1990s without long-term thinking. I realize that these two (positive and normative) questions look

7. See note 2.

too ambitious since the competence of economics to explain how the economy actually functions is admitted to be extremely fragmentary and limited, and its ability to produce recipes for making the economy work better is even more fragmentary and limited. And as a follower of Kornai, who stresses the importance of strict adherence to positive analysis, I am probably running the risk of forgoing this basic approach in my work. But it seems to me a challenge to try to present my observations on these questions following a line of thought that comprises generalization, assumption, assertion and norm.

It is obvious that the East European policy makers cannot promise to solve their economies' problems; however, they can do many things that can help to reduce them. Let me suggest a partial list of sensible things to do. The first is to conduct the economic transformation according to the specific conditions in their countries and guided by the principle of *what is good for their economies and societies.*

Another important issue is the need for a long-term *programme* encompassing the main challenges and the necessary policy responses in terms of priorities and strategies, and an alternative programme for the changes embodied in the reform. As the American economist W. Diebold stressed in the late 1940s, 'No society can survive without long-term thinking'.[8] Without vision there is no progress. The medium- and long-term development programmes should be the compass of the East European policy makers on the new road on which they are embarking now. Without such a compass they can easily lose the vision of the future in the day-to-day politics of the present. The main constraint to this challenge is obviously the lack of politicians of high calibre in most of the countries in the region.

Another issue is to reconsider the polemic about the *role of the government* in transition. Government intervention should help to expand overall demand. I am not advocating here the return to predominance of government involvement in economic affairs as in, say, Oskar Lange's terms, or, as the Austrian-born American economist von Mises has wittily put it, the Santa Claus approach to economic order.[9] Von

8. Susan Strange, presidential address, International Studies Association annual meeting, Chicago, IL, 23 February 1995.
9. Ludwig von Mises in a letter to Friedrich von Hayek, 27 July 1944 (Hoover Archives, Stanford University).

Mises was very clear in his views on government involvement and in a letter to Hayek of 1946 he writes: 'Laissez faire does not mean: let the evils last; it means let the consumers decide... There is no middle way. Either the consumers are supreme or the government.'[10] Yes, indeed: less government, in comparison with the communist economic order, should be a goal of the transition, but the goal should not be government withdrawal from economic activity in the transition stage. Strong government is actually needed. This was stated also in a lecture by the Nobel laureate Douglass North at Stanford University in October 1995, when he remarked: 'laissez faire means chaos'. Let me refer also to the statement of one of the prominent young American economists, the Harvard professor of political economy L. Summers: 'We have lost sight of the role of government's supporting hand in our enthusiasm for the "invisible hand"; some government intervention is good and that is true in the United States as it is in Mali' (*Business Week*, May 1992, p.78). And this is true also in Eastern Europe.

The sound *education* of the present workforce through retraining and of the future labour force (that is, children) should also be on the priority agenda. By definition education has only a very long-term effect on productivity since it matters, for example, only after the children become workers. The declining standards of education right across Eastern Europe and the increased poverty, affecting more than 50 per cent of the population, will play a significant negative role in the growth of productivity in the years to come. A slowdown in productivity because of inadequate or poor education is a phenomenon which should not be put off for the future: instead, steps for radical corrections in this regard should be taken immediately.

Government initiative is needed in envisaging, formulating and implementing these policies. Such an initiative is very much needed also in implementing *industrial policy* in the post-communist countries. Some respected economists such as the Washington-based John Williamson argue that it is now too late to secure the benefits of government initiative in Eastern Europe. I would suggest that it is not too late for such initiative and I attempt to explain why in the following sections.

10. Ludwig von Mises in a letter to Friedrich von Hayek, 8 March 1946 (Hoover Archives, Stanford University).

3. WHY INDUSTRIAL POLICY?

My reading of the literature on the East European transition is that, like the issue of payments union, the term 'industrial policy' is not fashionable in our professional circles[11] and particularly not liked by the policy entrepreneurs whose short answer is 'the best industrial policy is not to have an industrial policy'. And this is, of course, nonsense. The question of industrial policy has been on the political agenda in the US, Western Europe and Japan for a long time. The term industrial policy is relatively recent, however, and nearly all the works on the subject have been published since 1975.

3.1. Definition

I would briefly define my understanding of industrial policy as a political issue in a broader sense, namely as a set of selective measures adopted by the state to influence directly the structural composition of production (including not only industrial organizations) and the natural monopolies (rail, airlines, banks, saving loans). My definition of industrial policy is broad and does not stress the selective character of such a policy; I will return to this point below. Jozef van Brabant also defines industrial policy for Eastern Europe in a broader sense, emphasizing the need of mechanisms for policy coordination and implementation: '... I view industrial policy as a strategy formulated and possibly initiated, by the state (or on its behalf) that encompasses mechanisms by which the actions of various layers of decision making about resource allocation in an economy can be coordinated, monitored, evaluated and fine-tuned' (Brabant, 1993, p.49). Western analysts' definitions vary from underlining that industrial policies are concerned with promoting industrial growth and efficiency (OECD, 1975, p.7) or policies aimed at directly affecting the structure of industry, to 'any policy that involves a conscious attempt to alter the composition of either the outputs produced in the non-governmental sector of the economy or the inputs used to produce the output' (Watson, 1983, p.2).

Western definitions of industrial policy emphasize its selective character. As mentioned above, I avoid this point in my definition, because I put more emphasis on the *non-selective, non-discretionary*

11. See note 3.

and *transparent* character of *governmental* action in the long process of transformation from a formerly centrally planned to a market economy at the present difficult stage of economic reform (which can be best described as semi-chaos). And non-selective industrial policies, such as, for example, export-promotion services, some tariff- and non-tariff trade policies, help the process of emerging markets in post-communist Europe, or they help to deal with market failures in a *systemic* way.

Another point I want to stress here is the *political* aspect of industrial policy since it requires *governmental* action. And like any government policy, three main questions arise:

- What do governments do?
- Why do governments do the things they do?
- What does government action alter?

These three questions indicate the relationship between the economic rationality (or irrationality) of industrial policy and its political rationality (or irrationality) in certain cases and certain areas.

But let me briefly answer the question, why have an industrial policy? I partly answered it by defining the present stage of economic reform as semi-chaos. And the de-industrialization of Eastern Europe seems to be a mistaken development strategy in the long term. Another point to be added in this regard is the issue of the need of a programme of reform, as stressed in the second part of this chapter and in my previous work.[12] And I would again cite the American economist W. Diebold who stated that 'No society can survive without long-term thinking'.[13] This applies also to the needed industrial policy.

3.2. Types, Instruments and Targets

Industrial policy is implied where there is a market failure (for example, caused by externalities in production or consumption, market

12. These issues are discussed in, for example, the following works of mine: 'Economic Policy in Eastern Europe: What Can Be Done and What Should Be Done?', paper prepared for the International Studies Association annual meeting, Washington, DC, March 1994, and the European Association for Comparative Economic Studies annual meeting, Budapest, September 1994; 'Eastern European Economic Transformation', op.cit.; *Bulgaria in a Time of Change: Economic and Political Dimensions*, edited collection (Aldershot: Avebury, 1996), chap.7.
13. See note 8.

power deployed by producers or consumers, and asymmetric information between buyers and sellers) leading to distortions and divergence between private and social costs or benefits, economic inefficiencies and misallocation of resources. This is, and should be, a case for governmental intervention.

Two main *types* of government industrial policy can be identified:

- regulatory - to remove market imperfections;
- developmental - to change market outcomes.

Developmental industrial policy is necessary, for example, in three cases:

- to reduce the power of large transnational corporations (moving for profit considerations from one to another country);
- to narrow the economic horizon of the market and in particular of financial institutions; and
- to reverse biased allocation of industrial production.

A developmental industrial policy is particularly important where market forces provide inadequate incentives to invest in sectors essential for economic performance and productivity, such as high-risk, new-technology industries, or in cases where a biased allocation of industrial production preferring the centre to the periphery can be observed. The latter is relevant for Eastern Europe at present. Protection and strategic trade policy is another aspect of industrial policy which is also very relevant for Eastern Europe, and which falls between regulatory and developmental policy as well as between direct and *indirect* industrial policies. The *instruments* used can be the following:

- government enterprises;
- direct financial or technical assistance;
- tax allowances;
- tariff protection;
- regulation of competition, privatization and foreign investments.

I should stress here that the belief that the former state-owned enterprises cannot be well managed in the new market environment is an ill-placed perception, which to me relates to a 'free market madness'.

There is no doubt that a great many of these enterprises are relics of communist central planning and should be liquidated or privatized, but there are a great number of state enterprises which can be efficient and competitive. They all vary across countries and a more specific discussion of this issue is beyond the scope of the present study. And there is another point regarding industrial policy: in all the East European countries a rush was observed after 1989, not only to discard import quotas and other non-tariff barriers, but also to lower tariffs to negligible levels. Strategic trade policy, and particularly export-promotion services, are very much needed in Eastern Europe. And as the evidence from post-Second World War economic growth in the West shows, this was achieved mainly by expanding exports. A further point: capital controls, for the reasons explained in section 1, should also be on the government agenda. In other words, just as industrial policy is needed in Japan, the European Union and the US (for example, US government purchases of the output of companies in the Silicon Valley and in North Carolina), it is needed far more in the slump economies of post-communist Europe.

Policies to increase *productivity* growth should also be on the priority list of the East European policy makers. The depression in Eastern Europe has made these countries poor and only growth in productivity can make them a better place to live in. In the long run the rate of growth in living standards in the domestic economy is almost exactly equal to the annual increase in productivity, or, to express it differently, to the annual increase in the amount that an average worker can produce in an hour. And since the main source of productivity increase comes from continuous technological progress, policies in this regard are also urgently needed.

These observations indicate that the possible programmes for industrial policy (with central government being their principal author) in Eastern Europe can identify their *targets* by asking the following questions:

1. who is mainly affected by the policy?
2. toward whom is industrial policy directed?

These questions may be approached in various ways. At the sectoral level, it is important to specify which *branches* of industry or the economy are being targeted by the government. *Geographically*, the question should be asked whether industrial policy favours poorer or richer regions. At a more specific level, the influence of *size* and *ownership* is also of importance.

I should stress here that, although the central government can and should initiate the programmes for industrial policy, *local* and *regional* government action should also be encouraged.

3.3. What can Eastern Europe Learn From the Experience of Western Europe, Japan and the US?

The answer to this question is obviously a topic for a book-length manuscript. I will make only a few observations here.[14]

1. The underlying values of industrial policy are growth, efficiency, (workable) competition and innovation.
2. On the domestic level government intervention is higher in Europe and in Japan and clearly lower in the US.
3. Among the industrial policy instruments used, the most important in the West are, in order, tariffs (average tariff about 4 per cent of GDP), direct financial assistance (about 3 per cent of GDP), tax allowances (about 1-2 per cent of GDP) and government enterprise (responsible for some 5 per cent of employment and 15 per cent of investments).

14. Some publications on industrial policy in Western Europe, the USA, Canada and Japan include: F. Duchene and G. Shepherd (eds), *Managing Industrial Change in Western Europe* (London and New York: Pinter, 1987); J. Frommer and J. McCormick (eds), *Transformations in French Business: Political, Economic and Cultural Changes from 1981 to 1987* (New York: Quorum Books, 1989); D.B. Audretsch, *The Market and the State: Government Policy Towards Business in Europe, Japan, and the United States* (New York: Harvester–Wheatsheaf, 1989); S.J. Warnecke and E.N. Suleiman (eds), *Industrial Policies in Western Europe* (New York: Praeger, 1975); G. Hall (ed.), *European Industrial Policy* (London: Croom Helm, 1986); F. Gerard Adams and Lawrence R. Klein (eds), *Industrial Policies for Growth and Competitiveness: An Economic Perspective* (Lexington, MA: Lexington Books, 1983); P.R. Beije, J. Groenewegen, I. Kostoulas, J. Paelinck and C. van Paridou (eds), *A Competitive Future for Europe: Towards a New European Industrial Policy* (London: Croom Helm, 1987); W.G. Watson, *A Primer on the Economics of Industrial Policy* (Toronto: Ontario Economic Council, 1983); *Une Politique industrielle pour la France* (Paris: La Documentation Française, Ministčre de la Recherche et de l'Industrie, 1982).

Industrial policy in some developing and newly industrialized countriés is discussed in, for example, *Une Politique industrielle pour la France*.

In the late 1970s and in the 1980s a substantial reduction of tariffs has occurred (although with a simultaneous increase in non-tariff barriers, such as numerous quotas), counterbalanced in part by an increase in subsidies (approximately 1–1.5 per cent of GDP or even more). There are differences among countries. Before entering the EU Austria had the highest tariffs in Europe; high tariffs are observed also in Australia and New Zealand. Tariffs are particularly low, however, in the Scandinavian countries, Switzerland, the US and Japan. Industries that are most spared from the liberalization process are those with a large number of employees that also face stiff foreign competition; financial assistance is directed to industries in which the unemployment rate is high, and government enterprises are present in the most highly concentrated sectors.

4. The central government has prime responsibility for industrial policy, although with the trend towards regionalism, the role of regional governments has grown to some extent.

5. State intervention is primarily aimed at 'problem' industries and industrial policy attempts to support declining industries and regions first, and then technology.

6. Large enterprise and domestic capital are favoured. A good example in this regard is the US government policy in North Carolina in the 1980s entailing the purchase of the big domestic companies' production. However, a new interest in small businesses can be observed, and foreign capital is treated in a relatively neutral manner.

7. Industrial policy is strongly directed towards regional development. This is particularly true in the case for direct financial assistance (for example, enterprises located in rural areas in Western Europe and in the US).

Towards whom is industrial policy directed? In all these countries agriculture and light industry (clothing and food) are probably the two main targets of industrial policy. The clothing industry is usually protected by the highest tariffs, and agriculture by the strictest quotas. Agriculture, shipbuilding, aeronautics, data processing and steelmaking are favoured with direct financial assistance. The mining industry is favoured by the tax system. And government enterprises are located primarily in the transportation and energy sectors, and also in the steel and auto industries.

The term 'industrial policy' is not used in all Western countries. This is the term applied in the US, Britain and Japan. In Germany the term *Strukturpolitik* is used and in France the term 'planification à la française'. The main objectives of the German *Strukturpolitik*, for example, have been cutting back declining sectors and encouraging innovation and efficiency in the growth areas. While some type of competition policy is common in Europe, Japan and the US, the role of anti-trust policy has a unique position in America. The general approach towards industrial policy in Europe and Japan has been to build cooperative relationships between government and private enterprise, while by contrast, the adversarial relationship between the public sector and private business in the US is exemplified by the country's anti-trust policy. The so-called 'fair trade policy' in Japan and EU competition policy are also typical examples of industrial policies as well as foreign trade policies and exchange rate policies in their international dimension.

It might be interesting to mention here a few points concerning industrial policy in Japan, where the government and particularly the Trade and Finance Ministry (MITI) worked on development programmes in the late 1940s and in the 1950s. Some scholars (Patrick, 1994, p.234) consider Japan as 'probably the most successful case of industrial policy in recent world economic history'. A so-called Industrial Rationalization Council was set up as an advisory board under MITI in 1949 with the aim of facilitating consensus among the government, private firms and labour on how best to implement industrial rationalization plans. Another important organization in shaping Japan's industrial policy was the Japan Development Bank. But in principle four major players were involved: the Economic Planning Agency, MITI, the Ministry of Finance, and the Bank of Japan. In 1963 the government selected two industries for protection: first, industries with high income elasticity of demand, and second, industries with rapidly growing productivity (Morita, 1995, p.6). This was in principle a policy where government resources were channelled to the potential winners. In the 1980s the focus of government attention shifted towards macroeconomic problems (specifically, the huge budget deficit) and 'administrative reform' (for example, reducing subsidies to agriculture and to the Japan National Railways). In the 1990s attention has shifted to 'structural reform' to deal with the consequences of the speculative stock market and land price bubbles of 1986–90, and the appreciation of the yen. Government resources go now more to the losers, rather than to the potential winners, with government loans, for example, going to small businesses, rather than large concerns, and almost no subsidies to industry, but still substantial government subsidy to agriculture.

As regards the European countries, even before the Second World War the states of Western Europe were economically and politically too small to deal adequately on a national basis with the domestic impact of changing patterns of international competition. But Belgium, for example, did that and achieved a high level of growth. This requires forgoing the ambition of imitating the industrial structure of nations such as the United States, and includes allowing and even encouraging a greater degree of foreign investment and ownership as well as even more reliance on export markets. Such small countries are in the position of trying to manage both the speed at which they become intertwined with the international economy and the impact of the dependencies which result.

All of that indicates that, in order to be successful, industrial policy presupposes the *development of institutions* for a *forward-looking strategy*. And since industrial policy is a political issue in the EU, in the US and Japan, its logic might be best described as the *politics of compensation*. The government removes with one hand the resources and conditions that allow industry or part of the economy (such as agriculture) to prosper and gives them back with the other in the name of social objectives. For example, subsidies to industry also compensate in part for the reduction in tariffs. Because of tax allowances on the other hand, investors hold a privileged political position in the development of industrial policy. Another reason behind increase of subsidies, for example, is the rapid rise in unemployment, which increased after 1974 in the EU and the US.

The American economists Lester Thurow and Robert Reich designed in the 1980s the so-called strategic trade policy concept. The strategic trade policy of the Clinton administration is clearly a good example of strong government involvement in formulating economic policy. Another good example is the manner in which the trade dispute (or trade war) between the US and Japan was settled in the summer of 1995.

4. Industrial policy, Privatization, Foreign Investments and the Left Governments in Eastern Europe

I now turn to the question of whether the elected socialist (that is, former communist) governments in much of Eastern Europe would be able, first, to work out their vision for industrial policy, and secondly to implement it. Again, this is in itself a topic for a book-length study. I am discussing it here, since if I am arguing that industrial policy is important to deal with the reform in a systemic way, and that in essence industrial policy is a political issue, I need to approach the question of what might be expected to be done in the next few years of the transition.

Let me begin by stressing again the importance of industrial policy as a part of a broader vision, or a programme for economic transformation.

Industrial policy should also be part of the general vision of reform and privatization. Another aspect of industrial policy is that it should be part of the overall foreign investment strategy (if any) of the country. Foreign investments (both direct and in the form of equity) are an important channel of funds to the depressed economies of Eastern Europe at present since they bring new capital, know-how and managerial skills. Three main channels of foreign investments to Eastern Europe and the former Soviet republics can be identified: venture capital, multilateral companies and bank loans. In some of the East European countries - for example, Poland and Ukraine - investments by expatriates are also large, but this cannot be seen as a trend right across the region.

Foreign investors inspire a great deal of mistrust in post-communist Europe, which is to some degree understandable, since these countries were isolated from the world economy for so long. Neither should we forget that even in the West (for example, in Canada) 'multinationals are one of the institutions Canadians trust the least', according to a Canadian study (Blais, 1986, p.39).

The leftist governments in Eastern Europe might contribute in some countries to a deepening of sentiments against foreign investors, and these sentiments will be stronger if there is no clear vision of privatization. Moreover, it would be a poor economic policy if the extreme solutions were adopted, such as introducing direct and indirect regulations which pose obstacles to foreign investors or adopting a policy which does not treat domestic and foreign investors equally.

It seems to me that the experience of Japan with respect to industrial policy might be of interest for the East European policy makers: first, in selecting industries with high income elasticity of demand, and secondly, in selecting industries with rapidly growing productivity (see Morita, 1995). There is another point to be made here in this regard: industrial policy requires the existence of a strong government (as in Japan, the US and most EU countries). This is a matter of concern in the case of the East European countries, since they do not possess strong governments. This situation might create an environment where even a good programme for an industrial policy might in reality prove to be economically and politically irrational in most cases and in most areas.

CONCLUDING REMARKS

This chapter attempted to advocate the need for industrial policy in Eastern Europe, as a part of a long-term vision of reform. There is, however, no great hope that such policies will be introduced in a systemic way. The governments in post-communist Europe seem to over-regulate without focusing on the main economic objectives of the transition and without elaborating a comprehensive programme for the transformation or a separate programme for industrial policy.

It should not be forgotten that industrial policy in the West after the Second World War was characterized by a whole series of measures intended to slow the decline of industries or regions in difficulty. This strategy should be applied also in Eastern Europe after the trade liberalization of 1990–91 since the public there desperately wants and expects to see a happy marriage between the advance of reform and stability. One should bear in mind that a market economy brings growth and potential prosperity, but also disequilibria. Serious thought should be directed also towards agricultural policy in the East European countries as they attempt to join the European Union. As is well known the East European countries have a substantial part of their GNP produced in the agricultural sector and for that reason (among others) are not favourably regarded by the Brussels policy makers as potential full members of the Union. As regards the structural interventions needed in the East European countries, I should emphasize here that these interventions should be directed towards the following: (1) to deal only with sectors and not with single firms; (2) to be temporary; (3) to be taken only in cases where adjustment caused major social hardship; (4) to help firms to help themselves; (5) not to suspend the function of markets; (6) benefit recipients to meet performance goals in order to justify the government support received (tax money).

I would like to conclude optimistically that some of the East European countries may have a record of industrial policy in the years to come. Since industrial policy presupposes the development of institutions for a forward-looking strategy, the success of such a policy will depend on the speed of institutional change and the creation of new institutions and organizations. And as the institutional economics teaches us, institutional change is typically incremental and is path-dependent. That all indicates that my optimism does not apply to all of post-communist Europe.

REFERENCES

Blais, Andre (1986). 'Industrial Policy in Advanced Capitalist Democracies', in Andre Blais (ed.), *Industrial Policy* (Toronto: University of Toronto Press), pp.1–53.

Brabant, Jozef M. van (1993). *Industrial Policy in Eastern Europe: Governing the Transition* (Dordrecht and Boston, MA: Kluwer Academic Publishers).

Lazear, Edward P. (ed.) (1995). *Economic Transition in Eastern Europe and Russia: Realities of Reform* (Stanford, CA: Hoover Institution Press).

Morita, Ken (1995). 'Can Japanese Experience of Industrial Policy Be Helpful for Post-Communist Transition Economies?', paper prepared for the International Studies Association annual meeting, Chicago (February).

OECD (1975), *Objectifs et instruments des politiques industrielles: une étude comparative* (Paris: OECD).

Patrick, Hugh T. (1994), 'Japanese Industrial Policy', in Morris Bornstein (ed.), *Comparative Economic Systems: Models and Cases*, 7th edition (Boston, MA: Irwin), pp.223–35.

Robinson, Joan (1973). 'What Has Become of the Keynesian Revolution?', in Joan Robinson (ed.), *After Keynes* (Oxford: Basil Blackwell). pp.1–11

Watson, William G. (1983), *A Primer on the Economics of Industrial Policy* (Toronto: Ontario Economic Council).

Zloch-Christy, Iliana (1991). *East–West Financial Relations: Current Problems and Future Prospects* (Cambridge and New York: Cambridge University Press).

9. Can Japanese Experience be Useful for Transforming Economies?

Gabor Bakos

After the fever of rapid liberalization calmed down, the transforming economies of Eastern Europe now face the challenge of embarking on a new growth path. For this, of decisive importance will be technology and innovation. In modern market economies research and development (R&D) is not a pure market element because of its high expenditures, long time span and high risks. Japanese experience is useful in identifying how companies may be helped in developing their technologies through cost- and risk-sharing.

1. TRANSFORMATION AND R&D

Technology policy and innovation were considered as a special and separate branch of the national economy under the centrally planned system. Although there was a large network of research institutes under the Academies of Science, researchers were separated from production and the lack of a market made companies uninterested in innovation.

With systemic changes from 1990, Central and East European countries could no longer maintain their large academic research network and it collapsed because of the worsening government budget deficit. Earlier, in the late 1980s, the ratio of R&D spending to GDP was almost 3 per cent for Russia and 2.5 per cent for Hungary, a level comparable to that of developed Western countries (for example, the USA and Germany, both at 2.4 per cent in 1994), but in the early 1990s it fell back drastically to a level of 0.3–0.4 per cent. Many academic research institutes disappeared, talented researchers went abroad, and others found jobs in different activities.

As for manufacturing, domestic companies experienced the pressure from unfolding market forces and competition from imports. Left without a conscious development strategy and industrial policy on the part of the government, many of them collapsed. Domestic firms privatized through foreign investors managed to survive, but most have been reduced in size. Joint ventures or foreign firms in the first period concentrated on acquiring market shares rather than producing new goods. When buying out a domestic company, they immediately acquired its sales network, through which began to market their Western-made products, thereby making domestic engineers idle.

In the wake of rapid marketization any role or guidance on the part of the government was deemed undesirable and a monetarist policy alone prevailed to manage macro-economic equilibrium. The monetaristic approach maintains that liberalization together with privatization will stimulate market competition, which in turn will automatically lead to restructuring and new technologies.

After six years, however, the need for a new development strategy is being felt both on the national and on the micro levels. Foreign companies, which earlier were interested in acquiring new market shares, by now have settled down and become interested in the development of production. They are now beginning to build up their R&D potential and to expand local production. As an example the case of the Hungarian Tungsram company may be mentioned. After being bought up by General Electric, the new owners recently began to revive the Hungarian research laboratory and already a few new products have appeared. Again, when the Japanese Suzuki opened its factory, it prompted the Hungarian government to work out a strategy towards the automotive industry and to provide some protection for the new industry.

Can Japanese experience be useful in helping to speed up development in transforming economies? For a long time, the Japanese system was considered to be a special Asian type of market economy, which could hardly be applied elsewhere. Recently, however, numerous examples have proved its viability. For instance, the largest Japanese direct investment, Magyar Suzuki (Hungary), indicates that the Japanese work system, management and supply network (the *shitauke* system) are fully applicable and work efficiently.

2. JAPANESE EXPERIENCE

In Japan, technology policy was always considered to be a key to economic growth but at the same time it was a field closely tied in with industrial and financial policy. When after the Second World War Japan faced the immense task of rebuilding the economy, it connected reconstruction with importing the latest technology, which was supported by a selective loan policy. The two main pillars of the unprecedented Japanese development are probably a conscious technology policy and a sound, supportive financial base. Therefore, in the following argument we shall concentrate on the technology policy and the financial background, which through a low interest rate policy channelled funds to industry. Also, the seed money approach will be taken up, to discover how the government mobilizes private money and initiates large projects with small investments.

2.1. Government Guidance

2.1.1. Coordinated and integrated

Today R&D projects involve large costs and high risk, a long time span before commercial exploitation. Therefore private companies are willing to start research projects, especially in fundamental research, if the government shares the risk with them. Typical fields that need governmental guidance are energy, especially nuclear power, space research, and public goods such as health and education.

In Japan there are three main organizations responsible for national science and technology policy: the Ministry of Education (Monbusho), mainly for basic research; the Science and Technology Agency (STA), also mainly for basic research; and the Ministry of International Trade and Industry (MITI), mainly for industrial R&D.

The need for cost- and risk-sharing was recognized very early in Japan, when soon after the war MITI was established. MITI *coordinated technology policy, industrial policy and external economic relations with supportive financial policy* (with the Ministry of Finance). In Western Europe or the USA the coordination of technology policy at the national level was started much later, only in the 1960s. The MITI employed highly skilled engineers who started the postwar reconstruction with a pragmatic approach, first strengthening the economic base (energy, steel) and developing demand-elastic branches, such as textiles and machinery. Already during the reconstruction period, technology was considered an important priority, and reconstruction was to be realized by importing the latest technology. For this a priority rationing of foreign currency and import tax exemptions were applied (Odagiri and Goto, 1993; Wakasugi, 1986). The role of MITI is important not only for supporting technology but also for integrating the key strategic lines, namely technology, industrial policy, foreign trade and a supportive financial policy.

Another line of coordination is the so-called *consensus-creating activity*. From the early 1950s MITI set up study groups, research groups and deliberative councils (*shingikai*) to discuss and work out development plans (see Figure 9.1). In the *shingikai,* academics, industry officials and representatives of consumer associations were invited so that MITI could collect opinions from the broad public, on the one hand, and popularize new ideas, on the other (the mechanism of the *shingikai* is depicted in Figure 9.1). One of the most influential deliberative councils in the 1950s was the Industrial Structure Advisory Council, having altogether 18 subcommittees. The system of *shingikai* is being used even today, and in the early 1990s there were 33 regular councils attached to MITI alone (other ministries also have their council systems). The *shingikai* system is a viable way for sounding the trends in the development of companies and is a channel for dialogue between the government and the private companies.

The MITI runs a number of industry-related R&D programmes, ranging from energy to biotechnology and embracing a wide field of R&D. The main motivation and the organization of these programmes is aimed at providing a *connection between basic research and industry*.

This connection is helped mainly by the Agency of Industrial Science and Technology (AIST) located in the MITI. Of the total 13,000 personnel in MITI, 3,591 are in the AIST. But the administrative staff in the AIST is relatively small (388), and the main body is the research staff of the 15 research institutes under the AIST, together employing a staff of 3,203.

The research institutes under the AIST maintain contacts with industrial companies in their field of research activity, conducting joint research with them and picking up progressive ideas for further research. These ideas are forwarded to the AIST for additional

Figure 9.1 Vision formulation and shingikai

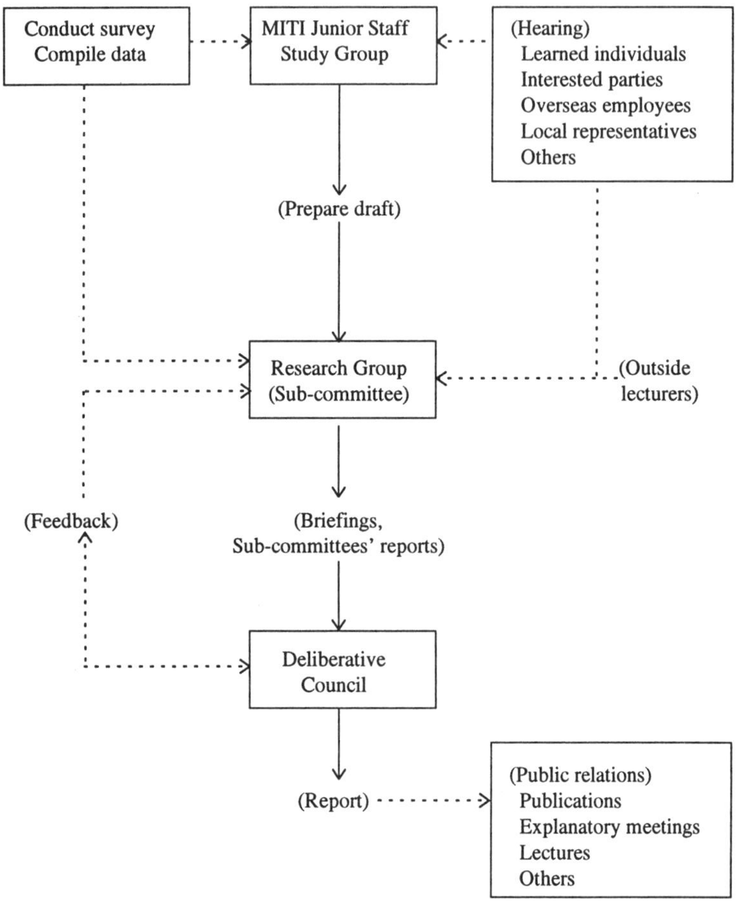

Source: Goro Ono, *Jissenteki sangyo seisakuron* (1992).

consideration. Several departments of the MITI are also involved in R&D: for example, the 'Machinery and Information Industry Bureau' actively took part in the fifth-generation computer project.[1] These administrators play an important role in coordinating R&D with industrial policy, in the preparation of projects, in establishing the financial background (preparing arrangements with the Ministry of Finance) and in coordinating trade (import) policy. Recently, the 15 specialists from the AIST who are responsible for the 15 research institutes, have been regularly invited to the meetings of the Industrial Policy Bureau.

This pattern of organization and its working ensures a continuous flow of new R&D ideas from private companies and from the AIST research institutes associated with them, to the upper level organs which can help the realization of these ideas through industrial policy, financial policy and trade policy coordination. Therefore, if one were to ask how the MITI can identify new ideas for further R&D and implementation, the answer is clearly that the MITI has no need to identify them at all, because the new ideas are supplied by the private companies themselves. MITI thus has only to select the most promising ones among them, which of course is again not an easy task. This approach of guidance is probably different from the early postwar period when industrial policy was first conceived and technology for its effective realization was promoted accordingly.

One could ask, why are private companies willing to disclose their ideas? Since basic research is expensive and risky, private companies refrain from investing in this field. However, when their ideas could be realized in a government-financed project, they are ready to participate also with an investment contribution. There is also an information flow among private companies, so that basic research is in fact not a business secret. This explains also why there are several research associations of private companies whose task is to solve fundamental problems. The keen competition begins after the result of the basic research has been

1. Its activity is formed with the aim of implementing technology policy and promoting cooperation for that purpose: 'The Machinery and Information Industries Bureau works closely with other bureaus to plan and implement policies needed to build an environment conducive to the healthy development of the machinery and information industries which play a major role in the knowledge-intensification of Japan's industrial structure' (MITI, 1992, p.14).

achieved. From this stage they compete in commercialization to be first on the market and to turn the idea into business results.

The government promotes the *transfer of research results* of government research institute to the private sector. Historically, in the 1950s, the government set up research institutes to achieve new basic results and then opened them to private companies. A classical example is the computer industry, which was started in government laboratories (Fransman (1990) gives a detailed description of the process). Recently joint research with private companies has been promoted, whereby companies are provided access to government research facilities, and from 1996 government researchers can transfer to private companies for research.

The STA is responsible mainly for basic research. Under the STA there is a large research institute called the Japan Science and Technology Corporation (JST, formerly JRDC), which was set up in 1961 for transferring technology from national laboratories to industry. Today about half of its activity is basic research, while the other half is more or less evenly distributed between technology transfer and research cooperation (inviting foreign researchers). The institute continues to introduce the results of basic research from its own facility as well as from other national laboratories into industry and to help their commercialization.

2.1.2. From selective to functional approach

In technology policy during the 1950s and 1960s the selective approach prevailed. At that time the most promising growth industries, such as the iron and steel industry, chemicals and machine-building were selected as priority fields, tax breaks, subsidies and accelerated depreciation and preferential credits were used as tools. In general, it is maintained that preferential guidelines were set according to selected branches, which would mean the same beneficial treatment for all companies within the respective branch. Thus, the Japan Development Bank, the most powerful distributor of government credits for development purposes, received general guidelines from the government concerning which sectors to prefer and it then operated autonomously in evaluating projects when granting credits to companies. However, the MITI took care of aligning the organizational structure of industry by sponsoring mergers, reorganizations and rationalizations in order to avoid excess competition. Typical examples are the shipbuilding and steel industries in the 1950s. Such organizational measures helped to direct financial resources to selected groups of companies.

Selective guidance was supported by trade protectionism for 'infant industries'. When, towards the mid-1960s, according to the GATT agreement, Japan was to open up to the world markets, this was changed to a 'timed protectionism', announcing a time-span after which domestic manufacturers must face international competition. This stimulated machinery and car manufacturers to speed up technology development and was important in facilitating export-led growth.

The selective approach was first changed by the adoption of the Large Scale Projects in 1968, which led in a few years to the Vision approach from 1970. This new approach means that the government selects central problems of the given development period, which have general relevance for the society as a whole or for several industries. Examples of such central problems are pollution and energy saving. The ambitious super-express project (*Shinkansen*), which started in the 1960s, also belongs to this new, functional approach. Its aim was to connect large cities and speed up development of regional areas along the new lines. Looking at this modern transport system, the complexity of the project becomes apparent: elevated concrete structures with rail tracks, a highly effective telecommunications system, stations with adjoining service areas - all of these requiring new resolutions from engineers and industries.

The functional approach is in a sense not much different from the selective one, because here again branches selected together have priority. What is different, however, is the perception of priorities. Earlier, in the selective approach separate branches were deemed to be essential for the economic base and to be key industries generating growth in other fields. The functional approach has a more complex perception, where through the problem selection many related industries are selected and beginning from the project conception a wide measure of coordination is required.

2.1.3. Visions

The vision approach was started in 1970, when the MITI prepared a significant report on necessary changes in economic and technology policy, entitled 'The Basic Direction of Trade and Industry in the 1970s', which was generally called the 'Vision for the 1970s'. This Vision proposed a basic shift from the capital-intensive heavy industries to knowledge-intensive industries. There are 'visions' for five and ten years. Visions are worked out using the *shingikai* method, that is inviting academics, industry and consumer representatives to sound out and discuss lines of development. These visions are important, because they serve as a guideline for forming more details policies (Uekusa, 1988).

The long-range forecasts of future science and technology developments can also be considered as an orientation both for governmental organs and for companies. The National Institute of Science and Technology Policy (NISTEP) of the STA regularly - every five years - prepares a comprehensive 30-year forecast for new discoveries and research achievements. This long-range forecast is unique, for in the USA or Germany similar forecasts have a time horizon of only 10–15 years. Another organ, the Economic Planning Agency (EPA), also compiles technology forecasts for the next 20 years; the latest of these published in 1993, runs up to 2010. These forecasts are prepared by several committees embracing academics and researchers from a number of universities and institutions. The forecasts contain expected technological novelties for both the whole world and Japan. Not only the probable date of the discovery, but also the commercialization is forecast. Such forecasts are useful for companies to form their development and business strategies and make early preparations for subsequent commercialization. Thus, for example, even if a widely usable superconductive material has still not been discovered, all the big Japanese electrical manufacturers have already conducted applied research, into how and in which products the new material could be used.

2.2. The Seed Money Approach

As is widely known, the government's share of 20 per cent of total R&D expenditures (compared with 36 per cent in the USA and Germany and 45 per cent in France) and about 1.5 per cent of industrial R&D expenditures is the lowest among Western countries, while governmental guidance is the most comprehensive and powerful in Japan. How is it possible with such a small money to exert such a great influence? For this enigma the 'seed money' approach provides an explanation.

Seed money means that the government with relatively small sums initiates R&D projects which would otherwise be too risky for private companies and hence they refrain from starting them. Given the starting push, companies join with their own capital contribution. Later, the project is carried on by the companies. The positive consequence is that the ensuing R&D results will soon be introduced by companies into production: in other words, the commercialization phase is shorter and more efficient.

There are various ways of combining public money with contributions from private companies, and the case of Key Technology Centre and the New Energy Development Organization (NEDO) will be discussed below. Also, the so-called Brain programme (a follow-up programme to the Technopolis) will be assessed, giving new insight into the mechanism of 'seed money'. Here the 'third sector company' is a special feature, meaning not the usual services, but a mixed public–private company carrying out and managing the project.

2.2.1. Japan Key Technology Centre

This facility was created jointly by the MITI and the Ministry of Post and Telecommunication in 1985 and belongs today to the MITI (more specifically, to MITI's AIST). Its purpose is to provide help, especially to small and medium firms, in developing new technologies, and to promote international cooperation. Its activity extends to capital contribution, loans and research services (Kiban, 1996).

1. Capital Investments

If a minimum of two companies establish a joint R&D company, the Centre will contribute 70 per cent of the capital required (excluding land purchase). The projects must be in key technologies at the basic or applied level, and have a lifetime no more than seven years (in special cases ten years). The investment contribution means that when establishing the R&D company in a form of shareholding company, the Centre will acquire 70 per cent of the shares capital. Preferred key technology areas are mining, manufacturing, and telecommunication and broadcasting technologies. After realizing the research project, the R&D company will be dissolved, with only an office working with few personnel remaining to manage the patent diffusion.

2. Loans

Loans are provided for applied research, up to 70 per cent of the project (excluding land). The project's lifetime is five years. The pay-back period is ten years with five grace years. The interesting feature of the loan is that interest is not charged if the project fails. But if the project succeeds, the interest must be returned. To assess the failure or success, the Centre undertakes an investigation and evaluation of the project. Depending on its degree of success, different interest-grades will be applied: that is, the interest rate will be multiplied with coefficients from 1.0 (complete success), to 0.75, 0.5, 0.25 and 0 (failure). Loans are provided for the same areas of activity as investments.

As can be seen, investment contributions are intended to help mainly basic research, made jointly by several companies, while loans are aimed at applied research, and are intended to help individual companies.

This specification indicates the government's understanding that in basic research it is more appropriate to pool the companies' resources without fearing competition among them, whereas loans can rather help the commercialization of new technologies at individual firms. Next, we briefly review the development of investments and loans provided by the Centre (see Table 9.1).

Table 9.1 Investment and loans by the Centre (million yen)

	1985	*1987*	*1990*	*1992*	*1994*	*1995*
Investments	2,000	17,300	21,700	22,000	20,900	20,600
Loans	2,000	7,700	6,300	6,500	7,200	7,600
Total	*4,000*	*25,000*	*28,000*	*28,500*	*28,100*	*28,200*

Table 9.1 clearly shows a firm increase in investment contribution. This is an interesting phenomenon, bearing in mind that companies are usually not very willing to conduct joint research. But, on the other hand, they can find the conditions on which an investment is made more favourable since it is not repayable, whereas a loan is in any case repayable. Furthermore, on the MITI's side there was an intention to give preference to investment contribution, because the government's support was deemed most efficient when assisting the risky fundamental research. Now, however, this view has become controversial from the financial viewpoint.

3. Mediation in arranging joint research
The Centre provides a mediation service for private companies wishing to conduct joint research projects with national research institutes. It helps to find suitable partners and prepares the joint research contract between the partners. Also, private companies can commission the Centre to conduct research, and the Centre then brings together experts from the government, industry or academic research to perform the task.

4. Japan Trust Fund
This is a special fund created by donations from private companies. The profits of this fund will be used to invite foreign researchers in key technologies.

5. Research information service
The Centre collects and provides to private companies research information in key technologies. The *capital flow of the Centre* (Figure 9.2) shows the sources and the uses of the capital. The Centre has a basic capital and a circulating capital, as depicted in Table 9.2.

Table 9.2 Composition of basic capital (million yen)

Investment from private companies	5,054
Investment contribution from Japan Development Bank	4,200
Government's investment contribution	10,900
(Loans for patents*	2,600)

* After completing the research, the result will appear in the form of patents. This special loan is provided to the company for the period from patenting until royalties are received from licensing the patent.

The basic capital consists of contributions from private companies, the JDB and the government, made in the form of deposits and securities. The basic capital has been stable throughout the Centre's history, and its function is such that the interests and dividends that it brings in are fed back to the circulating capital and are used mainly for running the Centre and for its activities other than investment contributions or loans to companies.

Figure 9.2 Capital flow of the Key Technology Centre

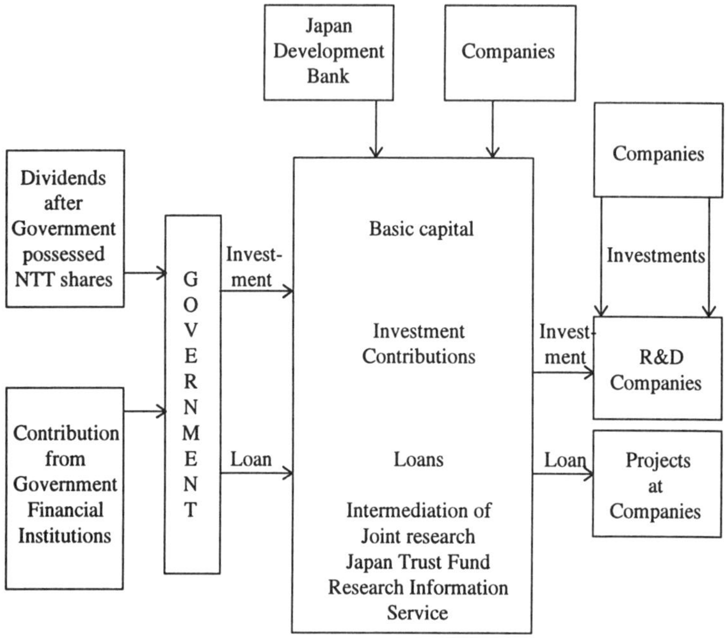

The sources of circulating capital are twofold: dividends from the NTT shares in the possession of the government and contributions from governmental financial institutions.

Why is the capital flow pattern interesting? Because, although on the input-side there is the government, the Centre has no connection with the ordinary government budget (for example, with the use of tax revenues) but is completely fed back to the market (as dividends, interest or bank loans).

2.2.2. NEDO (New Energy Development Organization)

The NEDO, established in 1988, is an organization which promotes mainly two activities: establishing research facilities for the private sector and running international joint research projects.

1. Research facilities

In 1988 the Law for Consolidating Research and Development Systems Relating to Industrial Technology was enacted to start a research facility development programme. The main purpose of this was to develop research facilities for new industrial technologies that would be too expensive and risky for private companies to undertake. The procedure for establishing a facility runs as follows. First, the NEDO creates 'Research Facility Development Corporations' for the organization of each research facility, then these corporations carry out the establishment of the facility. The corporations have a form of stockholding company whose members are the NEDO itself, private companies and local government. For example, the Ion Engineering Centre consists of 66 members: NEDO, Osaka Prefecture, Kyoto Prefecture, Nara Prefecture, Kansai Electric Power Company, Nippon Steel Corporation, Hitachi, Matsushita, Mitsubishi Electric Corporation, Sumitomo Electric Industries, Osaka Gas Company, Kubota Corporation, Kobe Steel Ltd, and so on.

The financial scheme for establishing a research facility (centre) is interesting, because it uses a combination of different resources (see Figure 9.3). The project's value consists of half direct investments and half loans. Within the one-third investment share, private companies usually take more than fifty per cent. The loans of the Japan Development Bank and the Hokkaido Finance Corporation are interest free (however, there is a 1 per cent administration fee) for 15 years including a three-year period of grace. As for the private bank loans, a special governmental financial institution (Sangyo Kiban Seibi Kikin, or Industrial Basic Equipment Fund) provides the necessary guarantee for the loan.

Figure 9.3 Financial scheme of NEDO

	Investment *Half*	Loan *Half*	
Two-thirds	NEDO	Japan Development Bank Hokkaido Tohoku Development Public Finance	*70%*
One-third	Local government Private companies	Private banks	*30%*

As can be seen from Figure 9.3, private companies need to contribute only a marginal part, especially if this is shared by many (40–60) companies. The lion's share remains, in any case, with the government, with 70 per cent of the total costs, allocated through the NEDO and the JDB.

Since 1988 the following five research centres have been set up:

	Institution	*Profile*	*Total costs (billion yen)*
1.	Ion Engineering Centre Corporation, Hirakata, Osaka Prefecture *Started:* 1992	Ion beam research for industrial use (new material creation, thin film formation, crystal growth)	7.8
2.	Research Centre for the Industrial Utilization of Marine Organisms, Kamaishi City, Shimizu City; *Started:* 1990	Marine biotechnological research biological organisms for industrial use	6.0
3.	Japan Microgravity Centre, Kamisunagawa-cho, Hokkaido Prefecture *Started:* 1991	Using an abandoned coal mine to test electronic materials, metallic materials and bio-technology processes in 10-second microgravity	5.2
4.	Ultra-High-Temperature Materials Research Centre Ube, Yamuguchi Prefecture Tajimi, Gifu Prefecture *Started:* 1992	Developing ultra-high-temperature resisting materials	4.5
5.	Applied Laser Engineering Centre, Nagaoka, Niigata Prefecture *Started:* 1992	Industrial application of laser technology	2.1

After opening, the maintenance costs are covered by the participating companies.

In addition, from 1992 a think-tank-like organization (Kenkyu Kiban Chisetsu Katsuyogata Sendoteki Kibanchosa Jigyo, or Softo-Hojin). was attached to every research centre This consists of researchers and professors and its work is to monitor the research, to collect new ideas for further research and to forward these to NEDO.

2. Grants for international joint research

The aim of the grant established in 1988 is to promote international joint team research in the field of industrial technology, in the following areas:

Area		*Field of research*	*Grant in 1992 (million yen)*
Materials		Materials characteristics and their use	30
Energy		Practical research on power generation technologies using oil-alternative energy; environment conservation energy generation	30
Global environment	1	Basic research on conservation and improvement of environment	24
	2	Practical research on production, generation and use of oil-alternative energy, which contributes to the conservation of the global environment	30

Grants for 1993 totalled 913 million yen.

To form an international team, a minimum four members from two different nationalities are required. A research team can receive funding for up to three years. The procedure for awarding a grant is as follows: 1. NEDO announces the grant every year; 2. applications are received and circulated for peer review; 3. grants are made available. Interest in grants is quite large, the number of applications exceeding the number of grants by 6–10 times.

2.2.3. The Brain Programme

In order to stop further concentration into large cities and to help industries in rural areas, the government devised a comprehensive programme which was enacted in 1988 as the 'Key Facilities Siting Law' (*Zuno Ritchi Ho*), or as we will call it, the Brain Programme. It was, in fact, a follow-up programme to the famed Technopolis project (1981), which aimed at creating new model towns for combining comfortable living space with high-tech industries and academia. Technopolis was quite successful in strengthening university research centres but failed to link them to regional industries. This deficiency was to be corrected by the Brain Programme, which planned to set up 23 R&D centres nation-wide in rural areas.

To start the programme, MITI entrusted its realization to the Japan Regional Development Corporation (JRDC), a special organ belonging to the MITI. This form of the realization found wide application from the mid-1970s when the so-called large development programmes were started. One reason for this was that the organization and management of such large programmes already exceeded the capacity of MITI, and another was that the MITI itself, as an administrative body, had not the legal competence to activate investments. Therefore formally new 'executive bodies' were set up. As a result, by now a so-called organizational infrastructure has been formed to implement technology policy measures. In this sense, the JRDC can be considered as an 'extended hand' of MITI.

The JRDC was first set up in 1962, named at that time the 'Coal Mining Area Development Corporation', with the aim to creating new jobs in the areas of coal mines which at that time were to be closed, and to organize efficient employment for local population. Later, in 1974, it was reorganized as the JRDC and was entrusted with the relocation of industries among regions, with city development and, recently, with the Brain Programme. At present the basic capital of the JRDC, which is wholly owned by the Japanese government, amounts to 88 billion yen, and the organization has 711 employees.

Initially, the JRDC issued guidelines on construction conditions and on the desirable location of research centres for local authorities, which then prepared project proposals; after screening them, the JRDC selected the final 23 projects. Next, an executive enterprise, the so-called 'third sector' company (*dai san sekuta kaisha*), was set up for constructing the research facility. Contrary to general understanding, here 'third sector' does not refer to services, but to a mixture of joint ownership between the central government, the local government and the private sector. Such third-sector enterprises were set up from 1973 for public works relating especially to regional development like infrastructure, railway lines, metro lines, and later also welfare projects, information networks and so on. This new entity was introduced because in the fields mentioned the market mechanism does not work efficiently owing to the long time horizon of such projects and their indirect business character (Imamura, 1993). Third-sector enterprises in Japanese are known under different names, including *zaidan hojin, shadan jojin, kabushiki kaisha* (joint-stock company), *yugen kaisha* (limited company), and *kosha*. Therefore, not the naming but the capital pattern is important.

In the Brain Programme the third-sector company prepared and constructed the research facility, and after completion it became the owner of the facility.

What is interesting about this 'third sector' enterprise is its structure. The enterprise takes the form of a joint shareholding company, where the shareholders are the JRDC, the local government authority, the prefecture and private companies located in the area. In this way, a multi-holder enterprise is formed. Their number in the Kita-Kyushu Techno Centre has reached 85.

The JRDC provided a capital contribution of a standard 600 million yen[2] to each enterprise: this was the 'seed money'. Therefore, JRDC's share of the capital was dependent on the total volume of the basic capital. Among the fifteen enterprises that have been formed so far, in five the JRDC holds a majority of shares, with an average of 45 per cent (in the Asahikawa R&D centre alone it has a surprisingly high share of 60 per cent), in six enterprises the local government has the majority with 45–50 per cent, while in four the majority belongs to private companies. The majority holding of the JRDC practically means a certain supervisory role, reflected in the participation of its

2. This sum was decided by MITI and the Ministry of Finance, estimating the costs of a 2000–3000 sq.m. research facility (building). At that time (the mid-1980s) construction costs were in the range of 700–800,000 yen per square metre, in total 1.4–2.1 billion yen per project. The government granted support up to one-third ot this (600 million yen), while the remaining two-thirds was supposed to be contributed by local authorities and companies (Interview at Japan Industrial Location Centre, January 1994).

representative in the management's meetings of the enterprise (later of the R&D centre) held four times a year. Looking at the capital composition from another angle, it is apparent that the capital contribution of central and local government amounts to 60–85 per cent of the total, the rest being divided among many private companies.

Owing to the fact that a great part of the capital is contributed by central and local government, and the rest is shared by a large number of companies, the capital contributed by a single private company is relatively small (see Table 9.3). The final two columns of the table are especially interesting, showing the average capital contribution of private companies and their percentage share in total basic capital. As can be seen, the capital contribution per company ranges between 5 and 20 million yen (in only two cases is it above 40 million yen), which can be considered a rather low burden even for a middle-sized Japanese company.

Table 9.3 Capital composition of 'third sector' enterprises (million yen)

	*Basic capital**	*JRDC*		*Local government†*		*Private company*		*Number of firms*	*Average capital contribution‡*	
		Amount	*%*	*Amount*	*%*	*Amount*	*%*		*Amount*	*%*
Asahikawa	1,000	600	60	260	26	140	14	15	9.3	0.9
Hachinohe	1,281	600	46.8	520	32.8	261	20.4	23	11.3	0.9
Hitachi	2,050	600	29.3	720	35.1	730	35.6	16	45.6	2.2
Gunma	1,520	600	39.5	300	19.7	620	40.8	30	20.7	1.4
Toyama	1,740	600	34.5	800	46	340	19.5	14	24.3	1.4
Gifu	2,000	600	30	900	45	500	25	33	15.1	0.8
Hamanako	2,500	600	24	750	30	1,150	46	59	19.5	0.8
Wakayama	1,710	600	35	400	23.5	710	41.5	15	47.3	2.8
Tottori	1,559	600	38.4	624	40	335	21.6	26	12.9	0.8
Hiroshima	2,685	600	22.3	1,100	41	985	36.7	68	14.5	0.5
Tokushima	1,369	600	43.8	504	36.8	265	19.4	12	22.1	1.6
Kagawa	2,335	600	25.7	1,350	57.8	385	16.5	17	22.6	1.0
Kita-Kyushu	2,189	600	27.4	1,100	50.7	479	21.9	85	5.6	0.3
Kagoshima	1,361	600	44.1	556	33.6	305	22.4	20	15.1	1.1
Okinawa	1,282	600	46.8	230	17.9	452	35.3	31	14.6	1.1

* = without land † = Local and prefecture government together ‡ = per firm

Source: Author's computation based on JRDC data.

2.3. Policy-based Finance and Low Interest Rate

Japan used a special financial mechanism to influence economic developments, and the government's financial activity induced the private sector to achieve specified objectives. The need for such financial guidance is explained in the Annual Report of JDB and JERI (1993) as follows: '...if the private financial market were perfect (in terms of competition, information and freedom of transactions) policy-based finance would be unnecessary. In reality, however, there are limits to the perfect fulfilment of these conditions in the financial market. [Policy-based finance] aims to stimulate and supplement the activities of private financial institutions.' The government must have some rational reason for starting financial interventions, otherwise such actions would be widely challenged by the private sector. For this a consensus-building process is used involving the main participants (in the form of *shingikai*, or deliberative councils). Thus, when the government's action starts, private companies and banks, feeling the government's support, are also willing to make investment commitments and open additional credits. Actually, this is also a seed-money approach: the financial seed-money policy (or pump-priming).

2.3.1. Credit policy

In general, there are three types of directed credits: (1) firm- or industry-related credits; (2) credits provided on functional criteria such as the promotion of exports, or the stimulation of small and medium-sized companies; (3) credits directed to accomplish social objectives, for example the housing programme. Usually the credit lines are precisely specified as regards target, amount and conditions. Projects undergo stringent selection standards and permanent supervision during the implementation of projects. Continuous monitoring of the performance has enabled banks to take early measures if problems have occurred. As a result, loan write-offs have been very low: for instance in the case of the Japan Development Bank the share of bad loans was 0.09 per cent between 1951 and 1955 and further decreased to 0.01 per cent in 1955–65.

The government realizes the policy-based finance through three types of institutions:

1. First, through banks which are wholly capitalized by the government, such as the Japan Development Bank (JDB) or the Export–Import Bank of Japan. Although owned by the government, these banks enjoy autonomy and posses their own capital too.

The Japan Development Bank was set up in 1951 for the financing of priority industries. The JDB capital is leased on the postal savings system, namely the Trust Fund Bureau, a special institution of the Ministry of Finance. The JDB employed a highly skilled group of ex-managers from the earlier Industrial Bank of Japan and Reconstruction Finance Bank, whose high level of technical competence in evaluating projects exceeded private sector capacities (Aoki, 1994). The JDB provided loans of durations exceeding those of commercial and investment banks.

2. Second, through government finance corporations. There are eight such corporations: the Housing Loan Corporation, the People's Finance Corporation, the Small Business Finance Corporation, the Environmental Sanitation Business Finance Corporation, the Agriculture, Forestry and Fisheries Finance Corporation, the Japan Finance Corporation for Municipal Enterprises, the Hokkaido and Tohoku Development Corporation and the Okinawa Development Finance Corporation. In addition, the Medical Care Facilities Finance Corporation was active between 1960 and 1984.

These corporations also belong to the government, but unlike the former banks, they have limited autonomy and must obtain ministerial approval for projects and funding programmes.

3. Third, public corporations and government agencies. There were 18 institutions in 1991 belonging to this category (for example, the Overseas Economic Cooperation Fund). These agencies are involved in policy-based financing usually as a side-business.

The share of policy-based loans among all loans, including those from private banks and financial institutions, was 13.2 per cent in 1955 and dropped to 9.6 per cent in 1965. Thereafter, however, it again increased to 14.1 per cent by 1980, which was caused by the dramatic expansion of credits directed to 'Japan's lifestyle base', that is, housing and life infrastructure. These loans played a considerable role in creating new industrial equipment and technology. They accounted for about a third of new industrial equipment and technology in the 1950s (Table 9.4).

Table 9.4 Supply of new industrial equipment funds

	1952–55		*1956–60*		*1961–65*	
	Bn yen	*%*	*Bn yen*	*%*	*Bn yen*	*%*
Government funds						
JDB	244.1	15.1	299.9	5.9	672.7	5.1
Others	275.5	17.0	850.3	16.6	1,867.5	14.1
Subtotal	*519.6*	*32.1*	*1,150.2*	*22.5*	*2,540.2*	*19.2*
Private financial institutions	1,096.6	67.9	3,958.0	77.5	10,681.8	80.8
Total	*1,616.2*	*100.0*	*5,108.2*	*100.0*	*13222.0*	*100.0*

Sources: JDB, JERI

As for the priority pattern, industry and technology enjoyed an absolute priority from the 1950s (see Table 9.5). While their share was about 30 per cent in the 1950s, after 1965 it dropped gradually to 3 per cent by 1975 and remained at this level until the 1990s. Other tendencies are: (1) housing finance increased considerably (from a 6.8 per cent share in 1955 to 38 per cent in 1990); (2) financing of small and medium business maintained quite a stable share (38–40 per cent); (3) regional development rose in importance beginning during the 1970s.

Table 9.5 Changes of shares in Fiscal Investment and Loan Programmes applied to industry and technology (per cent)

1953	*1955*	*1960*	*1965*	*1970*	*1975*	*1980*	*1985*	*1990*
29.1	15.8	13.6	7.8	5.7	3.0	3.0	2.9	2.9

Sources: JDB, JERI

Policy changes are apparent also in the financing pattern of government financial institutions. Thus, for example, the financing pattern of probably the most influential institution, the Japan Development Bank, reflects the relevant shifts in policy priorities (see Table 9.6). From 1985, in order to revitalize economic activity, financing focused on privatization (Japanese National Railways and NTT – Nippon Telegraph and Telephone Public Corporation), new technologies like biotechnology and space industries, the development of railways (Shinkansen super-express lines) and regional development.

Table 9.6 Changes in government policies and responses by the Japan Development Bank

Period	*Policy objective*	*Response by Japan Development Bank*	*Priority fields*
–1954	Economic reconstruction	Reconstruct and modernize basic industries	Electric power, coal-mining, ocean shipping, iron and steel
1955–64	Catch up with developed countries	Foster infant industries	Synthetic fibres, petrochemicals, nuclear power generation, machinery and electronics industries
	Correct regional disparities	Develop the industrial structure	Petrochemicals, automobiles, spinning industry, ocean shipping
		Respond to regional issues	Regional development
1965–74	Promote national land development and social development	Promote urban and regional development	Urban redevelopment, modernization of goods distribution system, private railways, housing development
	Construct a welfare society	Improve national living standards	Pollution control, housing industry, food safety
measures,			
	Build a foundation for economic and social development		gas, natural welfare facilities
		Promote technological development	New technologies, domestically produced computers
		Secure a stable energy supply	National oil companies, domestic production of nuclear power generation equipment
1975–84	Ensure economic security	Secure a stable energy supply	Use of alternative energy sources, energy conservation
	Attain stable economic growth	Promote development of original technologies	Promotion of technology, promotion of information-processing and communications
	Improve national life	Consolidate and develop the living environment	Urban development, regional development, improvement of national life

1985–88	Promote economic restructuring	Promote industrial restructuring	Enterprise restructuring projects, regional activation projects, stabilization of the shipbuilding industry
	Expand domestic demand	Provide conditions for foreign and domestic competition	Promote facilities for imported goods and direct investments into Japan
	Stabilize and improve national life	Introduce private-sector vitality into the development of social sector	Key railway development and construction of new lines
			Promote private sector investment in regional economies, Kansai Cultural Academy and Research City, resort area development
		Promote information-related industries	New telecommunications companies, VAN
		Improve national welfare	Promote employment of disabled people, fee-charging homes for the aged
1989–	Build up the foundation for national living standard	Improve living standards and urban infrastructure	Social capital development, key transportation facilities, efficient goods distribution system, environmental measures
	Reduce international friction	Promote internationalization	Promote facilities for imported goods and direct invest-to Japan
	Balanced development among regions	Promote industrial restructuring	Enterprise restructuring projects, regional activation projects
		Revitalize regional economies	Regional development, forming multi-polar pattern of national land use

Sources: JDB, JERI

The loan distribution of the Japan Development Bank is presented in Table 9.7.

Table 9.7 Pattern of Japan Development Bank loans (per cent)

	1951 –55	*1956 –60*	*1961 –65*	*1966 –70*	*1971 –75*	*1976 –80*	*1981 –85*	*1986 -91*
Energy	40.8		25.4	15.0	10.0	25.6	43.2	29.7
Transport	22.3		33.1	35.5	17.7	7.2	9.2	13.3
Industry	10.6	71.0	14.4	8.4				3.5
Technology				8.3	11.2	11.2	11.6	5.2*
Pollution prevention					21.7	19.7	8.2	4.3
Regional development		2.0	17.8	15.9	15.3	14.8	11.1	10.8
Urban infrastructure				11.6	17.2	16.7	12.4	18.3
Other	21.6	4.4	1.5	2.8	6.9	4.8	3.3	2.5

* Together with 9.4% for 'information and communication facilities' this figure amounts to 14.6%.

Note: Shares do not add up to 100 per cent because of other items omitted.

Sources: JDB, JERI

2.3.2. Low interest rates

Japan, in common with other Asian countries, such as Korea, Malaysia, and Taiwan, used a policy of low interest rates to stimulate investments and technology. In general, positive real interest rates, as a rule, attract savings, while negative interest rates induce savers to spend rather than save their income. Since slightly negative interest rates do not influence savings substantially, the government can use the low interest-rate policy to channel savings to investments, because lower borrowing rates stimulate the demand for loans. However, when excess demand for loans appears, the risk of inefficient allocation is greater, so that this demand should be regulated through selection measures either by the government or by private banks.

Japan has been using the low interest-rate policy consciously for speeding up economic growth and industrialization. Low interest coupled with credit-channelling by government financial institutions into priority fields ensured the concentrated and efficient use of financial resources. Thus, low interest rates do not result in low growth but can in fact contribute to new investments and rapid growth. A World Bank study also states that 'generally, financial repression is associated with low economic growth, especially when real interest rates are strongly negative.' But there is no evidence of this in Taiwan, China, Korea and Japan (World Bank, 1993).

In Japan real interest rates between 1953 and 1991 were on average - 1.12 per cent. Real interest rates on deposits were negative until 1983 and thereafter they were positive but rather low. Interest rates were also highly stable, small adjustments occurring once in five years. The lending rates were different according to whether loans were provided by private or by governmental banks. Private banks charged a higher interest rate due to many restrictions affecting the private financial sector.

How could negative real interest rates be maintained for 30 years? There are several reasons. The most general one is Japan's high savings propensity (for education, health and housing), which causes savings to stay at a relatively high level even if conditions are not the most favourable. In addition, Japanese citizens have no choice to transfer their savings to foreign banks eventually offering higher interest. Another possibility for savers from the 1980s onwards would be to buy foreign bonds, but the Japanese generally refrain from that, counting on uncertainty of repayment from foreign countries or banks.

As a result, low interest rate loans contributed substantially to new investments and technology. There are, however, different opinions, also, concerning the efficiency of this policy. A quantitative macro-economic analysis reveals that excess loans to manufacturing did not raise productivity on a value-added basis (Hamada *et al.*, 1987).

3. LESSONS

In East European countries liberalization went together with almost totally free imports, which pushed domestic companies into a hopeless situation. Foreign investors were granted privileges to move in, resulting in financial discrimination against domestic firms. Even in Hungary, the most early and cautious reforming country, the systemic change caused a hidden shock, because the transition was not managed and even several years after the change there is still no development strategy (Bakos, 1994). According to the experience of Singapore, a foreign-capital-based liberal growth path can also be successful if there is a national priority of economic branches and conscious management of wages versus inflation (Goh, 1970; Cheah, 1996).

What Japan showed to the world was that it is possible to work out and to realize a national development strategy for the country's benefit. For this, extensive interest-harmonization and consensus-creation are necessary, involving a continuous dialogue between the top management and the industries, companies and citizens, who are 'managed'. The central institution of this process is the MITI, whose role changed over the time from strategy-making to rather a think-tank function. Is such strategic policy-making feasible in transforming economies? After similar offices were set up in South Korea, recently China introduced it, too, and in 1994 so did Hungary. *Focusing on technology catching up and coordination with industrial policy as well as concentrated financing would help restructuring.* A national development strategy is also an orientation for private companies to work out their business plans and an incentive to stimulate sluggish investments

The seed money approach in technology policy is particularly significant. By pooling and combining financial resources, the government is able to stimulate research and to share risks, especially in basic research. Private companies then join government-initiated projects and benefit from later commercialization of the result.

Using financial tools such as tax breaks, subsidies and early depreciation can be effective if inflation is kept down, and if tax burdens that are at present almost unbearable (because of the insatiable hunger of the central budget deficit) are eased. A supportive financial policy providing long-term and low interest rate credits is promoting research and technology projects at private companies.

For some countries, including Hungary, Poland, the Czech Republic and Slovakia - which, as discussed in chapters 5 and 6, are already associate members of the EU and will in a few years probably become full members - the further opening to the EU is on the agenda. This

new industries; however, a 'timed protectionism' might be accepted. Even if traditional tools of a national strategy such as import taxes and, subsidies might not be used openly in the future, a shift to more sophisticated methods, like the seed-money approach, information flow and technology transfer would be of great help

REFERENCES

Aoki, Masahiko (1994). 'Monitoring Characteristics of the Main Bank System: An Analytical and Developmental View', in Aoki Masahiko and Hugh Patrick (eds), *The Japanese Main Bank System: Its Relevance to Developing and Transforming Economies*, (Oxford University Press).

Bakos, Gábor (1994). 'Hungarian Transition after Three Years', *Europe–Asia Studies* 1994. no.7.

Cheah, Hock Beng (1996). 'Can Governments Engineer the Transition from Cheap Labour to Skill-based Competitiveness? The Case of Singapore', in Martin Godfrey (ed.), *Skill Development for International Competitiveness* (Cheltenham: Edward Elgar).

Fransman, Martin (1990). *The Market and Beyond* (Cambridge: Cambridge University Press).

Goh, Keng Swee (1970). *Decade of Achievement* (New York: Praeger).

Hamada, Koichi-Kuroda and Akiyoshi Mashiro-Horiuchi (1987). *Nihon keizai no makro bunseki* (Macroeconomic analysis of Japanese economy) (Tokyo: Daigaku Shuppankai).

Imamura, Tsunao (ed.) (1993). *Dai-san sekuta no kenkyu* (Research on the Third sector) (Institute of Economic Research, Hitotsubashi University, Tokyo).

Japan Development Bank (JDB) and Japan Economic Research Institute (JERI) (1993). *Policy-based Finance: The Experience of Postwar Japan.*

'Kiban gijutsu kenkyu sokushin senta' (Japan Key Technology Centre), *Information Bulletin* (Tokyo, 1996).

Ministry of International Trade and Industry, *Information Bulletin* (Tokyo: MITI, 1992).

Odagiri, Hiroyuki and Akira Goto (1993). 'The Japanese System of Innovation: Past, Present, and Future', in Richard R. Nelson (ed.),

National Systems of Innovation: A Comparative Study (Oxford: Oxford University Press).

Ono, Goro (1992). *Jissenteki sangyo seisakuron* (Pragmatic industrial policy) (Tokyo: Tsusho Sangyo Chosakai).

Uekusa, M. (1988). 'The Oil Crisis and After', in Masumi Komiya *et al.* (eds), *Industrial Policy in Japan* (New York: Academic Press).

Wakasugi, Ryuhei (1986). *Gijutsukakushin to kenkyukaihatsu no keizai bunseki* (Economic analysis of technology and research development) (Tokyo: Toyo Keizai).

World Bank (1993). *The East Asian Miracle* (Oxford: Oxford University Press).

Yoshino, Naoyuki (1993). *The Low Interest Rate Policy and Economic Growth of Japan* (Tokyo: Department of Economics, Keio University).

10. Venture Capital and the Shaping of Economic Development

Franklin Pitcher Johnson, Jr.

1. VENTURE CAPITAL

The phrase 'Venture Capital' in Central and Eastern Europe has come to mean almost any kind of private equity capital used for founding companies, for providing growth capital, for buyouts of existing owners, and even funding for privatizations of government-owned companies.

Its meaning in the United States, where the term was first used 50 years ago, is usually confined to founding and growth capital for young companies, and almost always involves the concomitant provision of help and advice from the investor. The usage of the term in Western Europe, where financing and helping start-up companies is an uncommon activity by 'venture capitalists', has come, by practice, to mean late-round financing and buy-outs. The definition of the term in any area is influenced by what it takes to raise money from investors in venture firms, including not using the term 'venture capital' at all. The market makes the meaning. Venture capital activities have been rapidly growing in the United States, where they contributed, for example, to generating almost $100 billion in sales the personal computer industry in the period 1981–90.[1] These activities are important also for developing a positive attitude to business, and public acceptance of a shift in career and risk taking in the US.

1. *The Economist*, 25–31 January 1997, p.19.

2. ENTREPRENEURSHIP

Venture capital, defined as the activity of providing capital and help to young and growing companies, means little without its existing in an environment where entrepreneurs can thrive. In much of the old Eastern bloc, prior to 1990, there was a history of substantial restriction or prohibition of entrepreneurial activity, and the concept of venture capital was meaningless. As a result, there was very little timely flow of technology from the laboratory into consumer goods or into capital goods for the production of consumer goods. As restrictions on entrepreneurial activity were lifted, entrepreneurs quickly arose, usually poorly capitalized, to fill market needs in infrastructure such as retailing, transportation, distribution, communications and consumer and financial services. Except in the computer software field, however, technological entrepreneurs have been scarce.

Unfortunately, in some countries, especially Russia, criminals and gangsters have stepped into the authority vacuum and have become 'entrepreneurs' in important segments of the consumer economy. They have used methods illegal in any society to restrict competition or to extract payments from other business people. The word 'entrepreneur' is hardly a positive one in such an environment, and economic freedom has been subverted.

There is an emerging agreement, however, in most industrialized Central and Eastern European countries that the development of industry which utilizes modern science and technology should have a high national priority because of the resulting economic and social benefits. No consensus yet exists, however, that the technological entrepreneur should be the primary agent for that development. The elements of a favourable entrepreneurial environment are not widely understood, and many governments in the old Bloc (to say nothing of some governments in the West) hang on to the belief that government activity should direct and control where the economy goes. Government direction and controls are antithetical to the entrepreneurial freedom to pursue markets, and inimical to the flow of venture capital to entrepreneurs, whether that venture capital be foreign or domestic.

A look at the relative success of entrepreneurial activity around the world in differing political and social environments clearly suggests a working hypothesis that is just as applicable to Central and Eastern Europe as to the rest of the world:

> A climate which actively nurtures entrepreneurial activity with a minimum of restrictions will be the most likely to produce the most rapid and long-lived growth of industry based on modern science and technology

Countries which have strong industrial bases utilizing the continuing advances of technology will have the exports and jobs to build strong economies. Well-financed entrepreneurs are the best builders of these bases. Countries without strong entrepreneurial segments will languish with stagnant economies, unemployment and uneconomic jobs, and capital leaving or seeking to leave the country.

One worldwide set of entrepreneurial conditions will not work in every country, because of history, custom and mentality. There are some general elements of a successful climate, however, which, when given local rules by people who know the country, can maximize the odds that a nation will have a thriving technological industrial sector. In a country making a transition to an economy based on private enterprise, entrepreneurship and venture capital, or contemplating doing so, there are three primary areas of consideration for the promotion of an entrepreneurial climate: political and social conditions, economic conditions and transitional actions.

3. POLITICAL AND SOCIAL CONDITIONS FOR ENTREPRENEURSHIP

Freedom of economic action is the central element of an entrepreneurial climate. Individuals and groups must be free to seek out markets which they believe they can serve profitably, with few restrictions, relating solely to socially undesirable goods and services. A second element, described by Milton Friedman, is civil freedom, that is the ability to conduct business and life safely, and with a system of laws that protect ownership of property and the right to speak out freely in the conduct of business, or on any subject. Most leaders believe these two elements are preconditions for thriving entrepreneurship. There is no consensus that a third element, political freedom, the ability to select one's government, is a precondition, although there is a widespread belief that entrepreneurial activity leads to democracy and political freedom because it places economic power and the habits of freedom of action in the hands of individuals. In the view of some, order and safety are at odds with democracy in the establishment of a good business and entrepreneurial climate. They cite Chile under Pinochet and modern-day China as examples of entrepreneurial success without political freedom. The view of the present author is that entrepreneurs thrive best when every dimension of personal freedom is maximized and that democracy itself is a worthwhile goal.

There also has to be a widespread understanding by the public of the social and economic roles of entrepreneurs. They not only respond rapidly to markets, but, as people striving for economic success from normally modest origins, they often provide a healthy turbulence in what otherwise might become a stratified and stagnant society. They build wealth for their country by trying to build wealth for themselves. In a transitional society, it takes education and time for the public, let alone the government, to see that the things entrepreneurs do can be congruent with national aims. There is also difficulty in some countries in persuading people to accept the financial success of others, even as they eagerly use their products and services.

Another required political condition is the existence of a set of business laws that permit entrepreneurs to function. There must be legal organizational forms such as corporations, proprietorships and various kinds of partnerships; trade and contract laws; anti-monopoly, fair-trade and competition rules; orderly bankruptcy procedures; and securities laws describing forms and conditions of investment.

A national pool of talent and knowledge must also be in place for entrepreneurs to thrive. Business education in marketing, production, accounting and finance; the development of engineers and technicians; and the continuing conduct of sophisticated research in at least some areas are all vital if the technological entrepreneurs of any country are to be successful in the international arena. As discussed in Chapters 1, 8 and 9 of this volume, governments have a key role to play in sponsoring education and research.

4. ECONOMIC CONDITIONS

A number of economic conditions must also be present to foster a productive entrepreneurial climate. A central condition is that entrepreneurs must be able to make and keep money, because that is central to why they do what they do. Of the things government can affect, the existence of moderate taxes is important at both the corporate and the personal level. When a young company begins to make money, its main hope of financing its growth comes from retaining its earnings. High tax rates on companies retard their growth. Likewise, high taxes on people lower their incentives to work, and prevent the formation of savings and capital which are vital to the formation of other new businesses. A social effect of high personal taxes is to keep ordinary people from rising on the economic ladder and to dampen the healthy economic competition that keeps a society constantly changing.

Many countries have chosen to tax gains on the sale of capital, such as shares in companies, at low rates so that individuals can form capital and can move investments from one form to another without much penalty. In this respect, the United States, which prides itself on being entrepreneurial, has higher capital gains taxes than some European countries.

The ability of employees to own shares in the companies in which they work has been a hallmark of some of the most entrepreneurial of societies. Options, which are one technique, give an employee the right to buy some shares at a fixed price at some later time. The existence of stock option programmes gives employees with little capital the chance to participate in the growth in value of their companies. This requires that options be legally permitted, and not taxed too heavily. The desire and need of entrepreneurs and other employers to share in ownership is obviously a vital condition as well.

Most businesses, however, require more capital to function and grow than the founders and retained profits can provide. The sale of shares in the company for cash is one way of generating needed capital, and this kind of capital is called equity. It is permanent capital; it does not have to be paid back, but it shares in the ownership. For young companies, equity is usually superior to debt because of the economic uncertainties typical of such firms. The constant need to pay interest and meet repayment schedules from borrowing money can mean danger to a company of any size. When companies have reasonably predictable operations, however, the 'renting' of money by borrowing it has a useful role.

When borrowing money is necessary and appropriate, lenders need to be available. Banks are the primary source of borrowings in most parts of the world, and an active banking system is necessary to support the community of businesses, large and small. In essentially every country, the government is involved in a central bank which facilitates the functioning of the banks that deal directly with that country's businesses and facilitate foreign trade.

There is a special kind of capital provider, and sometimes lender, to young and growing businesses in many countries. That institution is called venture capital. Venture capital firms normally provide capital and business expertise to young companies that need capital and help. They receive a share of ownership in these companies in return for their investment of time and money. The requirement for venture capital is so widespread that many countries have incentives or even support programmes to encourage the formation of venture capital companies which, in turn, foster the growth of young companies. Venture capital is also often provided by individuals as well. By itself, however, the availability of venture capital means little unless the other essential elements enabling entrepreneurship are present. Normally, private venture capital does not appear unless many or most of the other elements are in place.

When companies become large enough and predictable enough, their shares are often sold to the public in general or to professionally managed institutions. While the stock market is a very old phenomenon for big companies in many countries, the existence of a stock market devoted to young and small companies is new and has been a driving force in the encouragement of entrepreneurship. Such markets provide young companies with a means to raise substantial amounts of capital for growth and to provide the early backers, the entrepreneurs and the employees with a chance to sell some of their own shares. The business of investment banking is necessary for facilitating such activity and for the functioning of the markets for the securities.

Another element of the entrepreneurial climate is the existence of the infrastructure of firms and institutions providing services and goods that entrepreneurs need. These include professional service providers such as law firms and auditors; suppliers of office equipment, computers and the raw materials of production; good communications and transportation; various financial services; educational institutions; and others that enable the functioning of business. The lack of many of these functions has made the growth of entrepreneurship rather slow-going in the East European countries. Fortunately, the very lack of such amenities has created extensive entrepreneurial opportunities in those countries and the situation is improving rapidly.

For the technological entrepreneur in particular, the availability of large markets is important. Most technology-based products require that substantial sums be spent on development. Unless the customer base is large, the cost of development becomes too great on a per unit basis for the product to be priced in a competitive way. For these reasons, a national effort to understand the needs of external markets for technical products must be made and joint marketing among smaller firms may be necessary. Technology-based industry can be an important factor without substantial export activities in only the few largest economies. National policies which move in the direction of providing freely convertible currencies are another important factor in increasing trade in the technical sector and providing the necessary markets.

5. TRANSITIONAL ACTIONS

The above discussion represents a series of goals that are designed to be optimal to promote entrepreneurship, particularly technological and infrastructural entrepreneurship. For those countries whose societies and economies have been primarily socialist, and who have made a decision to adopt a private enterprise system, with emphasis on entrepreneurs, the transition to the conditions described earlier is a difficult one. Accomplishing the transition well is as important as setting the goals, and the transition clearly has to be custom-made in each country which chooses to attempt it. I present some necessary actions of transition in the following discussion.

The first series of steps must be devoted to minimizing social turmoil in an otherwise peaceful transition. The most visible agents of change are entrepreneurial merchants providing consumer goods and services to people. Emphasis should be placed early on permitting the opening of private shops, the privatization of existing state shops, and clearing the way for local and foreign private investment in firms involved in the importation and distribution of consumer goods. The removal of price controls and state-set prices on basic goods is always one of the toughest decisions, but it is a vital step in causing goods to flow and business to start. The pace of the phasing in of de-control on essentials and the protection of low-income people, as products meet market prices, is a delicate balancing act. Monetary and fiscal policy measures by the government to minimize inflationary pressures are part of the answer in keeping vital goods affordable but still plentiful.

Putting farming and light manufacturing on an entrepreneurial basis comes a close second in importance, because these activities are the sources of the local goods available to the people. The more supply that can be encouraged, the more free-market prices will be held in check. Consumer goods and services are the best area in which to get the market economy going and at the same time to give the people a sense of change in their lives. The example of how this was accomplished in the Czech Republic, Poland and Romania is a useful exercise for other countries considering a change to a market economy. These countries had both success and set-backs in their administration of change.

Another important step in securing public support for change is the encouragement of widespread public and employee ownership of business. This can be done by one of several privatization voucher schemes for larger businesses and by encouraging all businesses to have a scheme for employees to share in the ownership of the companies where they work, including entrepreneurial companies.

An immediate national investment in education is required to teach the skills of business and technology in schools and universities, and, in more general forums, the understanding by the people of free markets and entrepreneurial enterprise. To the extent it can be budgeted, increased national support for scientific research is also needed as the basis for the foundation of new industries in which the country may already have some expertise.

Whether in many stable capitalist countries or in formerly socialist countries in the throes of transition, the role of entrepreneurs - the people who form new businesses - is not often well understood or appreciated. They are essentially challengers of the *status quo*. States in transition have an unusual opportunity to make entrepreneurs a keystone of a new approach to their economies and societies. Not only are they the people who will provide the energy and drive to initiate and sustain change, but they will be the founders of the nation's industries of the future. What a government can do is set up an enabling climate and culture of encouragement and approval so that there will be plenty of people who come forth with the zeal, commitment and singleness of purpose to undertake the difficult and risky entrepreneurial struggle for personal economic independence.

6. PROGRESS IN CENTRAL AND EASTERN EUROPE

The progress along the pathway to an entrepreneurial economy and society, or even the commitment to build one, varies greatly among the old socialist bloc states. The differences are as great as the differences in the history, people and culture of the various nations. If movement towards the conditions to promote entrepreneurship as a fundamental social and economic goal can be measured as a dependent variable, then some correlative independent variables also can be identified, or at least hypothesized.

On the basis of the evidence available in early 1997, one such variable, and a positive one, is the degree to which democracy has become an open, effective process. Another positive one is the speed and fairness with which privatization plans have been adopted, and a simple, perhaps even simplistic one, is how far west the country is. Some negative variables are the degree of maintenance of bureaucratic regulations and controls on the formation and growth of businesses, the prevalence of gangsters and crooks in the economy, and the degree of corruption among government officials and business leaders. The leaders of countries, fairly elected or not, cannot do much about geography and the related geopolitical history, but the other variables, positive and negative, can be affected by vigorous political leadership. All too often, however, venal politicians are part of the problem, not part of the answer.

If one uses the willingness of private, or partially private, venture capital to flow into a country as a measure of the hard-eyed judgement of international investors concerning the chances of entrepreneurial success, then some data exist about the degree of progress. In defining venture capital for this purpose, private-equity firms set up to invest in existing businesses, usually young and growing, comprise the class. Firms set up to make more speculative investments in privatization vouchers, publicly-traded stocks or financial plays exist in most countries, but their existence does not say much about the state of entrepreneurship.

Government-related entities such as the American Enterprise funds supported by the United States, the DEG funds of Germany, the Phare programme of the European Union and various other smaller programmes have been active in Central and Eastern Europe.[2] Their presence, while making capital available, is no measure of the international investment community's judgement about hopes for entrepreneurship, but rather an attempt by these countries to support smaller private enterprise, without much thought about the sustainability of that sector.

The European Bank for Reconstruction and Development (EBRD), a multi-government sponsored development bank for the old eastern bloc, has taken the approach in the venture capital field that in most cases it will provide only 35 per cent of the capital of a venture fund, and the rest must come from other sources, mostly private, and that it will not make small, direct venture capital investments. The International Finance Corporation of the World Bank has taken a similar approach in the venture field, choosing to back professional venture teams with only a portion of the capital. For purposes of this chapter, therefore, funds partially backed by these entities, or guaranteed by the Overseas Private Investment Corporation (another US government-backed entity), are deemed to be private.

7. COUNTRIES

Western Industrialized

As the result of an unpublished paper[3] written in 1996 by a group of venture capitalists in Poland, more is known about venture capital

2. John Kreis *et al.*, 'Sources of Financial Assistance' (Washington, DC: Institute for Defense Analysis, 1995); from Internet page http://echs.ida.org/pilot/subg5/finance/index.html
3. Robert Manz (Enterprise Investors), David Hartford (Pioneer Investment), Neil Milne (Copernicus Capital), Jacek Witak (Renaissance Capital) and Steven Buckley

activity there than in any other country in the zone. In addition to describing the methods and problems of doing venture work in Poland, they point out the existence of nine venture firms investing solely in Poland, with about US$700 million under management, half of which is in a hybrid firm, Enterprise Investors, with capital from private sources, EBRD, and the US government-sponsored Polish–American Enterprise Fund. Other leading firms include Renaissance Capital, Poland Partners, Pioneer Investment and Copernicus Capital.

The authors also list nine more Central European funds which invest in part in Poland, with about US$750 million under management. The 1996 *Yearbook of the European Venture Capital Association* (EVCA)[4] lists six EVCA full members in Poland, all of which are included in the venture capitalists' paper (see note 3), and shows the existence of a Polish Equity Investors' Association as well, an additional indication of a well-developed venture market. On the basis of these data and my own observations (since I participated in the formation of financial institutions in Eastern Europe), Poland clearly has the most professionally-managed venture capital available of any country in the zone, and has been attractive to private, foreign investors because of the success of the privatization programme, the growth of the private economy, the availability of investment opportunity, a relatively low level of government interference in smaller businesses and a stable government. The left and right movements of the electorate so far have not bothered outside investors, because they see the entrepreneurial climate essentially unaffected. So far, many of the venture deals done in Poland have been in rebuilding the infrastructure of the country in distribution, services and light manufacturing. While venture capitalists have not done many direct privatizations, companies resulting from privatizations have been funded.

The Czech Republic is not close to Poland in the amount of venture capital available, but has a good reputation in the Western investment community. The EVCA *Yearbook* shows only two members, but there are at least four prive venture funds active there including Renaissance Capital, Trigon Capital and Fleming's Czech Fund. There is an active Czech Venture Capital Association. Given the strong funding flow to

(Poland Partners), 'Venture Capital in Poland', unpublished private paper (Warsaw, October 1996).

4. European Venture Capital Association, *1996 Yearbook* (Brussels: Ernst & Young, 1996).

Poland, it is highly likely that the Western backers of venture capital in Central and Eastern Europe will turn next to the Czech Republic, for many of the same reasons they have backed funds in Poland, although the market is much smaller. In the observation of the author, infrastructure, computer and financial services and light manufacturing have provided much of the opportunity.

There is probably more US$100 million available for venture investment in the Czech Republic, including portions of regional funds. As they are in Poland, venture managers are usually experienced in Western business and often have origins in the country. Slovakia, the divorced spouse of the Czech Republic, has little private venture capital activity, a quarrelsome and confused government situation, an on-again, off-again privatization scheme, and no clear commitment to an entrepreneurial environment. The country does have a Slovak Venture Capital Association, with five members, but potential activity there is dominated by government and bank-dominated entities. Slovakia is a clear exception to the notion of westernness in the zone being a positive correlative factor.

Hungary got off to a good start in venture capital investment early in the decade, but several shifts in government policy towards privatization and decontrol have slowed enthusiasm for this mid-zone country. Nevertheless, Hungary has a US$130 million private equity fund there (the First Hungary Fund), and several bank- and government-related funds, along with a Hungarian Venture Capital Association. The American investor, George Soros, born in Hungary, has made sizeable grants there, and in other countries, to promote entrepreneurship and the private enterprise system.

South-Eastern Europe

Of the nations of the former Yugoslavia, Slovenia has a venture capital association and some bank-oriented funds, in a peaceful and encouraging environment for entrepreneurship. Serbia and Montenegro, Croatia, and Bosnia-Hercegovina have been war-stressed with most opinion favouring Croatia as an early emerger in entrepreneurship. Albania, the poorest country in Europe, has one venture fund sponsored by an Italian Bank and EBRD, optimism on the part of the people, expressed in polls in 1996, that things will get better, but a fragile democracy. Small-scale entrepreneurship abounds, but there is little progress on the important elements of an entrepreneurial society, some of which require governmental action.

Romania is in the throes of a tardy privatization scheme, but is considered the next likely place for outside venture capital, following the election in 1996 of a supposedly progressive government, and in view of its good natural resources and size. Until changes are made, however, heavy-handed government regulatory activity remains inimical to large-scale entrepreneurial activity. Also, a few local businessmen have arisen to dominate important segments of the economy, which causes concerns of monopolistic behaviour and suppressed competition from potential new entrants in these fields. Romania has two or three private venture firms and probably less than $10 million under management.

Bulgaria also has been slow to privatize and is considered over-regulated and bureaucratic by many potential foreign venture investors. There are at least two bank-related private venture firms. The government has set up units to encourage foreign investment, but has done little to foster an entrepreneurial environment. Local businessmen have set up some rather powerful economic units that provide an anti-competitive element. In addition some business people speak openly about the need to buy 'insurance' to protect their businesses and persons. Nevertheless, because the scientific and technical expertise of many potential entrepreneurs is good, there is some optimism in the country and abroad that there will be solid opportunities for entrepreneurs and venture capital if the government can get out of the way. There is further optimism in this regard since the 1997 elections.

Moldova, rich in agricultural resources, has little organized venture capital, but deals do surface from time to time for private investment. The large Ukrainian-based private equity firm, Western NIS Enterprise Fund, however, states that it is looking at deals in Moldova.

Baltic Countries

Estonia, Latvia and Lithuania have attracted private venture capital from a fund set up by the Finnish firm, Sitra, and EBRD, with capital of about $10 million, and from the Western NIS and Baltic States Fund. These countries have been working to liberalize the entrepreneurial environment with educational programmes and progressive changes in regulatory affairs.

Russia and its Neighbours

Despite its famous gangsterism, heavy bureaucracy and political and social turmoil, Russia's sheer size, its well-advanced privatization scheme and its reservoir of scientific and technical talent have attracted foreign venture capital. Much of it, like the eleven regional funds such as the St. Petersburg and Smolensk Regional Venture Funds and the Russian–American Enterprise Fund, is sponsored by governments or the EBRD. More than any other country in the knowledge of the author, Russia has attracted large numbers of private foreign investors, many of whom have become on-site investor–entrepreneurs. Much of this activity has revolved around privatization schemes. The private–EBRD Russian Technology Fund in St. Petersburg is working on start-ups and young technology companies. There are several other funds – such as the Russia Partners Fund, the New Russia Small Business Fund, the Crystal Ventures Capital Corporation, and the Pioneer Direct Equity Fund – whose stated purpose is private investment in young companies. Altogether, however, Russia probably has a smaller amount of organized private venture capital for investing in and helping start-up and young ventures than Poland, but a larger amount of capital available for privatization schemes and larger-scale private investment.

As of early 1997, a Russian Venture Capital Association was being formed with 34 entities listed as potential members, eleven of which were the EBRD-related Regional Venture Funds.[5]

Ukraine has two venture funds operating in an uncertain political environment, including the Western NIS Fund. The country is one which is considered by many western investors to have strong economic potential because of its size, industrial background and technical knoweldge. There is no visible private venture fund based in Belarus.

8. CONCLUSION

The business of venture capital, the provision of capital and advice to new and young companies, is only one part of what is needed to

5. Likka Linnakko *et al.*, 'Memorandum of Organizing Committee, Russian Venture Capital Asosciation' (Helsinki: Nordic Russian Management Company, January 1997).

provide a healthy environment for entrepreneurial activity. Private venture capital firms must compete in world markets for capital which will be directed by its managers to seek the best possible return for the risk taken. Although Western government agencies are at present directing capital and reducing the risk for investors in the old eastern bloc, investments in the zone will ultimately have to compete for capital evenly and openly with the rest of the world. In order to be competitive in world capital markets in the future, countries in Central and Eastern Europe will have to build conditions that encourage entrepreneurs' activities, as well as providing honest and stable investment environments with minimum impedance to capital flow.

11. Comparison of German and Japanese Economic Linkage Policies

Randall E. Newnham

1. INTRODUCTION

How far does the reach of economic power extend into the world of political, territorial and security issues - the world of 'high politics'? This question has vexed analysts for generations. Yet finding an answer to it is today more crucial than ever, as countries which base their power primarily on economic strength, such as Japan and Germany, rise to prominence in world affairs. This chapter will discuss the role of economic instruments in an area which is perhaps the core of 'high politics': territorial control. Specifically, it will look at two cases in which states have attempted to use economic aid to gain territory. The two cases are the German–Soviet negotiations which preceded German reunification and Japanese–Soviet talks on the Kurile Island dispute. The crucial question to be examined is this: in what circumstances can economic aid be used to effectively 'purchase' land from another state?

In July 1990, the German Chancellor Helmut Kohl and the Soviet leader Mikhail Gorbachev agreed on a plan for German reunification. Essentially, the USSR bowed to all of Kohl's demands: Germany would be reunified rapidly under the West German political system and would remain in NATO. To many observers, this breakthrough marked the real end of the Cold War. In return, Kohl offered an unprecedented economic aid package, valued at about 50 billion DM (30 billion dollars).[1] Apparently, economic linkage was successful in this case.

1. Estimates of total German aid vary widely; this amount reflects those measures discussed in detail at the July 1990 meeting. However, Germany offered other aid

In March 1991, the secretary-general of the ruling Japanese Liberal Democratic Party, Ichiro Ozawa, travelled to the USSR. Like many previous Japanese envoys, he sought to win Moscow's consent to the eventual return of four tiny Kurile Islands to Japan. Ozawa reportedly brought with him an offer of some $26 billion in economic aid, an offer quite comparable to that made eight months earlier by Chancellor Kohl.[2] An unbiased observer would probably have expected Ozawa's mission to be at least as successful as Kohl's. After all, why should control over four small, isolated islands be worth more to the Soviet leadership than control over East Germany – the German Democratic Republic (GDR), the cornerstone of the Warsaw Pact military alliance and the CMEA (Council for Mutual Economic Assistance) trading bloc, a country of sixteen million people? Yet in fact, Ozawa's attempt to use Japan's economic power as Kohl had used Germany's was a failure. Gorbachev rejected the offer and no progress on the Kurile issue was made at the subsequent Soviet–Japanese summit in Tokyo in April 1991. After the collapse of the USSR, Japanese negotiations with the Russian President Boris Yeltsin were equally unsuccessful. To date, no significant progress has been made on the issue.

What factors can account for the dramatically different outcomes of these two cases? The cases were similar in many ways. Germany and Japan were both trying to influence the same leaders of the same country at about the same time. Thus, factors such as individual personalities and the political and economic situation in the state being influenced were relatively constant. Even the economic aid offered by Germany and Japan appeared to be similar in scope.

Indeed, as has been suggested, a good case can be made that the Kurile issue should have been easier to resolve than the German unification case. While some in the USSR did claim that the Kuriles had military significance, as will be discussed below, it seemed clear that East Germany had far greater significance. Some have stressed that the

both before and after this summit which can also be viewed as being linked – albeit more loosely – with reunification, as will be discussed below.

2. The specifics of the offer were reported to be as follows: $4 billion in emergency loans from the Japanese Export–Import Bank; $4 billion for relocating civilian and military residents of the islands; $8 billion in loan guarantees for private sector loans for Siberian resource development; and $10 billion in low-interest loans for general Soviet economic development (Gelman, 1993, pp.22–3). The offer's specifics and even its existence have rarely been discussed publicly by Japanese officials.

Kuriles could not be returned because this would represent a Russian retreat from the gains of the Second World War, a retreat which would throw all such gains into doubt. Yet was not the division of Germany and of Europe as a whole a far more significant result of the Second World War than the conquest of the tiny Kuriles? Finally, even the eight months which had elapsed between the Gorbachev–Kohl summit and Ozawa's visit might have been expected to work in Japan's favour. During those eight months the power of the USSR had declined noticeably and its need for outside economic help had risen greatly. One would expect that all these factors would strengthen Japan's bargaining power and make a favourable outcome more likely. Yet this was not the case.

The crucial factors which account for Japan's failure to recover the Kuriles and Germany's success in reuniting with East Germany appear to have been twofold. First, the issues of territorial sovereignty and self-determination were less favourable for Japan than for Germany – although, as we shall see, economic strategies can influence these factors somewhat, especially the latter. Economic linkage can be a powerful force, as the German case tends to indicate. Yet it is extremely difficult to use economic inducements alone to force a country to relinquish land which it considers to be legally part of its territory. This task is made even more difficult if giving up this land violates the wishes of the people inhabiting the land in question – that is, their right of self-determination. For these reasons, while it is conceivable that a state may agree effectively to sell colonial lands – as has happened several times in history – it will be extremely reluctant to sell part of its 'own' territory, inhabited by its 'own' people. However, as the German case shows, it is conceivable that a situation can be redefined away from the questions of territory and self-determination. The USSR had long believed it had a right to control the GDR and that it had the support of the people living there. However, Moscow was eventually convinced that this was not the case.

Second, the exact method of economic linkage used by Japan may have been less conducive to success than that used by Germany. Although the final economic packages offered by the two states were comparable, Germany had prepared the ground for its offer more carefully – through the use of what I refer to as 'general' economic linkage (Newnham, 1995, 1996). Germany had given the USSR trade credits and other forms of aid almost continuously since about 1970, and had been careful *not* to link this aid directly to the issue of reunification. Such indirect linkage aims to improve the general tone of bilateral relations, building mutual trust. In addition, by simply increasing the volume of economic ties, it increases the initiating state's potential future economic leverage.[3] Through such methods Germany was gradually able to improve its image in the USSR as both friend and an important trading partner, despite the fact that its actions against that country during the Second World War were much worse than those of Japan. When Germany then offered aid which *was* clearly linked to reunification (what could be called 'specific' linkage) it was successful, despite some lingering Soviet suspicions.

Conversely, Japan has always maintained a basically negative attitude towards providing aid for Russia and the USSR, as Germany did before 1970. What little aid has been granted recently has been limited and grudging compared to that given by other states, and thus has not been seen in a positive light by Moscow. The 'unity of politics and economics' (*seikei fukabun*) which connects aid directly to the Kurile issue has never been abandoned. In short, Japan has almost always used 'specific' linkage rather than 'general' linkage. Thus the image of Japan in the USSR remains quite negative, despite the fact that the conflict between the countries during the war was quite limited. It is therefore not surprising that Ozawa's attempt of March 1991 to link the issues was viewed with greater suspicion than Kohl's offer had been.

In this chapter, the German reunification case and the Kurile Islands case will be examined in more detail in an effort to probe the limits of economic power in the world of 'high politics' and security issues. It will be shown that in each case economic aid played a crucial part in the respective German and Japanese strategies for influencing the USSR. The reasons for the success of the aid strategy in one case and its failure in the other will then be discussed in more detail. While the role of economic instruments seems to be increasing steadily, it is still not an easy matter to use them effectively in the most difficult territorial disputes.

3. This point was made by Hirschman ([1945] 1980) in his classic study of German trade with Eastern Europe before the Second World War. Hirschman showed that nazi Germany deliberately offered generous trade deals to these states, which served gradually to increase Eastern Europe's economic dependence – and political dependence – on Germany.

2. ECONOMIC LINKAGE TECHNIQUES: THE GERMAN CASE

Before the role of economic linkage in German–Soviet or German–Russian relations can be examined, it must first be shown that an economic imbalance exists between the two countries which would allow linkage to take place. The political importance of such imbalances has been noted by authors ranging from Hirschman ([1945] 1980) to Keohane and Nye ([1977] 1989), who coined the useful term 'asymmetrical interdependence' to describe such one-sided economic ties. A clear economic asymmetry has in fact existed between the countries concerned for a very long period. It is not without reason that the Oder River, Germany's eastern border, is often referred to as 'Europe's Rio Grande'.

The great economic gulf between Germany and its eastern neighbours can be seen in a number of indicators such as per capita GNP, where Germany enjoys an advantage of five times or more over Russia depending on the measures used. Russia, with a population roughly double that of Germany, has an economy which is roughly half as large.[4] Furthermore, Russia has an economy which is not only smaller than Germany's but much less developed. Thus Russia has long tended to export low-value-added raw materials and semi-finished products to Germany, while importing machinery and other high-value-added products, a trade structure which is generally agreed to be unfavourable. Also, Russia has historically played a much smaller role in international trade and finance than has Germany, a factor which serves to magnify the importance of any given volume of trade, investment or credit for Moscow while minimizing its importance for Germany.[5]

Specific measures of the economic interaction between Germany and Russia also show asymmetrical interdependence. For the large, technically advanced and open German economy, trade and investment ties with Russia have been relatively insignificant. For the backward, closed economy of Russia the same ties have been vital. This can be seen, for example, in examining the two countries' relative dependence

4. Germany's GNP was estimated at 1.3446 million million dollars in 1994, while Russia's was about 721.2 thousand million (*CIA World Factbook*, 1995).
5. In 1994, for example, total German trade turnover amounted to 799 billion (thousand million) dollars, while Russian trade turnover was only 83.7 billion (*CIA World Factbook*, 1995).

on bilateral trade, as measured by the percentage of each country's trade conducted with the partner in question. The trade dependency ratio for Russia in its ties with Germany has generally been between five and ten to one, meaning that the same volume of trade is five to ten times more important for the Russian economy.[6]

Germany has generally been the leading trading partner of Russia and the USSR since the creation of the German Reich in 1870. This is the case today and was true almost continuously before the Second World War. Even during the period 1945–89, when the USSR made a great effort to insulate itself from Western influence by directing trade to its CMEA partners, West Germany was often Russia's leading Western trading partner.[7] Since economic ties to the West were vastly preferred by both the population and the leadership of the USSR – as shown by their insatiable hunger for Western currency, consumer goods and technical products – relative West German influence was higher than even its high share of Soviet trade would indicate.

In addition to trade, Germany's role in other forms of economic ties to Russia, such as credit and investment, has served to increase German influence. Germany played a large role in investment in Russia before the First World War, and has begun to regain that role today. Similarly, Germany has been an important source of financing for the overseas debt of both Russia and the USSR since German financiers floated large loans to support Russia during the Crimean War and the Russo-Turkish War (1877–78). That role re-emerged during the time of the Weimar Republic, and has again become prominent in the post-Cold War era. Thus Germany's relationship with its eastern neighbours – like the United States' ties with Latin America or Japan's links with its East Asian neighbours – remains a fruitful area for studying the relative effectiveness of various types of economic leverage in gaining political and security advantages in international relations.[8]

6. In 1991, for example, the year of the changeover from the USSR to an independent Russia, trade with Germany accounted for over 15 per cent of all CIS trade (twice the figure of any other partner). Yet for Germany, trade with the CIS amounted to only about 2 per cent of its total trade (*Statistisches Jahrbuch* 1992, and author's calculations). Since that time, with the total collapse of the CMEA trading bloc. Germany's role in trade with Russia has increased still further.
7. East Germany, in turn, was Moscow's leading trading partner in the eastern bloc.
8. Germany's structural economic advantage *vis-ŕ-vis* its Eastern neighbours is frequently an underlying theme in books focusing on Germany's foreign policy, such as Ash (1993), although this fact is unfortunately rarely placed in an explicitly

Successive German leaders, from Bismarck to Helmut Kohl, have always known of Germany's economic advantage over Russia and the USSR and have attempted to use it for political gain, but their linkage tactics have varied greatly (Newnham, 1995, 1996). Under the leadership of Chancellors Adenauer and Erhard (1945–66), West Germany sought to use its economic leverage much as Japan still does today. Germany maintained an essentially negative policy of denying government-backed credits to Moscow and limiting trade ties. It demanded that the USSR make concessions on issues such as the Berlin Wall and German unification before economic links would improve. At times this linkage was made quite clear, as when Adenauer imposed a short-lived grain embargo against the USSR in 1963 with the comment: 'we will sell you foodstuffs, but in exchange the wall must be taken down'.[9]

Germany's pressure tactics did induce Moscow to make concessions on some smaller political issues, but the central issue of reunification remained stalemated. By the mid-1960s many in Germany saw the policy of specific linkage as a failure. It seemed merely to deepen and sustain Soviet mistrust of Germany, playing into the hands of hard-liners in Moscow who portrayed West Germany as a neo-fascist 'revanchist' state. In addition, German leaders saw that the low level of German–Soviet ties permitted under the specific linkage policy was not valuable enough to Moscow to force major concessions. The new government of Chancellor Willy Brandt (1969–74) put forward a solution: a policy of positive general linkage.

Brandt proposed that Germany should expand trade credits and investment ties with the USSR without political preconditions. Yet this economic aid would not be apolitical: it would serve to address the two key shortcomings of the specific linkage strategy mentioned above. First, the new policy would build mutual trust and improve Germany's image in the USSR. Second, improved economic ties would raise Germany's economic value to the Soviet Union, increasing the value of the ties as potential political levers.[10] Together, these two factors would gradually soften Moscow's opposition to German political goals – such as reunification.

theoretical framework; a notable exception is Stent (1981).

9. Adenauer's remarks at a press conference in Berlin, 10 October 1963, as reported in *Frankfurter Allgemeine Zeitung*, 11 October 1963.
10. This argument was first made by Hirschman: see note 3, above. The basic principle was clear: economic ties must exist before they can be used as leverage.

In the end, a policy of general linkage did seem to contribute to German reunification. Certainly, though, the path from Brandt to reunification was not linear. Brandt's initial untied economic concessions to Moscow did help to obtain some of his immediate political goals. Notably, in the early 1970s Moscow helped West Germany to normalize relations with Poland and East Germany, which had been frozen since the Second World War. The Soviet side even pushed out long-time GDR leader Walter Ulbricht because of his opposition to improved ties with West Germany. German–Soviet economic ties deepened as Bonn provided generous export credits and entered into several massive deals to help develop Soviet natural gas fields and pipelines in return for gas shipments. West Germany seemed to have become a favoured partner for Moscow in the West.

However, West Germany's best efforts could not insulate it from the general East–West freeze of 1979–85. During these years the policy of general economic linkage seemed to have been discredited. Where was the Soviet goodwill which Germany had purchased with its economic aid? Still, West Germany had at least made progress towards changing its image in the Soviet Union, even if the political pay-off was slow in coming.[11]

Gorbachev's rise to power, however, soon restored West Germany's faith in its positive linkage policy. Here was a Soviet leader whose desire for economic and political reform would make him need German economic help and be willing to respond to such help with political concessions. Accordingly, West Germany was relatively quick to respond to Gorbachev's calls for aid. In early 1987, for example, in a major speech in Davos, Switzerland, German Foreign Minister Genscher urged the West to 'take Gorbachev seriously, take him at his word!' (Genscher, 1991, pp.137–50). During 1988 and 1989, as other Western states still hesitated to begin providing aid, Germany moved ahead with programmes of its own. In October 1988, Chancellor Kohl made his first visit to Moscow and offered the Soviet Union a loan of three billion marks (two billion dollars) (Ash, 1993, p.168). As had been the case in the 1970s, this aid was not linked directly to Soviet

11. The contribution of Brandt's 'Ostpolitik' to Germany's ultimate success in winning reunification remains controversial. While some authors have seen a clear contribution, others, such as Ash (1993), remain doubtful, asserting that German aid in the 1970s merely strengthened the conservative Soviet elite, actually postponing domestic and foreign policy reforms.

political concessions. Yet it was designed to encourage such concessions at some future date - a date which was fast approaching.

By the summer of 1989 the Soviet Union's East European empire, including East Germany, was beginning to show signs of crumbling. At an important summit meeting in Bonn in July 1989, Chancellor Kohl began to feel that Germany's policy of friendly support for Gorbachev was paying off at last. He and the Soviet leader took a private walk along the Rhine, in which the Chancellor talked at length about the inevitably of eventual German reunification. To his surprise, Gorbachev did not disagree; instead he began to talk of Russia's continuing need for German support. Kohl took this to be an indication of an implicit economic linkage: if Germany would continue to support the USSR, its friendship would eventually be reciprocated by progress on reunification. While the linkage in the 'walk on the Rhine' was subtle, the importance of the incident was shown by the fact that it was mentioned repeatedly in future private talks between the two leaders.[12]

During the difficult nine months between October 1989 and July 1990, as East Germany collapsed and German reunification became a real possibility, West Germany seized every opportunity to provide the USSR with various types of economic aid. For example, in January 1990 Bonn responded to a plea from Moscow by providing some 220 million DM (150 million dollars) in emergency food aid. The political importance of such a signal was clear, as Timothy Garton Ash notes:

> it would of course be quite absurd to suggest that German unity was bought for 52,000 tonnes of beef. but this was an important and very specific signal that the prospect of Germany being Gorbachev's greatest helper in his embattled attempt to modernize the Soviet Union was made not less but more real by the possibility of German unification. (Ash, 1993, p.350)

Finally, in the late spring of 1990, West Germany felt secure enough to begin to link its aid more closely to the issue of reunification. In May, Kohl dispatched a top aide, Horst Teltschik, to Moscow with a secret offer of a five-billion-mark loan (about three billion dollars). Kohl made it clear that the loan would be agreed to only if 'Two Plus

12. See interviews with Kohl and Gorbachev in Kuhn, 1993, pp.33–6. The 'walk on the Rhine' was alluded to in talks in the spring of 1990 concerning a large German loan to the USSR and again at the crucial Kohl-Gorbachev meetings in July 1990.

Four' talks on German reunification were concluded successfully. At the time, no other Western state would have considered such a loan. In return, Gorbachev agreed to set a date for a German–Soviet summit which was to resolve the remaining questions about unification - most notably Germany's membership of NATO and the withdrawal of Soviet troops.

As was noted above, it was at the July 1990 Kohl–Gorbachev summit that the German Chancellor won final Soviet agreement to reunification on German terms. The total economic package offered by Kohl was roughly as follows. Germany would pay for the living expenses of the Soviet troops in the GDR, for their transport home, and for new housing for them in the USSR ($10 billion). Germany would allow the USSR effectively to convert worthless rubles into German marks to continue existing trade agreements with East German firms after unification ($10 billion). Despite Soviet insolvency, Germany would continue to provide unlimited cover for Soviet purchases in Germany under the Hermes credit insurance programme.[13] To this must be added the credit promised in May 1990 and its associated interest costs, all guaranteed by Bonn (approximately $7 billion), and a number of smaller aid programmes. In return Gorbachev agreed to Germany's key political demands: the reunified Germany would remain in NATO and Soviet troops would be withdrawn. However, this crucial economic deal would probably have been less effective if Gorbachev had not already come to trust Kohl personally and trust Germany, owing to the friendship and support Germany had consistently demonstrated - in large part thanks to its economic aid policy.

In the ensuing months, Germany continued to provide new aid to the USSR and to Russia in order to secure the German reunification deal. In September 1990, just before the final reunification treaty was signed, Kohl increased the funding for the Soviet troop withdrawal in response to direct pressure from Gorbachev.[14] In early 1991, worried that the Supreme Soviet would not ratify the treaty, Germany offered still more

13. The German government issued new Hermes credits of 23.5 billion marks (about $15 billion) to the USSR from 1 January 1990 to 1 January 1992, but since these credits were issued continuously it is difficult to know exactly how much of them to attribute specifically to the July 1990 package. These figures and others in this paragraph are taken from *Antwort*, 1993, pp.55–6.
14. There were two tense Kohl-Gorbachev telephone calls on the eve of the signing of the 'Two Plus Four' treaty, in which Gorbachev threatened to derail the agreement if more money was not forthcoming.

aid. For 1991 and 1992 Germany halted its 'transferable ruble' offer, but agreed to substitute Hermes export credits on terms so generous that a special OECD exemption was needed before they could be offered. Bonn also agreed to set up a special foundation to aid Soviet victims of the Second World War. Finally, in December 1992, Kohl agreed to provide the new Russian government of Boris Yeltsin with 550 million marks in additional aid in order to speed up the troop withdrawal from the former GDR (*Bulletin*, 1992).

Throughout this period, Germany's behaviour in international organizations was an important part of its generous linkage strategy. Germany sought to increase its value as a friend of the USSR by inducing other Western states to aid Gorbachev. Germany's strong public advocacy of aid in the G-7, the European Community and other groups meant that it effectively received credit in Moscow for every dollar donated by these organizations. At the 1990 G-7 summit Germany was already pushing for aid to the USSR, and its efforts continued at the 1991 and 1992 summits (Meier, 1992).

In all, Germany has in recent years primarily used a conscious strategy of general linkage in giving economic aid to Russia and the USSR. The success of Germany's economic linkage policy can be seen not only in its role in promoting German unification, but in its role in promoting German–Russian friendship. It is striking to observe that Russia remains quite friendly with Germany, despite making huge political concessions to the Germans which might have been expected to cause great resentment. Meanwhile, although Russia has made no real concessions to Japan, Russian resentment of Japan is clear.

3. ECONOMIC LINKAGE TECHNIQUES: THE JAPANESE CASE

Like Germany, Japan is generally considered to be a leading example of an economic power, the type of country referred to by Richard Rosecrance as a 'trading state' (Rosecrance, 1986). Japan's economic development has followed a remarkably similar track to that of Germany, from crushing defeat in the Second World War to rapid, export-led growth, to a position as one of the leading economies in the world. Currently Japan has the second largest economy in the world and Germany the third largest.[15] Like Germany, Japan has made great efforts to atone for past militarism by keeping its armed forces relatively small and containing its military capacity within a tight alliance with the US.

The paradoxical nature of Japan's power - its great economic strength and relative military weakness - has made it, like Germany, a perfect test case for studying the role of economic power in world affairs. Thus, there have been a number of recent studies which have examined Japan's use of economic incentives and economic sanctions to achieve various national goals. To date, however, these studies have been limited in two ways. First, they have focused on Japan's Official Development Assistance (ODA), rather than including other instruments such as Export–Import Credits and the promotion of private investment. Second, they have focused only on the Third World. Many studies have concluded that in this area Japanese economic aid fulfils one of two purposes. Some have alleged that Japan's main focus is on promoting its own economic growth. Thus, aid is supposedly given mainly to countries which supply Japan with raw materials or provide expanding markets for Japanese goods (see Hook, 1995; Ensign, 1992). Others have pointed to Japan's role as a supporter of American political and security goals, an effort which aims both to mollify Japan's most important political and economic partner and to secure a generally peaceful environment for trade world-wide (Doherty, 1987; Chan, 1992; Yasumoto, 1986; Orr, 1990). Some have posited some combination of the two goals: Wan (1995), for example, sees Japan as simultaneously pursuing an 'earning strategy' to boost its economy and a 'spending strategy' to distribute some of its wealth to support common Western aims. Yet most of these analysts seem to agree that Japan is still hesitant to pursue its own, unique national political and security goals along the lines of more assertive countries such as the United States.

One purpose of the present analysis is to show that the prevailing model of Japanese economic power - focusing on official development assistance (ODA) and its use to promote the Japanese economy and placate the US - is adequate. These studies have generally ignored

15. The Japanese GDP was estimated at 2.5274 million million dollars in 1994, while the Germany GDP amounted to 1.3446 million million: *CIA World Factbook*, 1995.

Japan's occasional efforts to use its economic power to promote its own unique national security interests, just as Germany, the US and other states have done. The problem with the existing literature is one of case selection. Most works have focused narrowly on Japanese aid to the Third World. In ties with these countries, Japan does not see itself as having security goals which differ greatly from those of its Western allies.[16] Thus, its pursuit of economic goals and of goals which support Western and US interests is not surprising. However, in another area Japan's use of economics for its own unique goals in 'high politics' is clear: the Japanese–Russian dispute over the Kurile Islands.[17]

It has been clear for years that in Japanese–Soviet and Japanese–Russian relations Japan's economic power - including its ability to grant or withhold investment, credits and trade, as well as traditional development aid - is of central importance. Yet to date most studies on the Kurile dispute have been written by security specialists, who have often not given this vital economic basis detailed attention or attempted to explain it in theoretical terms.[18] Japan enjoys a clear economic advantage over Russia, as it does over many of its neighbours, which gives Tokyo the potential for using economic linkage should it so choose. This economic asymmetry is another point of similarity between the German and Japanese cases examined in this study. Like Germany, Japan is much more developed than Russia, enjoying particular strength in a whole range of technical areas where Russia is especially weak. Like Germany, Japan has a larger economy than Russia, and is even more dominant in areas such as trade and investment. As is the case with Germany, Japan's total trade is about

16. Even in cases where some subtle divergence has emerged, the disputes are more over tactics than over goals. Miyashita (1996), for example, highlights Japan's differences with the West over how to treat recalcitrant dictatorial states in Asia, noting that Japan is more inclined to use increased aid to win over such states than to use the aid embargo measures favoured by the US. It is ironic to note this in the light of Japan's reluctance to aid Russia, despite Western prodding. Yet both Japan and the US share the ultimate goals of promoting trade, democratization and stability in Asia, so these differences should not be over-stated.
17. It is striking to note that many books of Japanese foreign aid do not mention the Kuriles (or even the USSR), while detailing Japanese ties to far less important countries such as Sri Lanka: see Arase (1995); Orr (1990).
18. Typical are works such as those by Gelman (1993), which provides much useful economic data but focuses mainly on the impact of the Kuriles dispute on US–Japanese security ties, and Nimmo (1994) and Glaubitz (1995), which bury economic linkage in atheoretical, detailed historical descriptions of Japanese–Russian diplomatic ties.

eight times as large as that of Russia.[19] Thus it is not surprising that the trade dependency ratio (mentioned above for Germany) greatly favours Japan in its relations with Russia; such trade composes a far larger percentage of Russian than of Japanese trade. In 1994, for example, it amounted to a paltry 0.7 per cent of Japan's trade turnover (*White Paper*, 1995). However, Japan has often been Russia's second leading Western trading partner (behind Germany) and, as noted above, trade with the West has always been of disproportionate importance to the USSR and Russia. Furthermore, trade with both the USSR and Russia has often resulted in large surpluses for Japan, to the point that Russia now has a debt of some eight billion dollars to the Japanese (Kimura, 1996, p.25).

Like Germany, Japan has been aware for decades of the political significance of its economic advantage over Russia, but the sharp limits of Japan's willingness to aid Russia were clear and the linkage to the Kuriles was always present.

Mikhail Gorbachev's rise to power and his turn to a policy of radical reform in both foreign and domestic policy offered new hope of resolving the Kuriles dispute. Yet for much of the Gorbachev period, even as other Western states were becoming more and more generous with economic aid, Japan refused to loosen its specific linkage to the Kurile question. In the summer of 1986, for example, Prime Minister Nakasone made it clear that progress was needed on the territorial question before Tokyo would 'clarify, in return for this, an intention to respond to economic cooperation as much as possible' (Nimmo, 1994, p.61). Japan's negative attitude towards aid to the USSR can be seen quite clearly in looking at its standing among major donors to the USSR and then Russia. In January 1992, for example, the European Community estimated that of some $78 billion in world-wide aid offered to the USSR in 1990–91 Japan had proposed only $2.5 billion. This compares to $2.8 billion from South Korea and fully $45 billion from Germany (Hasegawa *et al.*, 1993, pp.181–2). In fact, even the $2.5 billion estimate is probably generous as it includes export credits[20] and such items as tax exemptions for private aid to the USSR in the

19. In 1994 Japanese exports totalled 395.5 billion dollars and imports stood at 274.3 billion. In the same year, Russian exports were 48 billion dollars and imports 35.7 billion (*CIA World Factbook*, 1995).
20. Admittedly, given the Russian government's current financial weakness, the loans may very well not be repaid.

category of 'government aid'.[21] Even the new Yeltsin regime, which led to a Russia which could not be blamed for the seizure of the islands, faced an iron front on economic matters in Tokyo.[22]

The differences between the German and Japanese cases are further illuminated by contrasting the behaviour of the two states when international groups such as the G-7 debated aid to Russia. Both states sought to magnify the economic message they were sending to the USSR (and later Russia) by inducing such groups to follow their national linkage strategies. The battle was played out at the 1991 London and 1992 Munich G-7 summits (Gelman, 1993, pp.40–63). While the Germans were pushing loudly and publicly for increased multilateral aid to Moscow in a further effort to win Russia's friendship, Japan was pushing just as strongly to stop any multilateral aid - in order to reinforce its own aid blockade against Russia. Not surprisingly, such actions reinforced the perception in Moscow that Germany was a friend and Japan was not.

4. CONCLUSION

As the previous discussion has shown, Japan can probably win the return of the disputed 'Northern Territories' only if it changes its economic linkage tactics. General aid (not directly linked to the return of the islands), given to Russia as a whole, might help to soften Russia's overall perception of Japan and its objectives. Certainly this tactic seemed to work well for Germany in negotiations over German unification. Japan must also succeed, as Germany did when promoting unification, in neutralizing the issues of territorial sovereignty and self-determination. As has been noted, additional general economic aid may

21. Japan's first significant offer of aid came in late 1990, when it offered $100 million in humanitarian aid - albeit in the form of a loan, which greatly diminished its value. Even this minor aid package was delayed for a full two years, during which the Kurile issue hung in the balance, before finally being awarded in late 1992, by that time in the form of a grant (Gelman, 1993, pp.44, 48, 74).
22. Yeltsin himself said that Russia might be more willing to settle the Kuriles issue if Japan were more willing to provide aid, that is, if Japan would provide at least some aid without obvious strings attached (*The Wall Street Journal*, 9 July 1992, cited in Gelman, 1993, p.60). Since at least the 1950s, in fact, Russian and Soviet leaders have repeatedly hinted to Tokyo that general economic linkage would be more effective than specific links.

in itself help to bring this change about. If this two-pronged approach is adopted the Kuriles problem will be drained of much of its tension. The case will become more like that of the Alaska purchase in 1867, the Louisiana purchase in 1803, or German reunification. The state giving up the territory in question will see it as a distant area which is not integral to its sense of sovereignty. It will see the 'purchasing' state as a friend which can be trusted with the additional territory, not as a dangerous rival. At that point a final package of specific economic linkage, directly linked to the return of the islands (such as that offered by Ozawa in 1991) may be more effective.

BIBLIOGRAPHY

Akaha, T. and T. Murakami (1993). 'Soviet/Russian–Japanese Relations', in T. Hasegawa *et al.* (eds), *Russia and Japan.*

Arase, D. (1995). *Buying Power: The Political Economy of Japan's Foreign Aid* (Boulder, CO: Lynne Rienner).

Ash, Timothy Garton (1993). *In Europe's Name* (New York: Random House).

Bulletin of the German Federal Press and Information Agency, 22 December 1992.

Chan, S. (1992). 'Humanitarianism, Mercantilism, or Comprehensive Security, *Asian Affairs*, vol.19, pp.3–17.

CIA World Factbook (1995) (Washington, DC: US Government Printing Office).

Doherty, E. (1987). 'Japan's Expanding Foreign Aid Program', *Asian Affairs*, vol.14, pp.129–49.

Ensign, M. (1992). *Doing Good or Doing Well?* (New York: Columbia University Press).

Gelman, H. (1993). *Russo-Japanese Relations and the Future of the U.S.–Japanese Alliance* (Santa Monica, CA: RAND Corporation).

Genscher, H.-D. (1991). *Unterwegs zur Einheit* (On the Way to Unity) (Berlin: Siedler).

Glaubitz, J. (1995). *Between Tokyo and Moscow: The History of an Uneasy Relationship, 1972 to the 1990s* (Honolulu: University of Hawaii Press).

Hasegawa, T. *et al.* (eds) (1993). *Russia and Japan: An Unresolved*

Dilemma Between Distant Neighbors (Berkeley, CA: University of California Press).

Hirschman, A. (1980). *National Power and the Structure of Foreign Trade* (Berkeley: University of California Press); first published in 1945.

Hook, S. (1995). *National Interest and Foreign Aid* (Boulder, CO: Lynne Rienner).

Keohane, R. and J. Nye (1989). *Power and Interdependence* (New York: HarperCollins); first published in 1977.

Kimura, H. (1996). 'Prospects for Growing Economic Interdependence Among Russia, China, Japan, and North and South Korea, and the Impact on Security', paper presented to the annual meeting of the International Studies Association, San Diego, CA, 16–20 April 1996.

Kuhn, E. (1993). *Gorbatschow und die Deutschen Einheit* (Gorbachev and German Unification) (Bonn: Bouvier).

Long, W. (1996). 'Trade and Technology Incentives and Bilateral Co-operation', *International Studies Quarterly*, vol.40, pp.77–106.

Meier, C. (1992). 'Russland als Weltwirtschaftspartner? Perspektive für Kooperation und Hilfe nach dem Münchener G7-Gipfel' (Russia as World Economic Partner? Prospects for Cooperation and Aid after the Munich G-7 Summit), *Reports of the Federal Institute for Eastern and International Studies*, Cologne.

Miyashita, A. (1996). 'Japan and Foreign Aid Sanctions: The Case of Democratization', paper presented to the annual meeting of the International Studies Association, San Diego, CA, 16–20 April 1996.

Newnham, R. (1995). *Deutschmarks and Diplomacy: Economic Linkage and German Reunification*, doctoral dissertation, University of California at Los Angeles.

—— (1996). *More Flies with Honey: Positive Economic Linkage in German Ostpolitik from Bismarck to Kohl*, revised version of a paper presented to the annual meeting of the International Studies Association, San Diego, CA, 16–20 April 1996.

Nimmo, W. (1994). *Japan and Russia: A Reevaluation in the Post-Soviet Era* (Westport, CT: Greenwood Press).

Orr, R. (1990). *The Emergence of Japan's Foreign Aid Power* (New York: Columbia University Press).

Rosecrance, R. (1986). *The Rise of the Trading State: Commerce and Conquest in the Modern World* (New York: Basic Books).

Statistisches Jahrbuch (various years). *Statistisches Jahrbuch der Bundesrepublik Deutschland* (Statistical Yearbook of the Federal Republic of Germany), various years (Bonn: Statistisches Bundesamt).

Stent, A. (1981). *From Embargo to Ostpolitik: The Political Economy of West German–Soviet Relations, 1955–1980* (Cambridge: Cambridge University Press).

Wan, M. (1995), 'Spending Strategies in World Politics: How Japan Has Used its Economic Power in the Past Decade', *International Studies Quarterly*, vol.39, pp.85–108.

White Paper on International Trade, vol.II (1995) (Tokyo: MITI).

Yasumoto, D. (1986), T*he Manner of Giving: Strategic Aid and Japanese Foreign Policy* (Lexington, MA: Lexington Books).

12. The Political Economy of Transition: The Case of Hong Kong

Gillian Youngs

Hong Kong has been one of the great economic success stories of the post-1945 period. It has been an emblem of the rise of the Asian dragons and the geographical expansion of the global growth economy to the East-Asian region. In moving from its British colonial to its post-colonial phase with its transition to Chinese sovereignty in July 1997, Hong Kong undoubtedly faces a number of challenges. The purpose of this chapter is to offer an assessment of the most important of these and to place them in the context of the territory's recent past and its future as a Special Administrative Region (SAR) of China. The uncertainties about Hong Kong's future cannot be understood in purely economic terms, not least because the change in sovereignty marks a move from a Western liberal democratic sovereign to a communist one. Thus many of the points which follow emphasize a political economy approach which recognizes the interaction of political and economic processes. The discussion will be divided into four parts. The first assesses the nature of Kong Kong's economic success, its transformation to a service based economy, and its role as economic gateway for China. The second section explains the main changes which are now under way in Hong Kong related to the transfer of sovereignty and the Chinese 'one country, two systems' policy. The third section considers factors of political economy affecting the development of Hong Kong into an information society. The final section addresses Hong Kong's international identity and outlines the *independence* issues relevant to its future.

1. CHINESE DRAGON

The statistics tell much of Hong Kong's story. Its rapid and sustained rise to the top of economic league tables is impressive in both its scale and its scope. The territory characterizes itself as 'a major international trade and financial centre'.[1] Recent figures marked it as the eighth largest trading entity in the world; the busiest container port in terms of throughput; fourth busiest airport in numbers of international passengers and second busiest in international cargo handled; fifth largest banking centre in terms of external banking transactions; fifth largest foreign exchange market on the basis of turnover; and second largest stock market in Asia in terms of market capitalization. The *World Competitiveness Report* 1995 issued by the International Institute for Management Development and the World Economic Forum ranked Hong Kong as the third most competitive economy in the world (compared with fourth the previous year) after the USA and Singapore, and the US Heritage Foundation rated Hong Kong for the second consecutive year as the freest economy in the world.

Hong Kong's has been a colonial success story, a Chinese territory under British control with a pro-business style of executive government which has been instrumental in ensuring its rapid growth and commercial openness. In the past 20 years the Hong Kong economy has more than quadrupled in size, with its Gross Domestic Product (GDP) growing at an annual average of 7.5 per cent in real terms - outstripping the Organization for Economic Cooperation and Development (OECD) countries and growing more than twice as fast as the world economy. Its recent transformation to a service-based economy is both reflective of developments in other advanced industrialized economies and linked closely to economic modernization in the southern part of China, which has been competitive in attracting manufacturing from Hong Kong. The tertiary services sector in Hong Kong - including retail and import-export trades; restaurants and hotels; transport, storage and communication; financing, insurance, real estate and business services - rose from 67 per cent of GDP in 1980 to 83 per cent in 1994. The last British governor of Hong Kong, Chris Patten, in explaining that about 70 per cent of Hong Kong's workforce was

1. *Hong Kong 1996*, p.48. Unless otherwise noted, the statistics quoted throughout this chapter are from this source; see also pp.48–50.

employed in the service sector, stressed the non-interventionist supportive form of government which had accompanied this development.

> There has been no grand strategy to bring it about. It has been led by markets, not by mandarins. It has been made possible by the skill of Hong Kong's entrepreneurs and by the flexibility of Hong Kong's work-force. The government's role has been to keep taxes low and control of public expenditure tight, while at the same time making the necessary long-term investments in the territory's physical and social infrastructure: a new airport, new container-port facilities, new roads, bridges and tunnels, land reclamation and major investments in education, skills training, research, housing, health care and the development of decent and affordable welfare services. (Patten, 1996, p.11)

With the focus on the transition of Hong Kong to Chinese sovereignty and, of course, the increased attention to China as a key major growth market, there has been stronger recognition of the regional links relevant to an understanding of Hong Kong's continued economic success, especially as a trading, and increasingly as a service, centre. With growth in the Asia-Pacific region in the 1980s, Hong Kong's trade with the region increased dramatically. Nearly 90 per cent of Hong Kong's re-exports involve China as either source or destination. Hong Kong's trade in services is concentrated in shipping, civil aviation, tourism and financial services. 'Off-shore trading, cross-border land transport services and other business services, including exports of construction, legal, accountancy, computer and management consultancy services to China and other East Asian economies, have all shown rapid increases' (*Hong Kong 1996*, p.51). Economic reforms in China since 1978 have contributed directly to the forces integrating the Chinese and Hong Kong economies in terms of production, trade and investment. For example,

> More than four million people are estimated to be working in Guangdong [province of China] for Hong Kong companies, either through joint ventures or in tasks commissioned by Hong Kong companies in the form of outward processing arrangements and compensation trade. This, in effect, provides Hong Kong with a substantial production base across the border. (*Hong Kong 1996*, p.54)

In 1995 China was Hong Kong's largest trading partner, accounting for 35 per cent of the colony's total trade value. As a source of, or conduit for, external direct investment in China, Hong Kong accounts for about three-fifths of the total. Recent assessments of the transition of Hong Kong from British to Chinese sovereignty have rightly highlighted the degree of interdependence between the economies as well as the significance to China's continuing economic development of both Hong Kong's integration into the world economy and its strong and expanding service sector.[2]

2. THE POLITICAL ECONOMY OF TRANSITION

In important senses the major questions and concerns about Hong Kong's future after its transfer to China can be summed up as matters of political economy. What effect will the transition from a liberal democratic sovereign to a communist sovereign mean for the SAR of Hong Kong as it will be identified from July 1997? Simply put, in the short as well as the longer term, will it be good or bad for business? There are two major themes which characterize the transition as agreed between the Chinese and the British governments on the basis of the maintenance of Hong Kong's existing way of life for a period of 50 years. These are the notions of 'a high degree of autonomy'[3] that the Basic Law, under which Hong Kong operates constitutionally from July 1997, allows the government of Hong Kong in areas other than foreign policy and defence, which are the preserve of Beijing. The second is the term originally applied to Taiwan and now applied by the Chinese government to Hong Kong, indicating the possibility of two distinct systems operating side by side without problem.[4]

The issue has to be the working of these two vague themes in practice. A number of aspects relating to the future governance of Hong

2. See, in particular, Yahuda (1996); also Wang (1996). On the situation in China see also Foot (1995, pp.194–222).
3. Article 12 of the Basic Law.
4. The general view, therefore, is of Hong Kong as a testing ground for the possible reintegration of Taiwan into China, linking the success of the Hong Kong experiment to China's wider unification interests. This point was affirmed by Shiu Sin Por, executive director, One Country Two Systems Economic Research Institute, in a presentation entitled 'The Final Months of the Transition and Beyond' as part of the Hong Kong Lectures, Fourth Series: The Challenge – Beyond 1997, at Hong Kong University, 16 November 1996. He urged Hong Kong people to see themselves as playing an active part in this broader mission. See also Yahuda (1996, pp.26–9) and Wang (1996, pp.41–61).

Kong are relevant to how such practice may develop. The Basic Law drawn up under Sino-British auspices provides the constitutional framework for governance in Hong Kong and this law locates the Chief Executive as a key link between Beijing and Hong Kong.[5] The power of interpretation and amendment of the Basic Law rests with the Chinese National People's Congress, which can also invalidate and return a law to the SAR if it does not conform with provisions affecting the responsibilities of China's central administration or its relationship with the SAR.[6] The Chief Executive's role in effectively integrating policy perspectives in Hong Kong with those in Beijing will be one of the pivotal factors shaping the level of harmony between the SAR and the central Chinese authorities. It is important in this respect to recognize the degree to which the future of Hong Kong is a matter of the politics *between* the SAR and Beijing and that these will be affected by developments in the political economy of both China at large and Hong Kong in particular.

The main structure of governance in the SAR as set out by the Basic Law has much in common with the previous colonial system,[7] featuring an appointed executive council in addition to a legislative council, with the latter including, in the near future, a proportion of directly-elected members and a commitment to eventual election of all members by universal suffrage.[8] The legislative council, being the arm of the administration with the closest associations with democratic principles, not surprisingly attracted closest interest in the build-up to the hand-over. China's decision to appoint a provisional legislature, as a stated reaction to pre-hand-over electoral reforms introduced by Britain for the existing legislature and viewed as contrary to Sino-British arrangements (Yahuda, 1996, pp.125–6; see also King, 1995, pp.118–22), was notable on two counts. First, it indicated China's willingness to interpret the Basic Law rather broadly in the sense that no specific mention

5. Article 48 of the Basic Law; see also the assessment by Yahuda (1996, pp.120–28).
6. Articles 17, 158 and 159 of the Basic Law.
7. Enbao Wang (1996, p.82), however, has argued for recognition of a distinct difference between the appointment procedure of the colonial Governor of Hong Kong and that of the new Chief Executive because the latter is subject to 'local selection through election and consultation'. As with top civil service posts, however, the Chief Executive is actually appointed by Beijing, giving it final vetting power: see Articles 45 and 48 of the Basic Law.
8. Article 68 and Annex II of the Basic Law.

of a provisional legislature is included.[9] Second, the 400-member selection committee appointed to elect the candidate for the first Chief Executive and to handle the establishment of the provisional legislature reflected the expected strong business emphasis within its membership (*Window* 1996b).

The question of business influence in the short- and long-term patterns of governance in Hong Kong remains a focal point for current and future thinking about the meanings of 'a high degree of autonomy' and 'one country, two systems' in both theory and practice. Much has been made of China's enthusiasm for the continued business success of Hong Kong, and the established patterns of interdependence between the Hong Kong and Chinese economies, outlined above, provide a strong logic for this position. But when we think of the business climate in Hong Kong, we cannot do so outside of sensitivities to broad issues of political economy in a Hong Kong–China framework.[10]

As far as major politics in China are concerned, focus has for some time been placed on the difficulties of transition which might arise upon Deng Xiaoping's death (Overholt, 1996). With regard to China's political economy, the huge internal challenges facing the country as a result of its continuing modernization and market privatization are clearly a key area (Agnew and Corbridge, 1995, pp.140–45; Jenner, 1992). Developments in 'grassroots democracy', despite continuing patterns of centralized political repression in China, have recently been receiving attention.[11] One factor that is particularly interesting in this respect is the direct association of these developments with the economic changes in China and the transition after 1978 from a command to a market economy in the countryside.[12] This is a strong indication of political change accompanying economic change in China.

9. The Democratic Party leader, Martin Lee, addressed this point at length in his comments to a symposium entitled 'Hong Kong Becoming China: The Challenge Ahead' at Hong Kong University, October 1996.
10. See Yahuda's analysis of this area (1996, pp.121–2).
11. *The Economist* (November 1996) reported that over 80 per cent of villages had elected through universal suffrage and secret ballot their own chiefs and village committees. The predominantly agricultural nature of China should be noted in this context. The report explained that there are around 900,000 villages in China housing possibly three-quarters of the country's 1.3 billion people: see Overholt (1996) and *Asiaweek* (1996).
12. *The Economist* (1996); see also *Window* (1996a).

It is evident that the return of Hong Kong has deep relevance to such forms of linkage, as the 'one country, two systems' prescription affirms. Hong Kong's established and outstanding success and characteristics as an open market economy are potential catalysts contributing to political change in China in direct and indirect ways. The 'one country, two systems' formula has two-way dimensions. As well as the notion that it incorporates protection of Hong Kong's 'way of life'[13] for 50 years, it also bears witness to China's belief in the need to counter influences which could prove disruptive to its control over change on the mainland, especially in the political realm. As Michael Yahuda (1996, p.121) has argued,

> In addition to the issues of national prestige involved in its recovery, Hong Kong is seen, on the one hand, as a source for enhancing the national economy and, hence the political authority of the ruling communist party but, on the other hand, it is also seen as an instigator of national disintegration by being an exemplar of Western cultural and political norms.

In the Basic Law, the 'two systems' are referred to in general terms as 'socialist system' and 'capitalist system'.[14] These are vague with respect particularly to political economy and they depend on interpretations of the essential qualities of those systems which are likely to differ from Beijing and Western standpoints.[15] This was already demonstrated in statements by key officials in the build-up to the transition, the priority from China's position being the economic aspects of Hong Kong's established way of life.[16] Debates within Hong Kong tended, by contrast, to emphasize the interaction of political and economic factors, the importance of the 'rule of law' and broad issues of freedom of speech and the press.[17] While the Basic Law sets out a framework for continuity in such areas, there is strong focus on, and, understandably, concern about, the importance of how this will actually work in practice.

13. Article 5 of the Basic Law.
14. Preamble to and Article 5 of the Basic Law.
15. Ambrose King's assessment (1995) of 'one country, two systems' as 'an idea on trial' is useful in this respect.
16. See *Asian Wall Street Journal* (1996b); also Yahuda (1996, p.108).
17. These issues were identified as priorities, for example by Martin Lee; see note 9, above.

This has been complicated by the politicization which has resulted from the actual transition process itself, which, for argument's sake, can be dated from the historic Sino-British Joint Declaration of 1984, and which has been intensified by the contribution towards a democratic culture in Hong Kong of the controversial electoral reforms of the early 1990s. Ambrose King's assessment (1995, pp.107–8) of this politicization as a divergence from the main historical pattern of political economy in Hong Kong is extremely helpful:

> Hong Kong had been predominantly an economic and administrative city before the question of 1997 was first raised. Hong Kong had long been a politically inactive and economically dynamic city, ruled and administered by a vast and efficient government bureaucracy. The colonial government never seriously thought of transplanting British or any other Western-type democracy into the colony. ... Through the extensive institutionalized process of consultation and absorption, Hong Kong has developed a unique political system. The continuing and timely absorption of potential political élites into the administration has made politics outside the government almost unnecessary.

Once the question of 1997 arose, politicization took the form of a 'political market' overlaid on an established 'economic market' with 'supply side' (British and Chinese government) as well as 'demand side' influences and with the effects being most profound in 'the middle stratum' of society (King, 1995, pp.108–9). A deep historical sense of this *politics after economics* character of Hong Kong is an important element in the context of considerations of Western norms, and, in particular, issues associated with democratic principles, in relation to the SAR's present and future.

3. THE NEXT ECONOMIC TRANSFORMATION: INFORMATION SOCIETY?

Leading up to the transfer, increasing attention was placed on the future of Hong Kong's economy, where its continuing dynamism would rest and how this might be best assured. In one way or another the prime orientation has been the continuance of the Western industrialized development model. Hong Kong has passed from the manufacturing to the service stage and the intensification of this process should lead to a fully-fledged information society.[18] The notion of the information society features a strong emphasis on processes of production, manipulation and distribution of knowledge. It is educationally and technologically oriented and highly dependent on computer and communications systems and their capacities to disrupt previously-accepted time and space relationships. Globally, the dominant service economies (notably the US), and of course their trans-national corporations, have been continually expanding the ways in which we think about knowledge as product (Strange, 1994, see also Youngs, forthcoming). Major growth has taken place in the range of such products and their significance to employment patterns and practices, production as well as consumption (Barnet and Cavanagh, 1994; Bryan and Farrell, 1996).

The critical framework for thinking through the challenges facing high-growth East Asian economies in making the transition to knowledge-based development has been the 'quality growth' rather than 'quantity-based' perspective:

> Quantity-based growth is growth fuelled by applying increasing amounts of capital and labour, and eventually it is likely to result in rapidly diminishing returns. ... By contrast, quality growth is, in essence, a matter of efficiency - the use of technology to devise new products, increase output and to reduce costs. Economists have calculated that most growth in, for example, the United States is of the quality variety, whereas most growth in Asia outside Japan has been of the quantity type. (Patten, 1996, pp.10-11)[19]

The potential for 'quality growth' is frequently tied to factors well beyond the economic: for example, to the combination of 'social and political liberty' with 'economic liberty' to promote 'inventiveness, creativity and technological flexibility' (Patten, 1996, p.11). Thus a causal relationship is drawn between the existence of Western-type norms of political, economic and social freedom and the possibilities for 'quality growth'. In this way, the debate about broad political aspects, such as freedom of speech and the press and also the rule of law in relation to the future of Hong Kong, becomes firmly a matter of

18. The potential for this form of development in Hong Kong was outlined by Charles Kao in a presentation entitled 'Revolution in Communications and its Implications' as part of The Hong Kong Lectures Fourth Series: 'The Challenge - Beyond 1997', University, at Hong Kong University, 2 November 1996. See also Ure (1995) on telecommunications developments in Asia and Peter Drucker's examination (1993) of 'the knowledge society'.
19. See also Krugman (1994b).

political economy. Thus, the economic destiny, or continuing success, of Hong Kong, is argued to be tied directly to political continuity, to continuing political *as well as* economic development along Western lines.

One of the factors in play in this respect is the distinctiveness of Hong Kong's political economy in the East Asian context, what might be regarded as its competitive edge in the information society stakes[20] and the long-term relevance of this to China's further modernization and competitiveness. Hong Kong can be argued to be the most Westernized economy among the Asian dynamos, and the question is how significant this will be in boosting its potential as an information society and what impact its transition to Chinese sovereignty will have upon this situation.[21] This is fundamentally a long-term issue but it assists the identification of what can be considered key structural elements in the further development of Hong Kong's economy. These include all forms of educational[22] and technological training, skilling and re-skilling, innovation and entrepreneurship. The input of trans-national business activity within Hong Kong is clearly relevant to such factors and it was frequently stressed in the build-up to its transfer to China that the stable legal environment offered by the territory was one of the prime bases for its high degree of attractiveness to companies, including, importantly, those investing in China.[23]

20. It is interesting to contrast the case of Hong Kong with that of Singapore. The latter has followed the most high-profile path of modernization through technological transformation in East Asia but under political conditions which are overtly authoritarian in the areas of control of information, the press and so on: see Da Cunha (1994). See also Krugman (1994b) on the input (growth-based) orientation of Singapore's economic expansion in connection with the points made in the previous section. See also Krugman's (1994a) broad attack on competitiveness as 'a dangerous obsession'.
21. China's efforts, as well as Singapore's, to control Internet access for their citizens gained front-page media attention in 1996: see *Asian Wall Street Journal* (1996a). Hong Kong's Internet environment was well advanced before the handover. It was not clear whether freedom of access would become an issue in the SAR.
22. Educational reform has long been a major policy concern in Hong Kong. See the report in *South China Morning Post* (1996) on plans to 'drag Hong Kong schooling into the 21st century' so as to equip it with 'thinking, communicative and problem-solving people'.
23. The relatively high degree of mobility possessed in the present global economy by transnational companies and skilled professional staff is relevant here: see Yahuda (1996, pp.123–4).

Central to the challenges confronting Hong Kong, then, are a combination of transition processes affecting its political economy in the widest sense. It is an economy moving through the advanced stages of the manufacturing to service transformation with all the qualitative issues which that raises for human and material resources. It is a polity undergoing a colonial to a post-colonial transition; one which, partly because of its particular circumstances, has engendered a politicization that is significant in the context of its long-term history. The political dynamics are complicated by the dramatic change in political cultures (Western capitalist to communist socialist) of the sovereign power to which it is subject, and also the working out in practice of the 'high degree of autonomy' and 'one country, two systems' in this context. Thus the main indications are that in thinking about the future of Hong Kong we should do so in terms of its 'economic system' being 'intimately linked to the social, legal and political systems' (Clark, 1989, p.170). Hong Kong's high degree of success and integration into the global economy provides it with institutional involvements and affinities with the dominant (neo-liberal) capitalistic principles which are likely to be influential not only in terms of how the SAR's self-image as a political economy develops in the future but the ways in which its international links and activities are influential in its formulation and maintenance.

4. BEYOND LOCAL AND REGIONAL CONTEXTS

This chapter has concentrated so far on Hong Kong's local and regional relations but its international identity, certainly in respect of its economic achievements, is a significant factor in addressing the future of the SAR. During the colonial period, Hong Kong's 'full autonomy regarding international economic and trade matters' (*Hong Kong 1996,* p.22) was an influential dimension of its development of a form of independent international presence. With representation through its economic and trade offices and industrial promotion units in Europe, North America and the Asia-Pacific region, an extensive international network of Hong Kong Trade and Development offices and Hong Kong Tourist Association branches, the territory has established a solid overseas institutional identity. Hong Kong's regional and global status as an economic entity has been reflected in its active representation and involvement in major organizations, including the Asia–Pacific Economic Cooperation forum (APEC) and the WTO.

One of the provisions of the Basic Law identified in the period leading up to the transition as central to future continuity for Hong Kong refers specifically to its external relations:

> The Hong Kong Special Administrative Region may on its own, using the name 'Hong Kong, China', maintain and develop relations and conclude and implement agreements with foreign states and regions and relevant international organizations in the appropriate fields, including the economic, trade, financial and monetary, shipping, communications, tourism, cultural and sports fields.[24]

There is no doubt that Hong Kong's independent international relations, if that phrase is used very loosely, have, as this section from the Basic Law indicates, a strong focus on economic affairs but are by no means restricted to this area. While the economic dimension has a prime influence, it is worth taking the wider picture into account when thinking about Hong Kong's long-term future and the contrasting influences upon it. This includes understanding participation in the global capitalist system in its fullest cultural as well as political and economic senses.

When considering Hong Kong as part of China, the broad impact on the former of its integrated participation in the global economy is certainly a key element of its distinctive identity as historically formed. I have argued elsewhere (Youngs, 1996) the importance of remembering that while under British colonial control Hong Kong did not stop being Chinese, and, as I have outlined above, the years leading up to the transition saw Hong Kong increasingly linked geo-economically with China and its controlled embrace of capitalism. But Hong Kong's historical, colonially-influenced experience of the free flow of ideas and products in the global system distinguishes it sharply from the larger Chinese experience with certain qualifications, for example, with regard to areas such as Shanghai and Shenzhen, which in different ways have been motors of the Chinese modernization process and thus at the

24. Article 151 of the Basic Law. Continued Hong Kong involvement 'in an appropriate capacity' with international organizations of which China is or is not a member is provided for in Article 152.

forefront of China's steps towards integration into the international capitalist system.[25]

The dominant cultural messages in this system are certainly Western, and economic consumption cannot be neatly separated from wider cultural contexts and connections, especially in relation to global communications systems and the range of information and entertainment products associated with them (Barnet and Cavanagh, 1994). It is helpful to think in terms of lifestyles, rather than just products, being sold because of the ways in which the desire for and experience of such products represent much more than material issues. Eating, drinking, smoking, driving cars, buying clothes, furnishing and decorating homes: these all rely on products but they are also features of the way we live our lives and the extent to which we live our lives through such products. Hong Kong's capitalistic characteristics are as much a part of its cultural make-up and its political economy as other major historical influences, such as its élitist colonial style of government and its longer associations with the mainland.

Its multiple institutional international links, formal and informal, and the reach of its market networks have, in many ways, brought Hong Kong into the world and the world into Hong Kong. Such is the necessary openness of a dynamic and high-achieving capitalist entity. However, the Hong Kong economist Edward K.Y. Chen stresses the importance of government action in shaping the future economic development with long-term strategy oriented towards the labour market (manpower policies), at trade, investment and competition policies, and at socio-economic policies (income redistribution).[26]

The profile of Hong Kong has been raised and made more complex by the range of interests and concerns generated by the long process of its transfer to Chinese sovereignty. If anything, more eyes of the world are upon Hong Kong than ever. It is interesting in this context to note the following call by independent legislative councillor Christine Loh (1996, p.235):

25. Shanghai has a history going back to the beginning of the century as a major international city and continues to have significance, including that as a financial centre. Shenzhen, as one of China's special economic zones, has featured as part of the country's recent economic advance: see Seagrave (1995) and Agnew and Corbridge (1995, pp.142–3).
26. Edward K.Y. Chen, public lecture, Harvard University, 21 October 1996.

it is important for Hong Kong to continue to develop and expand its international links because they have helped Hong Kong people to capitalize on many opportunities, ranging from economic to professional ones, as well as in research, sports and culture.

5. CONCLUSION: MULTIPLE IDENTITIES

I have drawn a picture of Hong Kong in this chapter which emphasizes its multiple identities because I assess that these sum up in large part the structure of influences upon it as a Special Administrative Region of the People's Republic of China in the coming years. Hong Kong's impressive economic record of the recent past and how, as a colonial territory, it has developed a restricted polity which has undergone rapid and partial politicization as part of the transition process, are elements guiding its future possibilities. Its economic links with China are already well advanced and will continue to grow, and this should be advantageous for both sides and for others. East Asia remains a high growth region which is becoming increasingly integrated into the wider global economy, and Hong Kong is a leading regional entity in this context. Its political transformation will be twofold, focused both on the progress of the terms of the Basic Law as they come to be applied in practice, and, partly associated with this, on its relationship with Beijing as the overall central authority. The 'high degree of autonomy' on the basis of 'one country, two systems' is a situation likely to remain 'on trial' (King, 1995) for some time to come. We can expect Hong Kong's future focus to be as it has been in the past: on economic success. But the above discussion has suggested that we should not consider this situation outside political influences which have become more pressing for a range of colonial and post-colonial reasons. A new Hong Kong is being born which is bound to feature many remnants of its past, positive and not so positive, but which will also produce new and unexpected trajectories. Many of these relate to the areas covered in this chapter, including the question of possibilities for deepening its service sector along information-society lines. This draws us into broad considerations about Hong Kong society and issues such as education and training, new technology-based creative and entrepreneurial skills, and so on. It also reminds us that an economy is not just a matter of the material processes that characterize it, but of the calibre, quality and capacities of the people who work and live in it. Hong Hong's rise to fame has encapsulated the business efforts of local and international participants. Much has been made of the attraction to trans-national enterprises of the political and legal stability as well as the economic opportunities which Hong Kong has offered. Quality of life - political, economic and cultural - cannot be measured in dollars alone, and neither can the future potential of Hong Kong.

BIBLIOGRAPHY

Agnew, J. and Corbridge, S. (1995). *Mastering Space: Hegemony, Territory and International Political Economy* (London: Routledge).

Asian Wall Street Journal (1996a). 'Cyber patrols: censoring the Net isn't easy, but it can be intimidating', 11 September, pp.1 and 11.

Asian Wall Street Journal (1996b): 'Qian tells Hong Kong to avoid political attacks against China', 16 October, pp.1 and 5.

Asiaweek (1996). 'People power' 18 October, pp.28–33.

Barnet, R.J. and J. Cavanagh (1994). *Global Dreams: Imperial Corporations and the New World Order* (New York: Simon & Schuster).

Bryan, L. and D. Farrell (1996) *Market Unbound: Unleashing Global Capitalism* (New York: Wiley).

Cheek-Milby, K. and M. Mushkat (eds) (1989). *Hong Kong: The Challenge of Transformation* (Hong Kong: Centre of Asian Studies, University of Hong Kong).

Clark, D.J. (1989). 'A High Degree of Autonomy Under the Basic Law', in Cheek-Milby and Mushkat (eds), *Hong Kong*, pp.153–88.

Da Cunha, D. (ed.) (1994). *Debating Singapore: Reflective Essays* (Singapore: Institute of Southeast Asian Studies).

Drucker, P.F. (1993). *Post-Capitalist Society* (New York: HarperCollins).

Foot, Rosemary (1995). *The Practice of Power: U.S. Relations with China since 1949* (Oxford: Oxford University Press).

Hong Kong 1996. Yearbook published by Hong Kong Government.

Jenner, W.J.F. (1992). *The Tyranny of History: The Roots of China's Crisis* (London: Allen Lane).

King, A.Y.C. (1995). 'One Country, Two Systems: An Idea on Trial', in Wang and Wong (eds), *Hong Kong's Transition*, pp.104–24.

Krugman, Paul (1994a). 'Competitiveness: A Dangerous Obsession', *Foreign Affairs*, vol.73, no.2, pp.28–44.

—— (1994b). 'The Myth of Asia's Miracle', *Foreign Affairs*, vol.73, no.6, pp.62–78.

Loh, C. (1996). 'The Commonwealth and Hong Kong', *The Round Table, The Commonwealth Journal of International Affairs*, no.338, pp.231–7.

Overholt, W.H. (1996). 'China After Deng', *Foreign Affairs*, vol.75, no.3, pp.63–78.

Patten, C. (1996). 'Asian Values and Asian Success', *Survival* vol.38, pp.5–12.

Seagrave, S. (1995). *Lords of the Rim: the Invisible Empire of the Overseas Chinese* (London: Bantam).

South China Morning Post (1996). 'Education off-target', 16 November, p.19.

Strange, Susan (1994). *States and Markets*, 2nd edn (London: Pinter).

The Economist (1996). 'China's Grassroots Democracy', 2 November, pp.27–8.

Ure, J. (ed.) (1995). *Telecommunications in Asia: Policy, Planning and Development* (Hong Kong: Hong Kong University Press).

Wang, E. (1996). *Hong Kong, 1997: The Politics of Transition* (Boulder, CO: Lynne Rienner).

Wang, G. and Wong, S.L. (eds) (1995). *Hong Kong's Transition: A Decade After the Deal* (Oxford: Oxford University Press).

Window (Weekly Hong Kong news magazine published by Asian Regional Projects). (1996a). 'Civil Rights on the Mainland' (Commentary), 8 November , p.31.

—— (1996b). 'SC Ready for Key Decisions', 8 November, pp.6–8.

Yahuda, M. (1996). *Hong Kong: China's Challenge* (London: Routledge).

Youngs, Gillian (1996). 'Democracy and the Political Economy of Transition in Hong Kong', discussion paper, International Studies Association–Japan Association of International Relations Joint Convention on Globalism, Regionalism and Nationalism: Asia in Search of its Role in the 21st Century, Makuhari, Japan, 20–22 September 1996.

—— (forthcoming). 'Political Economy, Sovereignty and Borders in Global Contexts', in J. Hoffman and L. Brace (eds), *Sovereignty Today* (London: Cassell).

Concluding Remarks

Iliana Zloch-Christy

This book has attempted to analyse some principal issues of the political economy of transition in post-communist Europe in the framework of the globalization of the world economy. The analyses in the individual chapters lead to the conclusion that international economic relations have become more global and more integrated in their scope in the past two decades. The international system is centred in the developed economies but it is global in character. It shows unprecedented dynamism - rapid technological change and increased economic efficiency. The transforming East European countries are attempting to join the integrated world economy, and they opened their economies after 1989 in terms of more open exchange rate policies and exchange controls, and no prohibitive tariffs and quotas, and they are facing the challenge of finding strategic alliances and attracting foreign capital. Their economic development varies across countries and depends on institution building (private property and market-based trade), geography (for example, their proximity to Western markets and their natural endowments), history, and human capital.

One of the most interesting issues in shaping economic development is the role of government, as was stressed in several contributions to this book (for example, Bakos, Lairson, Zloch-Christy). This role is particularly important in the present transition in post-communist Europe. Many Western advisers to Eastern Europe, and some East European politicians, seem to understate the importance of strong government in this difficult process and in designing strategies for industrial policy, privatization, foreign investment, management of the external debt, institution building and in general forward-looking strategies for economic development. For many of the policy makers in Eastern Europe, the illusion of the first years of transition in the early

1990s, that the beautiful simplicities of a market order and of the invisible hand would be established quickly, is over. Scholars and politicians agree that economic success depends on the quality of governance, the international economic environment and the creation of a competitive market economy. And the other lesson learnt is that to face these challenges there is a need of *strong* but *limited* government.

This is an old dilemma faced not only by the transition economies in post-communist Europe but also by the developed economies of the industrialized countries and of the developing world. In the case of East European countries, the goal of the transition should be less government compared to the communist economic order and central planning, but this does not mean government withdrawal from economic activity in the transition stage. Strong government is very much needed. This was stated also by the Nobel laureate in economics Douglass North at Stanford University in November 1995. He remarked, '*laissez-faire* means chaos'. Government guidance is needed and is important also in other regions, as is shown by Gillian Youngs's discussion of the experience of Hong Kong, a South-east Asian 'tiger' considered by many economists to be a model of a successful twentieth-century *laissez-faire* story.

Such guidance is important in designing manpower policies, industrial (competition) policies and socio-economic policies. It may be of interest also to mention here that the role of the government in economic activity is seen as important by some American economic policy makers, including Lawrence Summers and Joseph Stiglitz. The latter, a former chairman of the Council of Economic Advisors to President Clinton and now chief economist at the World Bank, states in the case of the South-east Asian economies that some observers and analysts give too much credit to market forces in explaining the miracle of their economic growth. He warns that 'because markets played such an important role, some observers concluded that their success was convincing evidence of the power of markets alone. Yet, in almost every case, government played a major role in these economies ... There is little doubt that government intervened in the economy through the market.'[1]

Now, a few further remarks on the globalization of the world economy. As in the late nineteenth and early twentieth centuries, the 1990s,

1. Joseph E. Stiglitz, *Whither Socialism?* (Boston, MA: MIT Press, 1994), p.14.

marking the end of the twentieth century, are a period of increased interpenetration of national economies. The *globalization* of the world economy can be characterized by the following main trends:

1. Every part of the world is involved in international trade.
2. There is a great acceleration of world economic activity (including trade and foreign investments)
3. A rapid increase of world merchandise trade is taking place, with rising ratios of world exports to world GDP ratios (for example, 1950: 7 per cent; 1973: 11.2 per cent; 1992: 13.5 per cent).[2]
4. There exist many international (WTO, IBRD, IMF), regional (NAFTA, EU) and bilateral agreements, which create an open trading system, although non-tariff restrictions have increased and political tensions pushing towards protectionism are present in the developed economies.
5. Rapid technological changes are under way, which further contribute to an open trading system, with production itself becoming multilateralized.
6. The world capital markets are becoming globalized, and there is a massive rise of capital movements.
7. There is increased international migration of labour.

The *reasons* for the globalization might be identified as follows:

1. A sustained period of peace after the Second World War among the most advanced economies (USA, Western Europe, Japan).
2. The almost hegemonic leadership (military and economic) after the Second World War of the United States. It made the first free-trade steps and contributed to the creation of an open trading system.
3. The advance of technology itself.

The chapters in this volume do not discuss issues regarding where future economic and political developments may go in Eastern Europe and in the world economy. We hope that the reader will be better served by a study comprising analyses of East European and Western experts than by works speculating on future developments.

2. Cited in Jeffrey Sachs, unpublished manuscript, Harvard University, November 1996.

Select Bibliography

Brabant, Jozef M. van (1996). *Integrating Europe: The Transition Economies at Stake* (Dordrecht, Boston, MA, and London: Kluwer Academic Publishers.

Okimoto, Daniel (1989). *Between MITI and the Market: Japanese Industrial Policy for High Technology* (Stanford, CA: Stanford University Press).

Scherer, F.M. (1994). *Competition Policies for an Integrated World Economy* (Washington, DC: Brookings).

Sen, A. (1987). *On Ethics and Economics* (Oxford: Basil Blackwell).

Stiglitz, Joseph E. (1994). *Whither Socialism?* (Cambridge, MA: MIT Press).

Weiner, Myron (1995). *The Global Migration Crisis: Challenge to States and to Human Rights* (New York: HarperCollins).

Yoffie, David (ed.) (1993). *Beyond Free Trade: Firms, Governments, and Global Competition* (Cambridge, MA: Harvard Business School Press).

Youngs, Gillian and Eleonore Kofman (eds) (1996). *Globalization: Theory and Practice* (London: Pinter).

Zloch-Christy, Iliana (ed.) (1995). *Privatization and Foreign Investment in Eastern Europe* (Newport, CT, and London: Praeger).

Index